9780695804718
AF574241

RANG

14
6

VICTORIAVILLE

KURT

SHERWOOD

21
C
2

SHER-WOOD
PARK
2

THE FASTEST SPORT

by Gerald Eskenazi

With Special Photography by Ken Regan and Melchior DiGiacomo

A Rutledge Book
FOLLETT PUBLISHING COMPANY
Chicago • New York

COLOR PHOTO SECTION

page 1: *Face-off! Jean Ratelle, New York, vs. Dennis Dupere, Toronto.*

page 2: *TOP LEFT: Bill Barber leads a Philadelphia Flyers rush. TOP RIGHT: Fallen Red Wing, victim of either a deflected puck or a high stick. BOTTOM: Goalie Ken Dryden, who later quit the Canadiens because of a contract dispute, deflects a long shot in a game at Minnesota's Metropolitan Sports Center.*

page 3: *The New York Raiders, before they became the Golden Blades and then the Knights of Cherry Hill, New Jersey, in a contest at Madison Square Garden with the Philadelphia Blazers, soon to move themselves to Vancouver. Raiders' Brian Bradley fights Blazers' Peter McNamee for position in front of the net.*

page 4: *Montreal's Pete Mahovlich tries to drive through Boston's Dallas Smith and Rick Smith. The two Smiths, the latter now with California, are not related.*

page 5: *TOP: Gordie Howe, the NHL's greatest scorer. Howe retired, then unretired when the WHA's Houston Aeros offered him a chance to play with his sons. BOTTOM: Penguins goalie Andy Brown determinedly watches a puck that missed the cage. Brown, although young, is nearly the last of hockey's maskless goaltenders.*

page 6: *TOP LEFT: Raiders' Gary Kurt falls to the ice to prevent score. TOP RIGHT: Bobby Orr, hockey's greatest star, finishes a rink-long rush by veering to center before Canadiens defenseman Jacques Laperriere (2) can reach him. BOTTOM: New York Islanders goalie Billy Smith reaches desperately to deflect Toronto shot as alternate captain Bert Marshall rushes to help.*

page 7: *Chicago's Keith Magnuson, who fights with anybody, squares off with Bobby Orr, who tries to avoid fights—he is too valuable to the Bruins to spend time in the penalty box.*

page 8: *Flyers' Bernie Parent, the NHL's stingiest goalie, makes another spectacular save.*

page 9: *TOP: New England Whalers' Mike Byers attempts a sweep check but cannot stop Blades' Gene Peacosh from slashing. BOTTOM: Billy Smith stops the initial shot, and Boston's Greg Sheppard struggles for the rebound.*

page 10: *After Flyers captain Bobby Clarke loses possession of the puck, Maple Leafs' Ian Turnbull tries to prevent bearded Bill Flett from making a centering pass.*

page 11: *TOP: Philadelphia's Ed Van Impe sweats it out in the cooling-off box. BOTTOM: Linesman Pat Shetler and referee Art Skov assist injured Brad Park of the Rangers.*

page 12: *TOP: The Minnesota rush stopped, Philadelphia's Ross Lonsberry starts a retaliatory surge past North Stars' Dennis Hextall. BOTTOM: California Golden Seals' Gary Croteau (18) and Ivan Boldirev (9) congratulate each other on successful scoring play.*

page 13: *Bill Macmillan of Toronto throws a hip check on Brad Park of New York, but the Rangers' rushing defenseman has too much momentum, and both players go flying.*

page 14: *TOP LEFT: Art Skov signals an infraction: elbowing. TOP RIGHT: The bent shaft is indicative of the power behind Pit Martin's slap shot. BOTTOM: Detroit's Doug Grant, stickless, relies on quick reflexes to stop Seals scoring attempt.*

page 15: *Golden Blades aren't enough to stop Whalers' Rick Ley from bringing puck up ice.*

page 16: *Quebec Nordiques' Serge Aubry uses both stick and skate to cover the corner.*

THE FASTEST SPORT

Photo Credits

Michael Albanese (More Than Meets the Eye) : 69, 113, 131
Paul Bereswill: 194, 196, 197, 198, 199, 200
The Bettman Archive: 27 top, 28, 29
California Gold Seals: 135
Culver Pictures, Inc.: 24-25, 31 bottom, 91 top
Detroit Red Wings: 225
John Devisser, in cooperation with The Hockey Hall of Fame: 32-33, 35, 38 bottom, 40-41, 44, 47, 49, 53
Diana DiGiacomo (More Than Meets the Eye) : 6 bottom
Melchior DiGiacomo: 1, 2 top left, 3, 6 top left, 8, 10, 12 top, 14 top left, 15, 16, 66-67, 77 right, 89, 103 top, 105, 109, 119, 121, 125, 137, 139, 142, 145, 148, 149, 151, 154-155, 159, 165, 167, 169, 206
Hockey Hall of Fame: 43, 48, 50, 55, 71, 81, 84 center and top, 99 top, 239
Los Angeles Kings: 123 top
Peter Mecca (More Than Meets the Eye) : 69, 77 left, 143 right, 162-163
New York Public Library Picture Collection: 27 bottom
New York Times: 202
Richard Raphael: 4, 6 top right, 7, 22-23, 87 top, 97, 101, 122, 140, 141, 157, 219
Ken Regan: 1, 2 top right and bottom, 5, 9, 11, 12 bottom, 13, 14 bottom and top right, 39, 79, 87 bottom, 95, 116, 117, 127, 129, 143 left, 161, 192-193, 201, 203, 204-205, 207, 208, 210-211, 224
Les Rosner: 171, 173, 175, 177, 179, 181, 183, 185, 187
United Press International: 31 top, 36, 37, 38 top, 70, 73, 80, 83, 84 bottom, 85, 91 bottom, 98, 99 bottom, 100, 103 bottom, 106, 107, 108, 110, 114, 115, 123 bottom, 128, 133, 134, 146, 147, 189, 191, 226-227, 229

Prepared and produced by Rutledge Books
For Follett Publishing Company.

ISBN: 0695-80471-5
Library of Congress Catalog Card Number: 74-77305
Printed in Italy by Mondadori, Verona.

This is a revised, updated version of the book that
originally was published under the title *Hockey*.

ACKNOWLEDGMENTS

The magnitude of this undertaking did not fully hit me until I went to the New York Public Library on 42nd Street and looked through the catalogue for "Hockey." No book had been written that combined behind-the-scenes looks, strategy, history and discussions on expansion. There was a biography or two, there was a how-to book or two, there was a collection of reminiscences. Furthermore, on checking facts as stated in the books, I discovered discrepancies.

I thus relied on other means of research, namely, talking to people, phoning people, writing letters, visiting, making appointments and reading old record books. Literally dozens of people willingly gave their encouragement and help. The first place I visited was the Hockey Hall of Fame in Toronto, where Lefty Reid, the Hall's secretary, gave me the run of the lovingly-put-together building and gave full access to the photographer.

Clarence Campbell, the president of the National Hockey League, spent many hours with me on the telephone during his business hours, feeding me valuable inside information as well as remembrances of hockey's past. The league's vice president, Don V. Ruck, personally contacted each club's public relations staff, told them of the project and asked them to give me their help.

The league also is fortunate in having as its publicity director and statistician the remarkably capable Ron Andrews. His office provided much of the statistics that appear in the book, in addition to many statistics of my own. For the first time a reader can find the goals-against averages for the Vezina Trophy winners each year as well as many more statistics never before tabled.

Since I live in New York, I called upon the Rangers for their help. In particular, Emile Francis, who was busy running the club from his office as general manager and then had to take on the added burden of coaching in midseason, squeezed in several hours to take me behind the scenes of a club. Bill Jennings, the Rangers' president, gave me valuable background information. Muzz Patrick, the Rangers' former general manager and coach, lent me valuable clippings and scrapbooks and spent time discussing Rangers of the past.

Each of the 12 clubs' public relations men were gracious and helpful, and I found all of them willing to please. Much individual time was given me by Conn Smythe, Frank Selke, Sr., Cooper Smeaton, Camil des Roches, Bruce A. Norris and Weston Adams, Sr.

I discovered that hockey people love to talk about their sport, including the reporters who cover it. To my colleagues, my thanks for their inside views; to my boss, Jim Roach, my appreciation for his permitting me to have the needed time; and to Rosalind, whom I remembered in the last line of the text, gratitude for keeping the children's noise level down for six months while I worked.

Gerald Eskenazi
Roslyn, New York

CONTENTS

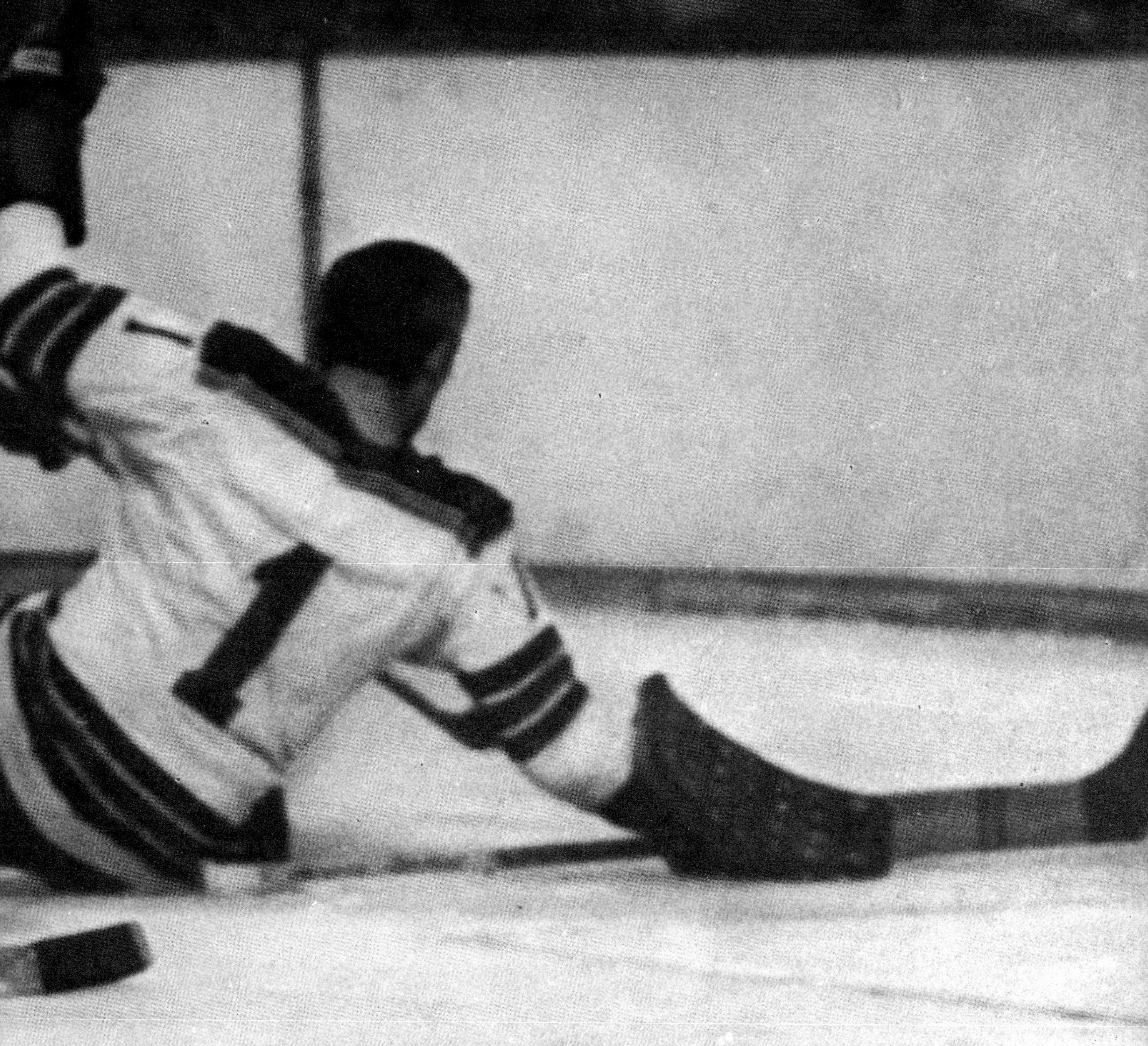

1

MAGAZINE SHIN GUARDS, TIN CAN PUCKS

how it all began

Not too many years ago hockey, for many Canadian boys, began on a Saturday night. Following a successful day of marketing, farmers left town, their wagons emptied of fruits and vegetables. Youngsters hurried after the wagons, waiting for the horses to leave a reminder on the road. Their object was to collect and hoard what they imaginatively nicknamed "horse apples." By morning, the apples had frozen solid and the local hockey team had a week's supply of perfect hockey pucks.

Through those long Canadian winter nights the young players would dream their dream—of golden days playing in the National Hockey League and making the Stanley Cup play-offs. Today that dream is real for more boys than ever. Even American youngsters, although they will never know the peculiar pleasure of chasing farmers' wagons, now hope to be selected by the NHL or World Hockey Association. For hockey has taken root in the American consciousness. Since the turn of the century it has been a way of life north of the border, but with the expansion of the NHL in 1967 and the coming of the WHA, the fervor now reaches across the United States, coast to coast, north to south.

The NHL plays to 90 percent capacity. In its debut the WHA did better than pro basketball in its first season. And in Montreal and Toronto, club owners love to tell stories of subscribers willing their season tickets to their heirs. The qualities that have elevated hockey into prominence in the United States —and made it Canada's national pastime, as well as a thriving sport in dozens of countries —are intimacy and immediacy. Explosive action takes place just yards away from the spectators.

The essence of the sport is a kind of controlled madness: white ice tinged with a bluish-gray hue, royal blue, crimson red, and candy-striped lines painted across the ice, team uniforms made unique by their handsome yet totally irregular design, the frozen black puck, the lashing sticks and, ultimately, the players themselves, doing a crazy ballet on skates, charging, pushing, rushing, in maneuvers executed beautifully, neatly, passionately. Add a crowd joined together not only by its excitement for the action but also by the confines of a closed arena, and the sport becomes a spectacle. Each game, each play, each second is pulsatingly different.

Because of the largely intuitive nature of its play, because of its color and dash and because of its basic simplicity, the game can be enjoyed at all levels. When the National Hockey League expanded, first doubling in size to 12 clubs then adding even more, there was little worry among the owners about acceptance by the additional United States cities. Even fans who have never seen a game can identify with the sport's basic thrust. And for those who know the game, there is the appreciation of plays executed by a skater rushing at 30 miles an hour or a stop by a goaltender of a hard rubber disk whipping goalward at 150 feet a second.

There are, too, those fans who enjoy hockey for its simple brute force and aren't happy unless they see a brawl. Hockey is the most fight-filled spectacle of any major team sport, leading to one theory of what the word "hockey" means. The Mohawk Indians, who played field hockey once, claim derivation from the Indian word "ho-ghee," which means "it hurts" (the losers were hit over the head). The French also claim credit for the word

PRECEDING PAGES: The 1927 Dartmouth College team practices on the boarded rink at Lake Placid. ABOVE: Greek hockey was played in 500 B.C. *RIGHT: A game of shinty in Scotland.*

LEFT: 1896 game at Yale, one of the first indoor rinks. BELOW: American pick-up game with a round puck. RIGHT: A 1900 game. Player number: unlimited; a goalie's pads: too little.

"hockey." They say it came from "hoquet," a crooked stick of the kind used by shepherds.

Wherever the word came from, it was waiting for someone to make it meaningful, which the Canadians did out of necessity. In the 1870s, Canadian winters were long and cold, much more so than today. The Industrial Revolution had taken the average man away from home for extended periods each day, expanding his human contacts, making him more sociable. In the spring, summer and fall there was baseball, football or lacrosse to sate his growing interest in sports. But winters were confining due to snow, cold and impassable roads. The population was ripe for a new sport, another activity that could keep it occupied.

Slowly but perceptibly, youngsters turned to the frozen ponds. It wasn't just to ice skate, however. Used to the challenge of team competition, they borrowed some of the rules of field hockey and adapted that sport to the ice. The first game with rules may have been played in December 1879, when two teams of students from McGill University in Montreal took to the ice, 30 on a side. Kingston and Halifax residents like to think that their cities had this honor, but it is known for a fact that McGill students actually played a rule-structured game.

Those first tentative steps were something special, although today's players probably wouldn't venture onto the ice under the old conditions. The scenes were wildly humorous. There were no covered rinks, no high boards. A border of wood, a foot high at best, surrounded the playing surface—mainly to keep the pucks from getting lost in snow banks. For want of a better name, the places where ice hockey games were staged were called "rinks." The word "rink" actually is Scottish and means a "course." Over the years it came

to refer specifically to a place where curling competition was staged. Since curling was played on ice, in a confined area, the British-oriented Canadians started to call ice hockey sites rinks, and the name has remained.

On the frozen rinks in the 1880s there were no goalies' cages. What served as a goal were two poles bored into the ice. The players shot between the poles. The pucks? Whatever was handy—a tin can perhaps, or a pine knot.

The equipment was borrowed from other sports. At first the goalies didn't wear protective padding. They didn't have to, for the players hadn't mastered the art of shooting a puck high. Every shot skittered across the ice. But when the players learned how to lift the disk with a backhander, the goalies were forced to go to cricket teams and borrow wicketkeepers' leg pads. As the shots flew higher, they had to find a baseball team and borrow the catchers' chest protectors.

Skates barely deserved the name. Players turned up for games in their street shoes, then clamped on blades (remember roller skating in the street?). When the game was over, they removed the blades and walked home in these same shoes. Their socks were soaked, of course, and their feet sloshed around inside wet, scraped, unrecognizable shoes.

Shoes were often completely ruined, for the clamps dug into the leather just above the sole and were screwed tight. Other skates were merely placed under the shoe and strapped on, but these were not nearly as secure. The blades were long and flat, fine for someone skating straight ahead, but treacherous for a hockey player having to take a sharp, quick turn or make a sudden stop.

If hockey had been a summer sport such as baseball, the boys could have played during the week. If it had been a fall sport, like football, they could have played when the days were longer. But school days were lengthened by tedious round trips on foot and short winter days. The choice then was either to get up before dawn or to play on the weekend. So the players took their equipment with them, joined the Sunday afternoon skaters and disrupted quiet weekend skating forever. Editorials in the papers spoke of "ruffians" who knocked a puck around on the ice, endangering the lives of men and women who happened to be there at the same time a game sprung up.

The players, unorganized and flexible in their rules, protected themselves in the same spirit. Those who couldn't afford good equipment used whatever was handy. For 25 cents in Eaton's catalogue they could buy a rock elm stick. The catalogue, sheared in two, became shin guards, held in place by rubber strips cut from a tire's inner tube. Shoulders were protected by Maclean's magazines.

Their sticks were coarse, too, but far more serviceable. Early pick-up teams used field hockey sticks that looked almost like shillelaghs, but by the time collegians were playing in the late 1880s, ice hockey sticks were being manufactured in Montreal. They were usually made in one piece, out of elm. To get the curve for the blade, the sticks were steamed and bent, a process which was used for half a century. It wasn't until the 1940s that sticks were made in two pieces. The first ice hockey sticks leaned heavily on field hockey tradition and were rounded where the blade met the stick. Still, most youngsters chose to make their own, for hockey sticks *did* grow on trees.

By the 1890s, hockey already vied with lacrosse in Canada as the national game. But because it was still being formed, with hit-and-miss practically the rule, it had quite a way to go. Slowly more changes were brought about. One change was made that, today, seems ridiculously obvious. Since the two poles ground into the ice served as goalposts, many spectators as well as the goal judge, if he stood at a bad angle, could not tell whether a goal was in fact scored. The deliberate hit-

Two games exhibit hockey's progression. Game at top is played with low boards, pick-up goalie, while below, spectators enjoy tiered seats.

and-miss decisions didn't help either. There were other problems. The home team had the option of changing referees as it wished. In one game, the home club changed referees eight times until it got an official who pleased the players.

Something had to be done. A genius named Francis Nelson, strolling along the docks one day, spied a pile of fishermen's nets. And in one of those inspired moments that change history, he decided to string such a net between two goalposts. Now there was no question of goal or no goal. It was either in the net —or it wasn't.

Suddenly, things began happening in hockey. In 1911, the sport was given a big boost by its principal rival, lacrosse. A riot at a lacrosse match in Toronto resulted in serious injury to many spectators. Lacrosse had been first in popularity, but in the Toronto match thousands of fans were involved in a frightening display of temper that sent many to the hospital. The public soured on the sport and turned its attention to hockey.

At the start of the century, businessmen began investing in closed rinks, moving the sport indoors. The continued acceptance was accelerated by more significant rule changes. Fred C. Waghorne, the acknowledged Grand Old Man of Referees, introduced several startling innovations. Referees at that time blew a steel whistle to signal a play stoppage. But it was cold outside in the middle of winter, and just as cold in unheated arenas. The whistle would often stick to a referee's lips, and when he tried to pry it loose, a week's application of Vaseline couldn't repair the damage.

Waghorne, goes the story, was passing a restaurant in Kitchener one day when a waitress rattled a cowbell to call in the diners for lunch. Waghorne borrowed the bell and used it in a game that night. It worked—sufficiently well to become standard equipment. In later years, when arenas became heated and Canadian winters grew warmer and plastic whistles were invented, the bell was discarded.

Waghorne is also credited with inventing

Canadian clamp-type skate, circa 1888

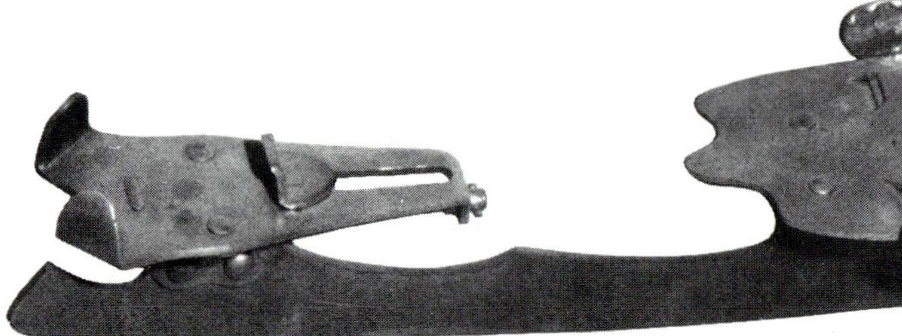

Improved clamp-type skate made in 1896

C.C.M. laminated model "Automobile F," 1905

United States "Torpedo" skates, made in 1895

An 1894 screw-on, with Canadian metal trim

1865 English, with wood top, metal trimming

Earliest type of ice skate was the 1860 Dutch

English or Dutch, 1850–1860, with heavy straps

One of the first boots, made by C.C.M., 1905

today's face-off. For years, the face-off was a painful experience for the referee, filled with danger, exasperating for the fans. The referee first placed the puck on the ice. He then leaned over the centers' sticks, grabbed one blade in each hand and placed them against the puck. He was then supposed to skate quickly out of the way, not unlike a man who has just connected a bomb fuse, and shout "Play!"

In theory, it worked well. But under heated game conditions the centers never waited for the referee to skate backward. As soon as their sticks touched the disk and one player felt the other's stick applying the slightest pressure, the fuse was triggered and they went for the puck. The referee wound up with scraped, badly bruised shins. A new face-off had to be ordered and the whole process would begin again.

Necessity, in this case, too, was to become the mother of invention. Waghorne had a particularly bad game one day in Paris, Ontario. All through the game, the fans for each team screamed for their center to beat the other man to the draw, and the centers obliged, cutting Waghorne's legs unmercifully. Waghorne was disgusted. He told the opposing centers to put their sticks on the ice 18 inches apart. Then he threw the puck between them, like a zoo keeper throwing a piece of meat to two lions, and let them do what they wanted.

Generally, there were nine men on a side. A goal judge stationed himself behind the poles. Depending on whose side his sympathies were with, and depending on the "crowd mood," he would or would not signal a goal, the actual shot sometimes totally irrelevant to the call.

A goal judge had to be ubiquitous when the action moved toward his end. His only protection was the goalie and his own reflexes. He stood a few feet behind the poles where he then had to avoid blinking, avoid getting hit by a stick or puck, avoid getting ground into the ice when the action was behind the goal. He signaled a goal by waving a white handkerchief which he kept in his shirt pocket. If he sensed a hostile crowd, the handkerchief remained tucked away. But cheating, for some reason, never became a major factor in those early contests.

The hit-and-miss nature of the game, coupled with its expanding popularity, cried out for formal action and finally, in 1885 in Montreal, a group of hockey lovers sat down to a constructive session. First, they named themselves the Amateur Hockey Association of Canada. Then, instead of the nine men that McGill's students had eventually written into the rules, they lowered the number on a side to seven.

That same year the first organized league, four teams in number, was formed in Kingston. It included Queen's University, Royal Military College, the Kingstons and the Athletics. The first championship game was won by the University as it defeated the Athletics, 3-1. The game was marked by the fact that each time a puck was shot on goal, play had to be stopped while the goalie located and replaced his skates. Goalie's skates then were those destructive clamp skates, and everytime the blade blocked a shot, it would fly away, tearing the sole of the goalie's shoe.

Military men learned the game and as their assignments shifted and they moved to the west, the north and the provinces, the game traveled with them. It caught on everywhere. In cities where there was no rink or even a frozen pond, the boys skated on streets. Oldtimers remember how pedestrians suddenly found themselves surrounded by small cyclones on skates, who would then test their skill by shooting the puck between the legs of passers-by.

The action on the ice was even more frenetic. Since many teams had to use public parks, they often had a bandstand or a flagpole at center ice, and the structures in the middle of the rink became the most hazardous feature of the game.

Spectators sat on snow banks, fortified with liquor. Toward the end of a game, after skates and sticks had churned the ice to mush, the fans would get soaked whenever a stick

RIGHT: A progression of sticks, including from the right: the oldest, pre-1850 (#1); Cyclone Taylor's famous curved stick (#6); 1930 stick (#7). All but last are 3½- to 4-feet long.

LEFT: See pg. 34. CENTER: Goalie's stick used continuously by Percy LeSueur of Smiths Falls and Ottawa, in all his games from 1904–1909. RIGHT: Black Hawk goalie gloves of 1920's.

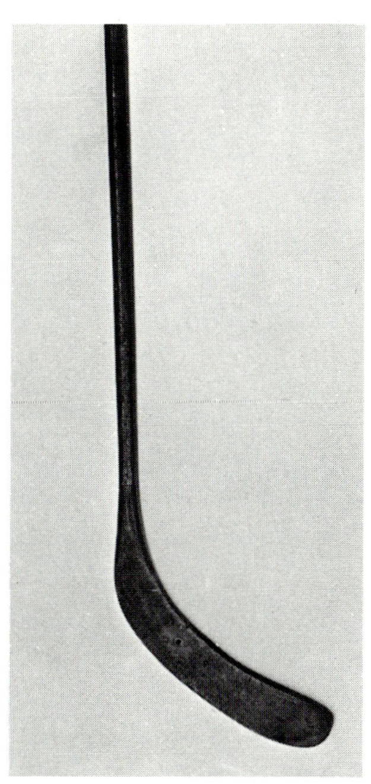

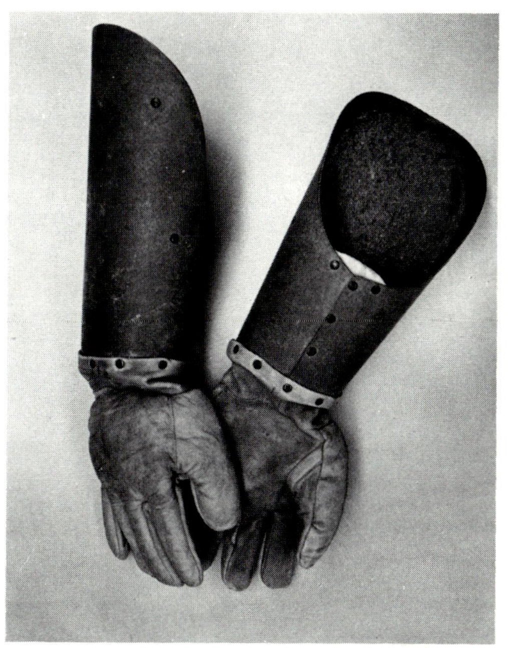

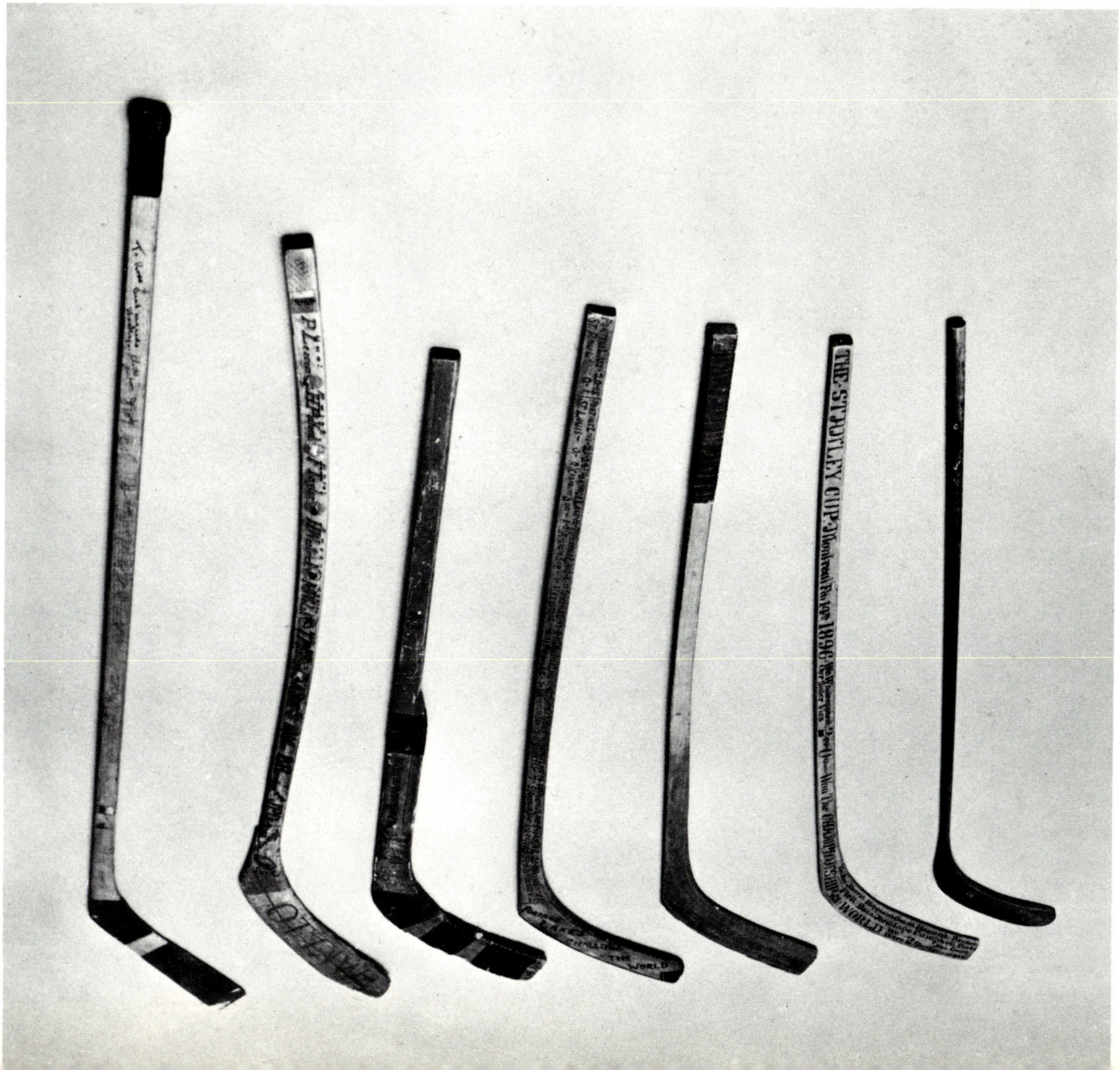

lashed at a puck that rested on one of the many soft spots. There was a special rapport between fan and player (common sense was all that separated them) and while plays were underway, spectators growled instructions.

The fans, for all their intimidating comments, gave the game one of its great traditions—the hat trick. Today, a player scores "the hat trick" if he gets three goals in one game and, in fact, a fan or two will invariably toss a hat onto the ice. But once upon a time, when a player got three goals, the fans would pass around the hat and proudly present the player with a monetary reward.

The term had its roots in cricket. If a bowler knocked down three wickets on three tosses, it was considered such an outstanding feat that his club presented him with a hat. The expression originally meant three consecutive goals scored by one skater, with no other goals in between.

The seventh player (or "extra" man by today's standards) was a rover. He would trail plays goalward, picking up what the trade now calls "garbage goals," taking unglamorous, close-in shots after most of the work had already been done. The defense was not aligned in its side-by-side formation as it is today. Rather one defenseman was called the point man, and the other defender was the cover point—he stationed himself in front of the point man. The theory was that if the attackers got past one defenseman another would be there to back him up. This was fine for that time, when forward passing wasn't legal and the defensemen didn't have to worry about the man who didn't have the puck.

Waghorne, who claimed he refereed more than 2,400 hockey games—the equivalent of calling a full present-day season's schedule for 30 years—also solved the problem of the split puck. It is one of the questions buffs like to bring up when they try to stump one another. If a man shoots the puck and it breaks (pucks fell apart easily 70 years ago) but half the puck goes in the cage, is it a goal? This problem presented itself in a game Waghorne worked, and after much deliberation he ruled "no goal."

His logic was unassailable. According to the rules, a goal was scored if any part of the puck was over the goal line. In this case a part of the puck clearly was in. However, a "puck," by official definition, had certain dimensions. Since the slab of rubber in the goal did not meet the specifications of what a puck was supposed to be, Waghorne reasoned there could be no goal, since the puck was no longer a puck.

When hockey moved indoors, many problems were solved, but many new ones were created. The lighting in many rinks was by oil lamp. Dick Irvin, an outstanding player who also coached successfully in the NHL, remembered his first impression of an indoor arena as one of lamps behind the goals throwing grotesque, dancing shadows on the ice. He was surprised that hockey was even attempted

LEFT: Harvard goaltender of 1919. Gloves were long and flimsy. Nets had yet to be widely used on goals. ABOVE: Hat trick customs, in one form or another, have continued.

under such conditions. Worse, there were low-hanging rafters, some draped with bunting. Shots that were deflected high vanished, never to be seen again. Some players mastered the art of shooting the puck high, where it temporarily disappeared, only to fall suddenly in front of the goal where a teammate was waiting.

In those cold, damp, dark arenas, where spectators sat bundled up, where long shadows crisscrossed the ice, the first professional Canadian barnstorming teams made their appearance. These first teams set patterns of play that were to last for many years, even though the reasons for their style had long disappeared. The defensemen, for example, never scooped the puck, pitchfork fashion, out of their own end. The reason: the puck might get lost in the rafters.

The game of hockey was crystallizing and it now had arenas where it could be showcased. In two decades a way of life had evolved. The public, and the sport, were ready for professional hockey.

Face-offs have changed remarkably between 1924 (above) and today (facing). Example: today's ubiquitous referees wear skates that allow them to move in on the action. RIGHT: Bells that replaced whistles in the early days of Canadian ice hockey. Steel whistles stuck to the referee's lips in cold arenas. It wasn't until heated rinks and plastic that whistles were revived.

NORTHLAND
VICTORIAVILLE

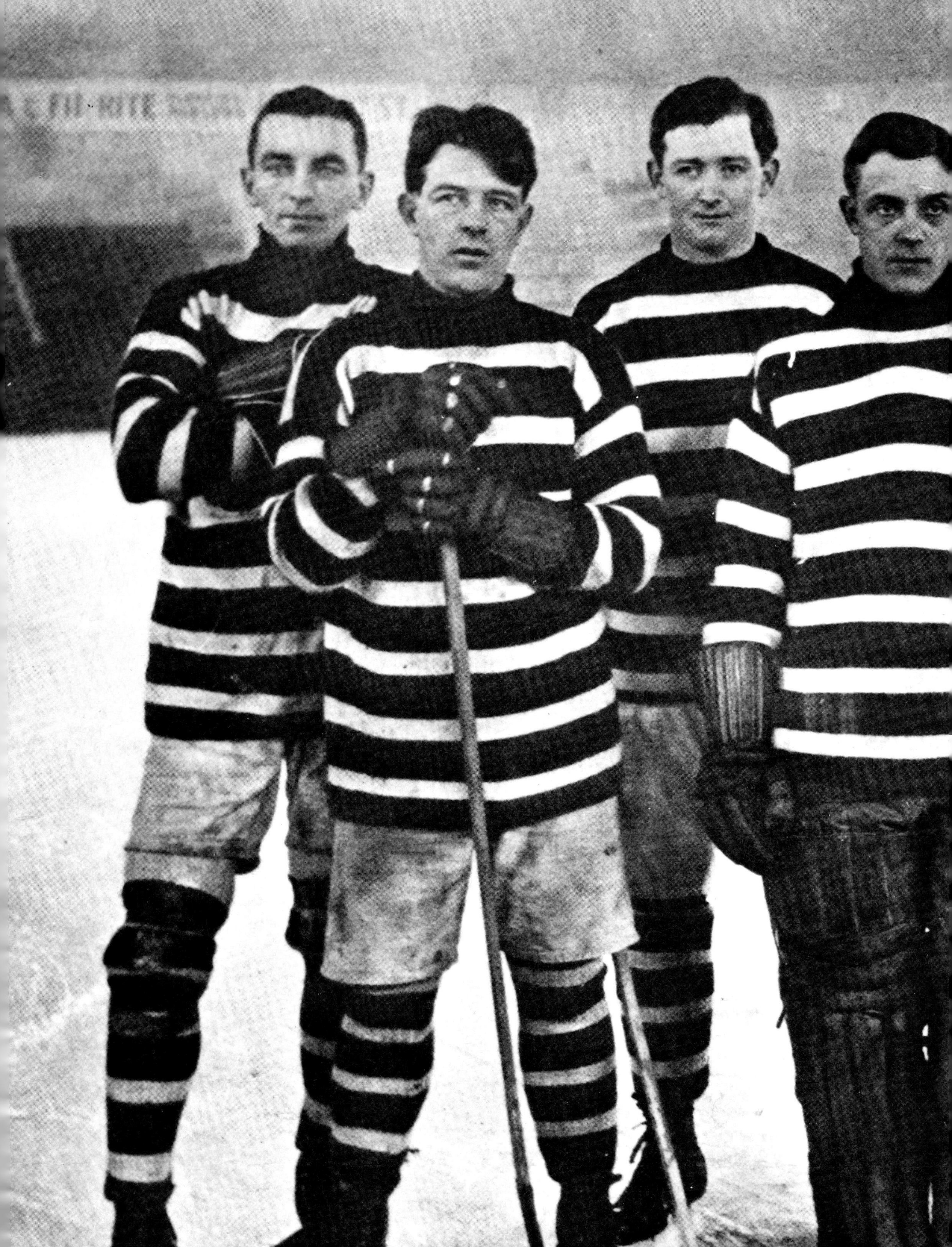
FIT-RITE

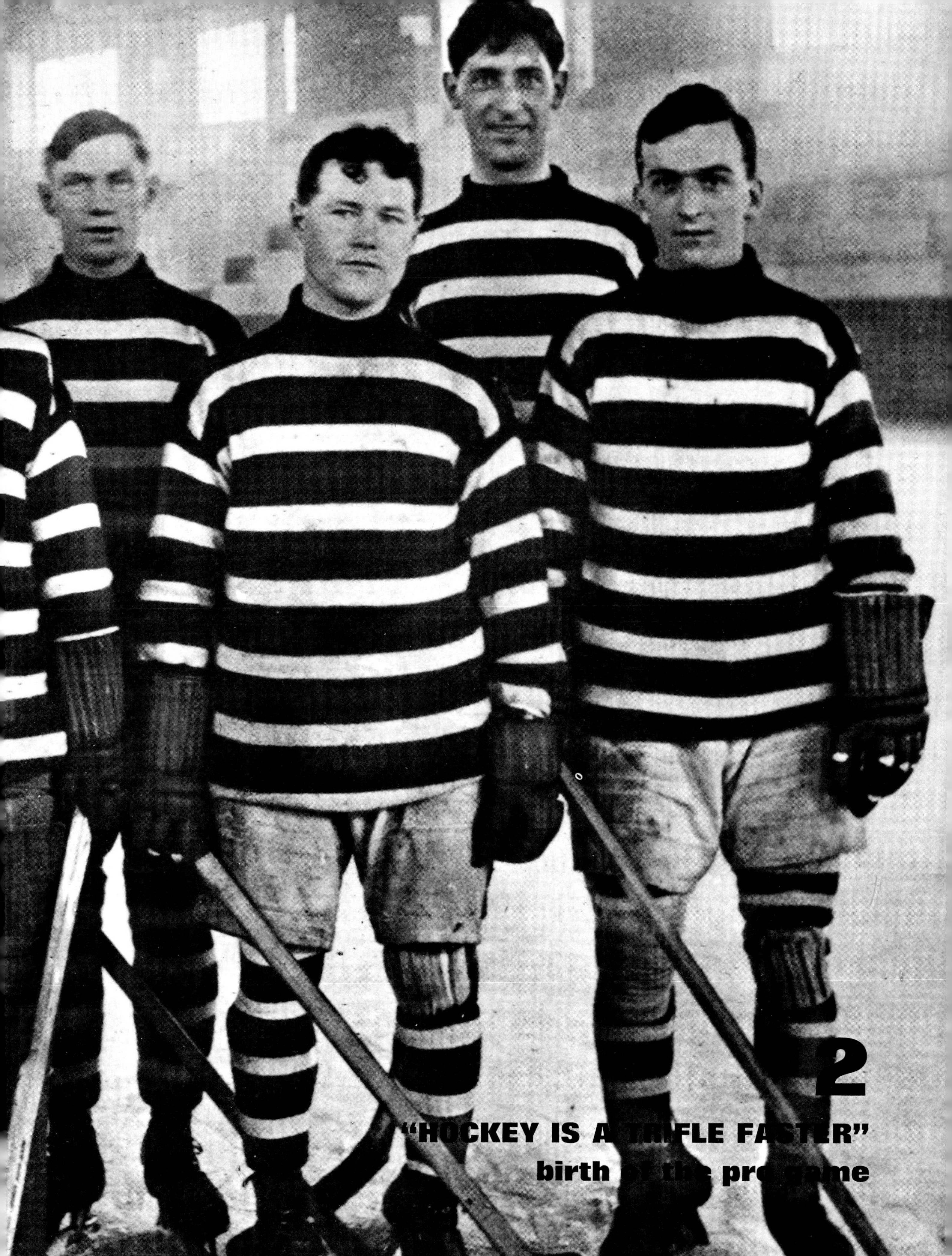

2

"HOCKEY IS A TRIFLE FASTER"

birth of the pro game

The first hockey leagues of any kind in Canada were amateur, not professional, and were born in the 1890s. In 1892, Canadian Governor-General Frederick Arthur, Lord Stanley of Preston, made a gesture that united all of hockey and resulted in one of the most glamorous events in the world of sports. Lord Stanley donated a cup which was to go each year to the amateur champion of Canada. It cost him ten pounds sterling ($48.67). In 1893, Stanley Cup competition began and, as the years went by, became almost mythically symbolic of the game of hockey.

For Canadians, the emotions surrounding Stanley Cup play far transcend the feelings that Americans have for the World Series. Ironically, Lord Stanley never saw a Stanley Cup game. Even the spirit he intended the Cup to give the sport backfired. He wanted it to go to the best amateur team, but competition for the Cup became so keen, the prestige accorded the holders of the Cup so great, that teams gradually relaxed their amateur standards and bought and paid the best players available.

By far the largest and most influential hockey league in Canada in the 1890s was the Amateur Hockey Association, a five-team league made up of the Victorias, the Montreal AAA, Ottawa, Quebec and the Shamrocks of Toronto. In 1899 dissension plagued the league, and out popped another league. There had been strong animosity between some of the AHA's executives and the Capitals, a club that wanted to be admitted into the league. When, due to a split decision, the Capitals failed to become members, Quebec, Victoria and Ottawa withdrew.

With the Capitals, they formed the Canadian Amateur Hockey League. The Shamrocks then joined the new league and the AHA was dissolved. The new CAHL soon found itself in the position of its predecessor (Montreal was the only AHA team not a member of the new league): that of being a closed corporation, permitting no new teams to join and break the stranglehold the CAHL held on Canadian hockey.

While Canadian hockey was in ferment, something major was happening below the border—acknowledged professionalism. The game had been popular for years in company towns, especially in mining and smelting areas. In 1903, a dentist named J. L. Gibson culled a team of Canadian imports, brought it to Houghton, a copper town (population 3,500) in Michigan's upper peninsula and named the team Portage Lakes. Thus hockey's first professional team was born in the United States. Americans were happy to pay to see a team they called their own, made up primarily of Canadians. More than 70 years later, the custom remains.

Dr. Gibson and his men barnstormed through other company towns, painlessly taking the local populace's money. His club was so good, and beat the other towns so badly, that they in turn began importing Canadians. As a result, the International Pro Hockey League was organized in 1904. Despite new competition from Canadian-dominated teams, Portage Lakes remained the best. In 26 league games, it scored 237 goals and gave up 48 while winning 24 games and losing only two.

The specter of American dollars luring Canadian boys away from what they considered simon-pure hockey visibly shook Canadian amateur teams. Playing for money was something that the owners just couldn't believe a player would do, although the morality at is-

PRECEDING PAGES: 1912 Victoria Senators at Willow Arena in Victoria. Second from right is Lester Patrick, point man of seven-man team. ABOVE: 1898 Montreal Victorias, Cup champs.

The Montreal AAA, Eastern Champions of 1889. Official positions were left and right wings, point, spare, center, goalkeeper, cover point and rover. Team wears official uniform.

sue was a bit one-sided, since the owners did considerably better than break even. It just seemed there was something indecent about receiving a salary to play a game. After all, hadn't Joseph Seagram, founder of the great whiskey empire, caused a scandal in 1893 when, in a joyous moment after his favorite team won an important game, he gave gold pieces to each of the players?

A group in Sault Ste. Marie, Ontario, however, saw nothing immoral about playing for pay, so the "Soos," as they were known, became the first Canadian team to acknowledge itself professional and join the new pro league. More great Canadian players drifted into professionalism, and Doc Gibson lured two now legendary names into his team—Fred (Cyclone) Taylor and Hod Stuart. These men, now enshrined in hockey's Hall of Fame, received up to $500 a game, an unbelievable sum then and highly desirable even now. Taylor and Stuart would play a game for the pros in the States, then skip back to Canada. Finally, they became regulars. Stuart's life ended within three years, in a dive off a pier. His name had meant much to other Canadian amateurs while he was alive, though, and his and Taylor's defection sent many hockey players searching for money.

A typical case was that of 18-year-old

Edouard Charles (Newsy) Lalonde. Lalonde, who may have been the greatest athlete the French-Canadian community ever produced, had been known as an outstanding lacrosse player (good enough to be voted, in a 1950 poll, as Canada's lacrosse player of the half century), but with rumors of "play-for-pay" being passed around, he struck out for more rewarding territories. When his friends in Ontario heard that Newsy was going to play for Sault Ste. Marie, they panicked. They told him that a professional hockey player's life was too rough for a teen-ager, that his growth as a player would be stunted by opposing sticks and undemocratic elbows. But Lalonde decided to go.

Riding all night and all day by train coach, he arrived in Sault Ste. Marie a half hour before his new club's game with Pittsburgh. Out of money (he hadn't eaten since breakfast), he hitchhiked to the rink. That night he scored two goals, both on defensemen's passes that hit him on the seat of the pants and ricocheted in front of the goal. Each time he spun around and poked the puck into the net. Lalonde had become a pro, and under circumstances that would be repeated many, many times in the future by other young, courageous hopefuls.

Newsy Lalonde was part of a breed of colorful bad guys whose names sound like a roster of Wild West outlaws—Sprague Cleghorn, Minnie McGiffin, Spunk Sparrow, Billy Coutu. Art Ross, whose name seemed tame enough but who nevertheless could be placed high on hockey's list of bad guys, was another one whose services were in demand in the United States. A $50-a-month bank clerk, he received as much as $1,000 a game to jump to a strange city for a one-night stand. His services went to the highest bidder. When the townspeople heard he would play for their team, they rushed to put down bets on the game and the gambling continued until the final whistle.

Ross, a hard-skating, explosive hockey player, seemed to create an urge to gamble. It was quite usual for fans at an Art Ross game to bet $40,000 among themselves while play was in progress. Years later, when the National Hockey League took in United States teams, Ross came out of retirement to build the Boston Bruins. He was so highly thought of that in 1947 the league accepted a trophy carrying his name to go each season to the league's leading scorer.

This collection of top names had the direct result of bringing about another major change in hockey. On the day after Christmas in 1904, Pittsburgh was scheduled to play at Sault Ste. Marie. But a Soo player never recovered from a holiday celebration and failed to show up. Normally, it would have been Sault Ste. Marie's bad luck to play with only six men, for teams didn't carry substitutes (another player meant another mouth to feed). Pittsburgh, though, had only six men due to an injury and so the squads agreed to play with only six to a side. The game was a success. Other owners naturally discovered that six-man hockey was a good game and so, to save money, discarded seven-man hockey forever.

But the pro league's success was to bring its downfall. Great players expected great salaries, and although the rinks were filled, capacity was limited. After 1907, the first professional hockey league in North America disbanded, a victim of expenses.

It didn't take long, though, for Canada to establish its first pro league and in 1908 the Ontario Professional Hockey League was formed. Two years later the National Hockey Association began, bringing with it a club called the Montreal Canadiens. They still are around, of course, and are the oldest professional hockey club. Others in the NHA were Renfrew, Haileybury, Cobalt and the Wanderers.

The Wanderers had a gentleman player named Lester Patrick whose father, Joseph, was a lumberman from Drummondville, wealthy enough to have retired at age 50. Lester's brother, Frank, was a gambler of sorts. Together, the three Patricks became famous for doing the unusual and the exciting. It came as no surprise, then, when in 1911 Frank brought up a preposterous idea with his brother and father. The Canadian Pacific coast, he stated, would like hockey. For some time, Frank told them, he had been thinking not only of bringing hockey to the west but of building artificial ice rinks and operating pro hockey teams. There were only eight artificial ice rinks in the world in 1911, and not one in Canada.

The Patricks reverted to an old family custom. Whenever a major decision had to be made, the three voted on it. Lester said no: the idea was unsound. Frank voted yes. Joseph broke the tie and voted with gambler Frank. So, late that year, the three went to Victoria, British Columbia, on a fact-finding mission. The population of Victoria was only 25,000, but a building boom was at its height. A Victoria newspaperman described it this way: "Men bought property during a drunken spree on Saturday night and sold it for a huge profit on Monday morning." But only one man in the speculative climate that engulfed Victoria was interested in joining with the Patricks and he bought just $500 worth of stock. The Patricks discovered to their sorrow that, except for a few expatriate easterners, no one on the coast had ever heard of ice hockey.

Their minds were made up, though. They decided that if they couldn't get anyone to take a chance with them, they would build hockey teams and arenas themselves and get back their investment at the gate. They went ahead and made plans for a 10,500-seat arena in Vancouver that was to be the largest indoor stadium in the world, and drew up other plans for a 3,500-seat arena in Victoria. They also formed the Pacific Coast Hockey Association with teams in Victoria, Vancouver and New Westminster (New Westminster was to play its "home" games at Vancouver, since the budget didn't allow for a third arena).

One problem remained—a remarkable parallel to the NHL-WHA wars 60 years later: where to get the players. The NHA had control of virtually everyone. The Patricks, though, learned quickly enough that most contracts of NHA players were valid for only one year and that many were mere handshakes. Good players often "made the rounds," playing for the highest bidder on "amateur" and professional teams. Armed with this knowledge, and cash, the brothers went searching with one guiding thought: they would find the best players in Canada and offer them double their present salaries. On January 2, 1912, their raiding completed, the Patricks opened the Pacific Coast Hockey Association with the first Canadian game ever played on artificial ice. A full house of 3,500 at Victoria saw New Westminster win, 8-3.

For many newspapermen, it was their first look at hockey. "With all due deference to cricket," wrote one, "we think hockey is a trifle faster."

Another reporter, commenting on New Westminster's goalie, Hughie Lehman, stated, "Lehman seems of ordinary size. Yet he fills the whole space whenever the puck comes his way. Wonderful power of physical expansion, that. Fine at a banquet."

Three nights later, Vancouver's massive rink opened before 10,000 fans. New Westminster won again, 8-3. The team without a rink was off to a good start.

Although Joseph Patrick left the job of running a hockey league to Frank and Lester and retired again, it was the beginning of an extraordinary decade, made even more unusual by the Patrick boys' consistent innovations. Much of the face of hockey we see today began with them. Before attempting any so-called far-reaching changes, they began with a seemingly simple one. The first players to take to the ice in the PCHA wore numbers. Even baseball and football players in Canada had not worn numbers before 1912. Fans at hockey games, and at other events, had been given programs that merely told them the players' positions.

Before too many games were played, the league had its first scandal, or at least what

The Portage Lakes team of Houghton, Michigan, champions of the International League. Portage Lakes was the first pro team. Most famous player was Fred W. "Cyclone" Taylor.

Trainer
D. Regan.
Goal
Fred W. Taylor.
Cover Point
CHAMPION
"Barney" Holden
Point
Goldy Cochrane
Rover
C. Bruce Stuart
Capt. Centre
Jack Descarie
'06
'07

BELOW: Hockey immortals Newsy Lalonde and Frank Patrick. Patrick was responsible for many of modern hockey's innovations. RIGHT: The 1918 Vancouver team, PCL champs. Among the notables are Jack Adams, fourth from left, Lester Patrick, next, goalie Hugh Lehman and Eddie Oatman, farthest right.

newspaper readers thought was a scandal. Because the games were close, as they usually are in hockey, some reporters called the Patricks' league a place where "syndicate" hockey was played. In answer, the brothers took out ads in local newspapers, offering $1,000 to any person who could substantiate a claim that a game was fixed. No one took them up on the offer, and the rumors quickly died.

During that first season, the Patricks envisioned still greater horizons. They wanted a Canadian version of the World Series and asked the NHA to send its eastern champions out west. But the rival league, still smarting over player raids—Lalonde and Cyclone Taylor were only two of the high-caliber players stolen—refused. Eventually the NHA and the Patricks got together, each agreeing not to raid the other's league.

The Pacific Coast league became a freewheeling loop, largely the embodiment of the men who headed it. The Patricks retained seven-man hockey, but in virtually every other aspect of the game they went forward. They permitted far greater mobility to make a save, thus extricating the already beleaguered goaltender from the ludicrous position of having to stop a small, black disk, shot at 80 miles an hour, from entering the far low corner of his net without taking his feet from the ice. PCHA goalies, now able to leap, dive, tumble or split, felt a new sense of freedom. As a result, they devised other new methods to win. A favorite tactic was to work the net loose, unscrewing the anchor that planted it into the ice. By the final period it was untethered and if the other team threatened, a flick of the elbow would send the net crashing down.

Progressive as they were, the Patricks never got around to removing the goal judge from the ice. The results were often humorous. One of those judges, John V. Johnson of Victoria, liked to tell the story of a game in which a fan directly behind him yelled over

and over again, "You're blind, Johnson." Johnson waited for his chance, and when at long last a shot came booming directly toward him at the perfect angle, he ducked. As the puck smashed into the fan, Johnson turned around and shouted, "Who's blind now?" The National Hockey League, after it was formed, finally decided to protect the goal judge from players' sticks and fans' abuse by placing him in a cage, from which he pressed a button that triggered a red light to signal a goal.

Frank and Lester always were on the lookout for ways to speed up the game and improve competition. During the Victoria-Quebec series in 1913 (ostensibly, it was for the Stanley Cup, but after Quebec lost, the NHA refused to part with it), 15 whistles were blown in the first five minutes for offside infractions. In 1913, a player was deemed offside if he was simply ahead of the puck carrier when he received a pass. To decrease the number of whistle stoppages, the Patricks painted two blue lines onto the ice, dividing the playing area into three equal parts with forward passing allowed in the center zone. The zones were introduced at Victoria in the first game of the 1913-1914 season and opened up the sport so much that soon forward passing was allowed in the defending zone and finally in the attacking zone.

The concept of intra-league play-offs also was a Patrick idea. Why, they reasoned, shouldn't a club that had a late start, perhaps through injuries or just poor play, have another chance at a title? After the end of regular-season play they permitted the second-best team to play off with the top club for a post-season championship.

Another PCHA innovation was the assist. Previously players never got credit for assists in point-keeping records. Now the two men who last handled the puck before the goal scorer were given one point each, provided no opponent had handled the puck in the interim.

None of these new ideas—numbering of players, freedom for goalies, blue lines, playoffs, assists—were adopted by the NHA, most likely because acceptance of such rule changes would have been tacit recognition by the NHA of the upstart league.

By 1915, the Patricks were ready to make still another daring move—the incorporation of a team from the United States. They got their opportunity that year when New Westminster dropped out and a club from Portland, Oregon, dropped in. The next year Seattle became part of the league and open warfare with the NHA broke out again, since players were needed from the east to stock the new team. It even was rumored that Cyclone Taylor would be transferred from the Pacific Coast Hockey Association to Ottawa of the NHA by the Department of Immigration. Frank reasoned that the leagues should live in harmony and asked the NHA to make a stock of its players available for a draft by the new Seattle club. The NHA replied, fine, if the Pacific Coast league would make its players available for drafting by the eastern league. That ended hockey's first draft.

While the Patricks' league was churning up excitement, the National Hockey Association was not exactly dormant. But the NHA's great turmoil was intra-league, filled with jockeying for position and behind-the-back maneuvering. The years following the NHA's formation in 1910 saw clubs dropping in and out of the league, names being changed, managements being shifted. The makeup of the league in its second year was Quebec, Ottawa, Wanderers, Canadiens (the Shamrocks resigned). Then Toronto and the Tecumsehs were added. In the 1914-1915 season the Tecumsehs renamed themselves the Ontarios.

That same season, Art Ross was suspended by the league for campaigning for players' rights, arguing that the league had no right to establish a maximum aggregate salary for a 12-team club ($35,000 a year). The owners, of course, wanted nothing to do with players' unions and acted swiftly at the first sign of dissension.

When owners got together on what was best for each of them financially, they often argued over tangential items. Toronto once complained to the league that in some cities team members were stoned by the fans. Officials worried because their dressing rooms were not out of bounds. A player or coach with a grievance could barge into a referee's room

FAR LEFT: Frank Calder, the National Hockey League's first president. LEFT: Cyclone Taylor, who sold his services to the highest bidder, sometimes for as much as $500 a game.

and knock him around. It was commonplace to see referees with police escorts.

The Ontario club changed its name to the Shamrocks for the start of the 1915-1916 season, and one Eddie Livingstone took over the ownership of the club. Livingstone also owned the Toronto team, a combination which was to work against him. As it was, he was disliked by many of the other owners.

World War I depleted professional hockey's ranks in Canada and at least two dozen NHA stars enlisted in the army. But the NHA found a way to combat the losses. The 228th Battalion, also known as the Northern Fusiliers, was attracting many players from the Toronto area. It seemed logical, then, that a club representing the 228th should join the NHA. To Americans, this must appear incredible. It is like the Great Lakes Naval Training Station football team of World War II years joining the National Football League. But the 228th applied to the NHA and in September 1916 was given a franchise. Gordon Keats, a fine player already under contract with Eddie Livingstone's Toronto team, enlisted with the Fusiliers and asked to play hockey with them.

Livingstone, angry since that very week his Shamrocks were forced to drop from the NHA (the league didn't want one man owning two clubs), and since Toronto had already been depleted by Patrick raids, accused the army of stealing Keats. He appealed to Major Frank Robinson, the NHA's president and an army man himself. The major sided with Livingstone and ruled that Keats, despite being in the army, should return to Toronto.

To confuse things in the league further, another move for a players' union was made, led by Cy Denneny, Toronto's star. Denneny had moved to Ottawa and wanted to play with the Ottawa Senators. He refused to report to Toronto. Ottawa made a variety of offers to Toronto for Denneny's services—money, players and combinations of both—but Livingstone refused. He suspended Denneny.

Two months after the season began, Denneny still was under suspension. The players let the owners know how they felt about that. They asked for a rule that would allow them to switch teams for a fixed transfer fee in the event that they changed homes. Transportation was not nearly as flexible as it is today, and a player who did not have his family with him might not see it for a season. But the rumor of unionism, not sympathy with travel conditions, made Livingstone react quickly. At the end of January 1917, he sold Denneny to Ottawa for Sam Herbert, a goalie, and $750—a record deal at the time.

Tempers of club owners were boiling and spilled over finally when several scandals erupted, scandals that brought into their maelstrom the army, the league and even the question of ethics. It was reported that Eddie Oatman of the 228th, tenth in the league in scoring, had not enlisted in the army at all but had merely been recruited and hired by the 228th to play hockey. Oatman claimed he had enlisted and passed his medical. He also said, innocently, that he was receiving $1,200 to play for the army and had a contract.

Actually, Oatman had joined the 228th from Portland of the Pacific league and had been recruited just as though the army was in the hockey business. For all Oatman's protestations about being a legitimate soldier, he was dismissed quietly from the service owing to "special circumstances" when the battalion arrived in St. John, New Brunswick, the last stop before it was shipped off to Europe.

Gordon Meeking was another player suddenly discharged when the 228th reached St. John. He had claimed he was promised a commission to play hockey. During the battalion's fervent recruiting he wore an officer's uniform, but as soon as the battalion arrived at St. John, Officer Meeking was unceremoniously told to put on a private's uniform. He was finally discharged for, of all things, being medically unfit. But Meeking did not go back to his home in Toronto, even to play

The 1925 New York Americans. Madison Square president Tex Rickard (with cane) sits in the middle, Colonel Hammond to his left. Emile Bouchard sits front, third from the right.

hockey. He stayed in Montreal, explaining sheepishly that he could not face all those friends and relatives who had given him a grand send-off to fight in Germany.

When the 228th left for overseas, it dropped out of the league. It had played half a season, won six out of ten games and averaged seven goals a game—highest in the league. Because league standings were thrown into turmoil by the departure of the Fusiliers, it was decided that the 1916-1917 season would be split into halves—the leader of the first half season would play the leader of the second half. Thus the first play-off in NHA history came about.

The Canadiens, the first-half leaders, defeated Ottawa in the play-offs and faced Seattle, a new member of the PCHA, for the Stanley Cup. The NHA promised that if their team lost they would positively give up their actual possession of the Cup. Seattle won, and the Cup crossed the border for the first time, something that Lord Stanley never imagined —or wanted. The 1916-1917 season had ended as strangely as it had started.

Split by greed, mistrust of Livingstone, and wondering just what effect the comic-opera capers of the 228th would have on hockey's long-term prospects, the NHA dissolved before the start of the 1917-1918 season. Quebec had dropped out after the previous season because it wasn't making money. Toronto had also left the league after the 228th disbanded because Livingstone claimed that all his best players were in the service. To keep Livingstone from coming back, the NHA decided to call itself the National Hockey League, drafting a new charter but maintaining the same constitution.

Major Robinson wanted no part of it, so Frank Calder, NHA secretary, was named the president of the new league which consisted of the Canadiens, Toronto, Ottawa and the Wanderers. Quebec was reimbursed for its players. Although they demanded $200 a man, they were in a tenuous bargaining position at best and probably received closer to $150. The players were then distributed around the league. The Toronto franchise ostensibly was in the hands of the owners of the Toronto arena that had bought out Livingstone. The NHL birthdate was November 26, 1917.

Everything seemed rosy. In fact, the first season actually went along without a hitch. By the time the 1918-1919 season rolled around, though, Livingstone was back in action, ready to sue for conspiracy. He also threatened to form his own league and raid the NHL. The trouble was that if he wanted to form his own league—with a team in Toronto, of course—he would have no place to play. The Toronto Arena owners ruled that only NHL teams could use their rink. Livingstone then attempted to resurrect the NHA, claiming that it died illegally, a maneuver that failed totally. The Wanderers meanwhile played in an adequate Montreal Arena. On the day after New Year's Eve in 1918, the Montreal Arena burned down, leaving the building—*and* the Wanderers—with smoldering ruins. With no place to play, the Wanderers withdrew from the league, ending a great era in hockey's short history.

The next year the Quebec franchise returned and, in a strange move, all the Quebec players who had been distributed around the league two years before were returned to the team. During the 1920-1921 season, when Toronto renamed itself the St. Patricks, back came Eddie Livingstone, this time threatening to form the Canadian Hockey Association. That same season the Quebec franchise was shifted to Hamilton where, the owners hoped, fans would turn out in greater numbers. To help the newly shifted team, the NHL allowed Hamilton to draft some of the stars in the league, one of whom was Babe Dye who immediately set about winning the scoring title. It was comparable to letting the Oakland Seals draft Phil Esposito. In January 1921, the Mount Royal Arena opened to house the Canadiens, who had been playing in the red at tiny Jubilee Rink. Ice hockey had seen its last smooth season for some time to come.

The 1921-1922 season saw the Canadiens sold for a mere $11,000. Even more significant was the formation that year of the Western Canada Hockey League, with Calgary, Regina, Edmonton and Saskatoon making up the teams. It made play-off arrangements with the Patricks' league, which had started to experience difficulties. The problem with the Pacific Coast league was at once similar to and different from the problem the old International Pro League had faced. The difficulty with the IPL was small arenas. With the Patricks' league it was large arenas—they were too big to pay their way for hockey alone.

Today's arenas, especially in the United States, are rarely empty. If hockey isn't being played, there is professional or college basketball to fill the seats, or an ice show, a circus, a political rally or a boxing match. The Pacific Coast league's arenas were used for league games perhaps 16 times a season. By the start of the 1923-1924 season, a change had to be made. Seattle dropped out, Vancouver and Victoria remained and were merged with the WCHL to form a new six-team league. The teams then shared arenas.

But it was only a matter of time before west coast hockey went under. Already the NHL was talking of expanding to the United States, moving to wealthy eastern cities, where money was plentiful. The Patricks knew they could not compete in this atmosphere. As it was, Frank and Lester were clearing perhaps $3,000 each a year from all their operations. In February 1924, the NHL agreed to discuss international expansion formally. At a league meeting the owners granted a franchise to Boston for the following season. At the same meeting the league accepted a trophy from Dr. David A. Hart,

The 1920 Winnipeg Falcons. Hockey rinks were beginning to come into their own. Note high rafters, long stands to the left.

father of the Montreal Canadiens' coach, to be presented annually to the player "most useful to his team."

During the next two years, the National Hockey League crystallized further, helped along by the demise of the league out west. A team from Montreal called the Maroons was made a member. The Maroons were founded by James Strachan and Donat Raymond, who wanted a club for Montreal's English-speaking community. Montreal and Boston both started play in the 1924-1925 season, a season that ended in a bitter mix-up having nothing to do with expansion.

Hamilton had finished first, but its players refused to participate in play-offs. They argued that they had signed two-year contracts with a schedule calling for 24-game regular seasons. Now the schedule had been increased to 30 games. They demanded extra pay, a demand that only now is beginning to be felt in other professional sports, most notably in pro football. Calder, furious at Hamilton's demands, ruled that Hamilton was not allowed to participate in the play-offs and that the league champion would be decided by a play-off between the team that finished second (the Canadiens) and the third-place club (Ottawa). The winner would meet the Pacific Coast champion for the Stanley Cup.

For the 1925-1926 season, the league accepted franchises in New York and Pittsburgh, Hamilton still being under suspension. Finally the league decided to drop Hamilton altogether and allow the New York entrant, the Americans, to sign Hamilton players. Pittsburgh's team was the Yellow Jackets of the United States Amateur League, but when they became National Hockey Leaguers, their name was changed to the Pirates, obviously borrowing the name of the baseball team.

The league on the west coast continued to have its troubles. The players wanted more money, equal to what the players in the east were getting. Frank Patrick desperately tried to convince the western players that reports of high salaries were unfounded. No one in the east, said Frank, received more than $3,000 a season. If that wasn't exactly the truth, at least it was at an honest appraisal of what the Patricks were getting out of hockey. So the next season, 1926-1927, the brothers sold their league to the NHL for $250,000, a good move for everybody concerned. The NHL needed western players to stock three new clubs—the New York Rangers, Chicago and Detroit. Among the players who moved east were Vancouver's Frank Boucher, who went to the Rangers, Bill and Bun Cook, from Saskatoon to the Rangers, and Eddie Shore, from Edmonton to the Bruins.

The National Hockey League now had ten clubs, divided into two sections. The Canadian division had the Toronto Maple Leafs

(who had changed their name from the St. Patricks), the Ottawa Senators, the Montreal Canadiens, the Montreal Maroons and the New York Americans. The American Division clubs were the Boston Bruins, New York Rangers, Chicago Black Hawks, Detroit Cougars and Pittsburgh Pirates.

That same 1926-1927 season, in which the NHL stood alone, also saw another major change—the Stanley Cup became the exclusive property of the league. Never again was it to be competed for by any team other than a member of the National Hockey League. The league had come to stay, and although four of the teams were to drop out over the next 15 years and no new teams added for 40 years, the circuit established itself as major league.

The National Hockey League, like any other established sports organization, has had internal differences of opinion over the years. There have been (and are) three distinct philosophies: one that seeks modernization and improvement, one that believes the existing structure is proven and not to be tampered with, and the third that has a middle-of-the-road attitude.

With the arrival on the scene in the early 1960s of two dynamic young club presidents, Bill Jennings of the Rangers and David Molson of the Canadiens, the modernization and improvement wing became stronger than ever. How, they reasoned, could the league call itself "national" if no west coast teams from the United States were represented?

Network television was becoming a factor in the economics of other sports, although the NHL was highly successful at the gate and could live without the additional revenue. But the major factor Jennings and Molson were concerned about, and about which they persuaded the league to bestir itself, was the very real possibility of a rival league being formed.

Baseball had been forced into expansion by the formation of the Continental League, which attempted to get a franchise in New York and which led to the formation of the New York Mets and their acceptance into the National League. Other franchises were granted by major league baseball, to prevent the Continental League from getting off the ground. Once baseball expanded, the upstart league's reason for existence disappeared.

Football had the American League competing with the tried-and-true National League, costing the NFL millions in bonuses and large salaries to lure players away from the AFL. Even before the AFL, another league had started in the 1940s and made inroads on the old league before it was absorbed. Basketball, too, had a history of rival leagues. The National Basketball Association was forced to expand, as were football and baseball.

Hockey obviously could not sit still. The areas of southern and northern California were ripe to become the focal point of a rival league, unless the National Hockey League got there first. Chicago and Boston were against the move. "We've got a nice little private club here," was the attitude of the Chicago management. The Bruins' owners, a line of descent from the original owners of the first United States club to play in the NHL, resisted. Traditionally, they have been against change. Detroit and Toronto were flexible.

There was another important person to convince—Clarence S. Campbell, the league president. Not particularly sanguine about the possibility of expansion, he was willing to be convinced. Campbell was an administrator, a remarkably capable executive. But he did not wield the power of a Pete Rozelle, the commissioner of football. Still, he was respected for his dignity, common sense and capability. He became the league president at the age of 41 on September 4, 1946, replacing Mervyn (Red) Dutton, who had become president in 1943, the year that Frank Calder died. Calder had been the president of the league since its birth.

One of the first items Campbell concerned himself with was the establishment of a pension plan for the players, now the strongest in any sport. Gordie Howe, for example, will receive more than $20,000 a year for life if he takes his pension at age 65. During Campbell's tenure the league started its annual all-star game, greatly increased the benefits for play-off money—and expanded.

When Campbell took over, he headed a league depleted by war. Returning players were too old. Attendance was not good. Under his leadership, during which referees gained new respect—and in turn gave the fans greater respect for the sport—the league prospered. In the years just before expansion the six clubs played to more than 93 percent of capacity. Some years Detroit had more than 100 percent of seating capacity as it sold standing room to accommodate the overflow.

Campbell had to be certain that in the face of all this success there was a real danger that a league might come in to compete with the six NHL clubs. Eventually he decided on expansion, but wasn't sure what form expansion should take. There were several possibilities.

The league could add to the existing structure, forming an eight- or ten-team league. Or it might break into two divisions. The first possibility was discarded, using baseball as an example with its clubs that drafted hand-me-downs and unproven minor leaguers. Invariably, the squads could not compete against the established clubs and finished down in their divisions. The governors did not like the idea of breaking up hockey's six established teams into separate groups. They should remain together, was the feeling.

In 1965, the league made its grand announcement. It would bring in six new teams and form a new division. Doubling in size surprised the sports world, surprise which turned to admiration for the greatest one-season upheaval in the history of any professional sport.

The league made the general announcement, sat back and waited for responses. The stipulation was that the city or group interested in a franchise had to have an arena in good repair seating at least 12,500 and had to show sufficient capitalization. The price: $2 million a franchise. The $12 million gross was to be divided among the six established clubs.

The reasoning on the new six-team division was logical. The new teams would compete mostly among themselves at first, without the pressures of trying to make it against clubs with whom they obviously would be overmatched. A team that starts a season knowing it has virtually no chance to make the playoffs will not perform well, and the fans will not turn out to see it play. A dozen cities applied for franchises, with at least 24 groups hoping to be among the six. In Los Angeles four groups vied for the honor of paying $2 million. The only Canadian city that made an effort was Vancouver, British Columbia.

The $2 million figure was arrived at in typical hockey fashion. "We just picked it out of the air," said one club owner.

Each of the interests made presentations to the league, submitting their structure and backing to the board of governors (the six established owners). Some presentations were elaborate, with full-scale models of proposed arenas. Some were unbelievably poor and at least one group came to an interview without knowing where its games would be played.

By February 1966, five franchises were issued—to Los Angeles, Minneapolis-St. Paul, Philadelphia, Pittsburgh and Oakland. At the final expansion meeting the Chicago management realized the forces of change had overwhelmed them, that their position was the minority one. At last, the Hawks proposed to the other owners that St. Louis be granted the remaining franchise. The reason? The Hawks owned the St. Louis arena. Here was a chance to unload the building. They sold it to a syndicate led by Sidney Salomon, Jr., and his son, Sidney Salomon 3d, who were awarded the final franchise.

League skeptics viewed the deal with alarm. They had complained in past years about the Norris family's dual dealings with the Red Wings and Black Hawks. This latest maneuver, they feared, only continued the Norris' game of playing both ends against the middle.

But the six clubs were set. All that remained was for them to get the players, provided for in the $2 million price. Players were to come from the rosters of the established teams. At a special draft, each old club was to "protect" two goaltenders and 12 players. The new teams were to choose a total of 20 players each, including two goalies; the old teams were to lose the same number. A new club chose a player from an established club. The established team was then allowed to "protect" its next player down the list. Then another selection was made, and another player protected. The procedure was to be repeated until the new teams arrived at their quota.

The date of the draft was June 6, 1967. The deadline for the $2 million each club had to put up was 2 P.M., June 5. A hundred newsmen converged on Montreal. The Queen Elizabeth Hotel, where the draft was to be held, was filled with cameras and equipment, reporters, interviewers, executives from the 12 cities as well as owners and executives from other leagues. The noisiest of the expansion owners was Jack Kent Cooke, owner of the Los Angeles entrant, who piqued everyone's curiosity by calling an expansion-eve press conference. An announcement posted on the press room's bulletin board warned that it should not be missed.

While newsmen flitted from room to

room at the hotel and milled around the lobby, seeking information that would give them clues as to which clubs would take which players, the new owners called little press conferences of their own, showing off their $2 million checks. Pittsburgh saved $400 a day in interest by drawing the money on the day due, instead of a few days earlier as most of the other clubs did.

The deadline for the money was fast approaching when rumors started that the Philadelphia money had not arrived. The Philadelphia contingent quite simply explained that a power failure had blacked out parts of New York, New Jersey and Philadelphia and that the Flyers could not wire the money from the Fidelity Bank of Philadelphia to the Royal National Bank of Canada.

Actually, the Flyers' entrepreneur, Jerry Wolman, the overextended, undercapitalized builder-investor whose plans included building the world's tallest building in Chicago, had gotten caught in a squeeze. Notes were coming due from all sides. His Philadelphia Eagles football team was in trouble; the Spectrum, the arena he was building in Philadelphia, was in trouble, and his Chicago skyscraper was in trouble. On top of all this, he had to come up with $2 million in cash. The league allowed Wolman a delay. The money arrived by noon, June 5.

Later that day Cooke strode into a huge room he had rented for the occasion. The sharp-eyed Los Angeles millionaire mounted a rostrum and announced grandly, "The Los Angeles Kings have just made a deal that will insure them the West Division championship." The reporters looked at each other and smiled. He hadn't even drafted one player yet. The deal that Cooke announced was the purchase of the Springfield Indians of the American Hockey League. Springfield was the private domain of Eddie Shore, who owned and operated the club and the arena. But the great Shore had recently suffered the latest in a series of heart attacks and realized he could not continue putting in an 18-hour day.

Cooke flicked a switch on a tape recorder, and over the speaker came the voice of Shore from a hospital bed. Shore sadly explained that failing health had forced him to sell. It was a grandiose performance by Cooke, worthy of Hollywood. The Springfield club, Cooke insisted, would enable him to bring up players to fill in if needed, players who were established and used to each other's styles.

The draft was staged in the Grand Salon of the Queen Elizabeth Hotel, with several hundred people filling every wooden seat. The man who would be drawing the names of the expansion clubs to determine the order of selection was Campbell, now the president of a league that for the first time was solidly United States-oriented. Campbell stood proud and erect on a brightly lit platform, warm from the hot lights of television and newsreel cameras. This probably was his proudest moment. He became a national figure in the United States to complement his stature in Canada.

Administration and organization always had been his strong suit. Even while he was attending the University of Alberta, from which he was graduated in 1926, he organized and ran the sprawling Edmonton Hockey League. He was a Rhodes scholar and attended Oxford University in England for three years, where he received a law degree. During World War II he served overseas with the 4th Canadian Armored Division and after the war was a member of the Canadian War Crimes unit. Then came his selection as president of the National Hockey League. Except for a strong fine he might levy, or the incident at the Forum when he was pelted with eggs following his suspension of Rocket Richard, Campbell's name never made United States newspapers with any regularity. Yet, there he was, the focal figure in the expansion draft.

The first club whose name he plucked out of the Stanley Cup was the Los Angeles Kings. Having the first pick, they chose Terry Sawchuk, the elderly, once-great goalie of the Wings who was playing for Toronto. That started a series of maneuvering and charges that became as much a show as expansion itself. The draft was on. It ended within six hours, surprising even Campbell who had thought the transfer of 120 players might take two days. For the brief period it was on, it was a sight to see.

For the previous six months, the clubs had gone over battle plans and dry runs. In the final week, promises had been made in back rooms, culminating months of wheeling and dealing. The established clubs could not protect everyone they wanted to, so deals had to be made beforehand. You leave my player alone, I'll do you a favor. Since an established club could do more for an expansion team than vice versa, the deals usually were honored. Newsmen chuckled during the proceedings when Wren Blair, the general manager of the Minnesota North Stars, often asked for a slight delay so he could talk things over with the Montreal Canadiens. It should not have been surprising that when the Canadiens left Claude Provost, one of the better left wings in the game, unprotected, no one gobbled him up.

Typical of what went on was the Boom Boom Geoffrion affair. Weeks before, Geoffrion had announced he would retire if he were drafted, actually a brilliant move by the Rangers. They knew an expansion club would think twice about taking the Boomer if he wasn't going to play. This meant the New Yorkers could leave him unprotected, while protecting another player. The last pick of the draft was Philadelphia's. They suddenly called a ten-minute time out. Speculation started. Would Philadelphia take him? At the end of the break, the Flyers announced they were selecting a Ranger—Terry Ball

"You can make deals and deals," said a relieved general manager, Emile Francis, "but when it comes down to it, you sweat. You never know." Somehow, Francis made all the expansion teams stay away from Geoffrion. He promised Minnesota favorable territorial rights. He promised Cooke a crack at promising minor leaguers. So all new teams had something to gain from the Rangers and held off on Geoffrion. In fact, Barry van Gerbig, a friend of Jennings, had told Jennings he would draft Geoffrion for the Seals to keep the Boomer away from Cooke, following speculation that Cooke would take the Boomer. The Seals did give Francis a moment's pause during one of their rounds. "We choose," said a Seals executive, "Boom Boom . . . Caron!" Everyone laughed, even Francis.

During the picking and choosing, Sid Abel of Detroit chewed his nails, Francis worked in his shirtsleeves, Billy Reay of Chicago was sullen. The new teams were apprehensive following their choices, as if they had second thoughts.

The Kings, meanwhile, were involved in a little game with the Toronto Maple Leafs. The Leafs' Red Kelly had announced his intention to quit and become coach of the Kings. Since Kelly did not want to play for Toronto any more and insisted he would not, it would be silly for Toronto to protect him. And they didn't—at first. Cooke expected to draft Kelly on the 18th round. But Imlach was talking about a double-cross. The Kings had grabbed Sawchuk from Toronto. The Leafs wanted Sawchuk back. Cooke was furious when Toronto protected Kelly after the eighth round. Everyone knew Kelly didn't want to stay in Toronto and at the age of 39 had a chance to start a new career as coach.

But Toronto did not want to give up Kelly for nothing (even though it *had* received $2 million) and demanded a trade with Los Angeles. They wanted a goalie. Leaf Johnny Bower was 42 years old and Al Smith, his back-up, was inexperienced. Two days after the draft, the Leafs and Kings got together. Kelly was traded, but not for a goaltender. He was exchanged for a minor-league defenseman named Ken Block. Los Angles got its coach, but the Leafs gained a defenseman for virtually nothing.

After the drafting was over and the cameras stopped grinding and the hot lights were turned down, the established owners left their seats, smiling. The broadest grins belonged to Jennings and Molson. They not only had seen expansion become a reality, but they had lost almost nothing from their own rosters. Some of the established clubs were also chuckling. Cooke had alienated many of them with his big talk. Just the day before he had said his new team could beat three established clubs. The owners, however, thought he had come out last in his selections. "Who did he pick?" asked one owner. "I never heard of any of them." Molson said with a grin, "It looks as if LA came off the worst."

If some of the owners knew what Cooke had done during the drafting, they might have gained new respect for him. The Leafs tried to turn and twist every way in order to get something for Kelly. They did, but not what they thought they should have received. Stafford Smythe, their president, nervously approached Cooke after the 17th round. "You draft Geoffrion," said Smythe, "and we'll give you Kelly for Geoffrion." Cooke replied, "Stafford, you're a wicked man."

Cooke knew what everyone was saying about his choices. He cautioned, "Look what Branch Rickey did in 1946 with the Brooklyn Dodgers. Who ever heard of Duke Snider in 1946?" he asked. He had a resigned attitude about all his deals. "It's the modus operandi everyplace else. So why not in hockey?"

The morning after, people could at last take a look at the new face of hockey. The schedule for the 1967-1968 season was expanded to 74 games from the usual 70. There was to be interdivisional play, with each club playing the others in its division 50 times (ten each) and the other division a total of 24 games (four each).

As expected, the East Division dominated the West Division—but not to the degree most people thought it would. Experts, including Campbell, felt that if the West could garner 25 percent of the possible points in interdivision games, it would be a competitively successful first year. It turned out that the new clubs captured 33 percent of the possible points. One club, the Kings, was almost .500 (10-12-2) against the East. One East team, the Leafs, lost more games than it won against the West.

In short order, people started to speculate how long it would take the new division to achieve parity. The first thing a new club had to learn was to work as a team, to form new allegiances. This the players did quickly. But the experts thought it would take at least five years before the West could consistently compete. There were two major reasons for this thinking. The East, first of all, had all the superstars. It also had the not-quite-superstars. If any were to come out of the West, they would have to be developed there. None came with grade-A credentials, except for a few goaltenders. Secondly, many future prospects were still under the control of the East Division and would be for another few years. The best players (on paper) still would be going to the East.

Still, the league believed it would have to give equal recognition to the West Division and make it part of the NHL tradition. Thus, the West vied for the Stanley Cup in its first season. In previous years the Cup final was between the winners of one round of play-offs —the first and third teams, the second and fourth teams. But at the end of the 1967-1968 season, the first and third teams and the second and fourth teams in each division played off, with the winners playing off again. The Canadiens were left from the East, the Blues from the West. In an extraordinary four-game series, the Canadiens won, but the Blues forced them into two overtime games and not one Montreal victory during the sweep was decided by more than one goal.

During the regular season, the West teams did considerably better at the gate for home games when the attraction was an East Division team, which came in with such built-in lures as Gordie Howe, Jean Beliveau, Bobby Hull, Rod Gilbert and Bobby Orr. After the first season of expansion, the West wanted a bigger share of the pie. They did not really believe they could win half their games against the established teams, but wanted the scheduling made equal.

The East rebelled, for some of the East clubs did not always play to capacity when a West Division team came to town. And teams in hockey do not share in gate receipts on the road. But the West had its way, and in the second year of expansion, 1968-1969, the schedule was increased to a record 76 games—almost half of them interdivisional. Now a club would play 40 games against its own division (eight against each other team) and 36 against the other division (six each).

The league, also needing equality for its all-star game structure, changed the format. The East played the West. Before the change the all-star game had been between the Stanley Cup defender and stars from other teams.

The sites for baseball and basketball all-star games are rotated from city to city. The NHL decided that for the time being the game would be held in the Cup defender's city. The league feared that if the game were rotated it might wind up in an expansion city, one without a hockey tradition. If that city's team were having a bad year interest would be low, attendance poor. It would be embarrassing, to say the least, to stage an all-star game before 6,000 people. The league was confident that the Cup defenders would be an East team for some time to come and it gave the defender the option of holding the game. Then, in 1969, the league reversed itself and voted for a rotating site starting in 1970.

The first East-West all-star game was held at Montreal on January 21, 1969. Curiosity was the major attraction. The East had Hull, Frank Mahovlich, Howe and Phil Esposito, including all the other leading scorers in the league. Its goalie was Ed Giacomin of the Rangers, considered the best in the sport. The East coach was Toe Blake, who had retired the season before after leading the Canadiens to the Cup championship.

The West was led by Scotty Bowman, coach of the St. Louis Blues, who had put up a valiant fight against Montreal in the Stanley Cup. In fact, almost half of the West squad was composed of Blues. Bowman and Blake each had seven choices of their own to fill out the squad, selected by a writers' poll, so Bowman filled his quota with four Blues. "I was almost embarrassed to tell Campbell," he said with a sheepish grin.

There didn't appear to be much doubt about the eventual result. The only question was, would the West make it respectable? It did, thanks largely to the East's superstars taking no chances on injury and to a masterstroke of Bowman's.

Blake went with the lines as selected by the writers. Bowman put out a sextet composed entirely of St. Louis players. This gave him an immediate edge in one important respect—all the players knew one another's styles and habits. Before the game was five minutes old the West took the lead on a goal by the first outstanding player to come out of the new division, Red Berenson. As the game went along Bowman threw out lines made up of players from the same team. A Minnesota North Star line and the St. Louis line scored all the West's goals and the Blues' Glenn Hall was outstanding in the nets. The final score was a 3-3 tie.

But there were to be precious few deadlocks in games between the divisions over the next few years. The West clubs had traded away too many draft choices.

Although the logical and patient among hockey observers had predicted a five-year wait for parity, many fans soon became distressed with the remarkable drop in quality. The grumblings came mostly from the established cities, where crowds remembered what the game had been like just a few short years before. Fans in the newer cities, most of whom had never seen big league hockey, didn't understand what the fuss was about. After all, they had never seen the Canadiens battle the Bruins in the good old days. Expansion hockey still was more exciting than the minor league version they'd witnessed previously.

In the first year of expansion, Campbell had hoped—indeed, would have been happy for —the West to take 25 percent of its possible points. The West surprised him and most others by gaining 34 percent. Perhaps things would continue in this surprising, happy vein. But no, the West started to decline after the first year, for a very simple reason.

As one general manager pointed out, "The first year all the guys had something to prove. They were called cast-offs and has-beens and guys who never-were. But they had pride, and they were motivated very easily. So many of them played above their heads. But you can't motivate guys in that way forever."

By the second year of expansion, the drop in motivation was apparent. The West captured only 30 percent of the possible points, and the next campaign the figure dropped to 28. It was apparent, at least to the image-conscious NHL, that something had to be done to shore up its sagging image. The West needed identity. And Canada still needed another NHL city.

The trouble with adding only one city was that it would create an unbalanced league of 13 teams. Any further expansion would have to include two clubs. Buffalo was a prime candidate. Buffalo interests also had taken a piece of the Seals in the hope if the franchise were displaced, it would wind up in Buffalo. So Vancouver and Buffalo, the prime cities for the next expansion, both had been involved with the Seals.

The opposition to Buffalo was more substantive than it may have appeared from the remarks of the late owner of the Hawks, James Norris, who had once said, "I don't want a town named Buffalo playing in my building."

By the end of the 1968-69 season, the league had made its decision. It was going to expand again and at the same time would upgrade both its West Division and its image in Parliament. It was done in a novel way. The Black Hawks had finished last in the 1968-69 campaign, but they still had drawing cards in Bobby Hull and Stan Mikita. If the Hawks shifted to the West Division, they would have a chance at making the play-offs and at the same time, another respectable established team would enter the expansion division. The new cities—Vancouver and Buffalo—would go to the East Division.

The price for these new franchises was put at $6 million apiece. In other words, the new franchise owners would pay a whopping total of $12 million, which would be divided among the existing 12 teams—$1 million each. That wasn't a bad investment return, especially for the newer clubs, who had only paid $2 million each two years before.

There were now two seven-team divisions, and a third Canadian team, Vancouver.

Predictably, the continued expansion generated a spate of new scoring records. Virtually every scoring mark has been wiped out since expansion began, and it is safe to assume that every year new teams enter the league more records will fall.

However much they inflated the established team's scoring, the new clubs in the 1970-71 expansion did give further stability to the league. The Canucks, as the Vancouver franchise was known, virtually sold out their arena from the beginning. The Sabres, in Buffalo, did so well in their first season that they literally raised the roof to add a few thousand more seats. The Buffalo team too, played before capacity houses. The league was so happy about the way its expansion had taken root that it planned for its next big expansion, in 1974. That would give the first six expansion teams eight seasons and Vancouver and Buffalo four full campaigns in the league. By then, Campbell said, the clubs would be nearly equal to the original six.

The 1971-72 season was in full swing when suddenly some people in California declared they were starting something called the World Hockey Association. Laughter and curiosity greeted the news. A rival hockey league? Where could it possibly get players? Hockey was not like football or basketball, for which the colleges turned out tens of thousands of boys a year, with hundreds ready to make the leap to the major leagues. Hockey just didn't work that way. Boys from the juniors needed time to develop—at least a year or two in the high minors.

Undeterred, Dennis Murphy and Gary Davidson, were looking into the possibility of starting a new league, to begin play in the 1972-73 season. They even named the cities in which the league would be represented—including New York, Los Angeles and Chicago. It was now 1971. In another year, they said, they would begin play.

Players were aroused but hardly overwhelmed. Even Campbell appeared less than concerned when he was asked about the new venture. He said diplomatically, "We're pleased that the NHL has done so well and has established hockey so strongly that other people want to get into the sport. We welcome competition." But then he added ominously, "But if they attempt to raid any of our players, we will fight them from the ramparts."

What at first had been a joke suddenly became serious. The WHA was gathering steam. Money was changing hands, and franchises were in fact created. Then the WHA announced it was going to have a draft, though it was not immediately clear of whom. The draft was held despite the disparaging remarks that greeted such seemingly hopeless selections as Winnipeg's Bobby Hull and Miami's Bernie Parent. It was all a joke, of course. The WHA, believed many, was simply seeking the publicity value.

Perhaps its most important franchise would be in New York. It granted one to a Long Island lawyer, Neil Shayne, a talker in the Jack Kent Cooke mold. Shayne said he would try to place a team in the new Nassau Coliseum, in the heart of Long Island. A New York franchise has always been critically important for a new league.

No one should have been surprised at what happened next, a step of major proportions that began an even more radical phase in the NHL's and hockey's development than did the 1967 expansion. The week after the WHA meeting the NHL announced it was going to expand in 1972, two years earlier than planned. And it was going to expand in New York and Atlanta. For the first time, big league hockey would be coming to the Deep South. And for the first time in 30 years, since the New York Americans folded, there would be two NHL teams in a metropolitan area.

Shayne was furious. He fired off a host of multimillion-dollar law suits—against the Coliseum, against Nassau County, against the NHL, against the Rangers. He charged that although it was a municipal building the Coliseum had not granted him playing dates because it was in collusion with the NHL.

In addition to expanding to 16 clubs in 1972, the NHL said it would bring in two more clubs in 1974 and that by the end of the decade it thought it might have 24 teams. Again, the NHL was "fighting from the ramparts." Part of the WHA sales pitch had been to entice medium-sized cities, such as Kansas City, Washington and San Diego, to put in with them and become big league. Now suddenly, the NHL was offering these areas the hope that one day they could join the world's strongest sports league.

There still was infighting going on when the 1971-72 season ended, no one had really much of an idea of which cities the WHA was going to start with. Though there was some wild talk and that secret draft of players, the WHA had no commitments. That quickly changed.

The Leafs' goalie, Bernie Parent, was the first to go. The Miami Screaming Eagles of the WHA offered him about a half million dollars to play for five years. He accepted. The salary was unheard of in hockey except for a Hull or Howe. And anyway, how could he leave? The NHL had its reserve clause.

Many people believe that a gentlemen's agreement existed in the NHL, that under no circumstances would the teams pay their players' exorbitant demands to keep them from jumping. Parent wanted $100,000 a year from the Leafs. They refused. He jumped. Parent, though only one player, gave the NHL cause for concern. In a grand news conference, the Bruins announced they had signed Bobby Orr and Phil Esposito to long-term contracts. The Rangers signed their goalies, Gilles Villemure and Ed Giacomin, to multi-year deals. The Flyers got Bobby Clarke for a few years.

Most of the players, however, waited and watched. And finally it happened. Hull made the leap. It was an incredible deal, of such magnitude that it had to be signed in two countries. He received a million dollars in cash for jumping to the Winnipeg Jets. Even if he didn't play one game for the Jets, that is, if the reserve clause had been held valid by the courts, Hull would have kept his million. In addition, he signed to play and coach for 10 years for a total of $1.75 million. In all he would receive $2.75 million for jumping. The new league was for real.

Those who knew it best were the players. Now they really did have a wedge. Even those under long-term contracts demanded renegotiation. At first, the teams refused. But the new WHA teams were continuing to make attractive offers. The Rangers' Brad Park and Vic Hadfield were offered $1 million apiece for four years to jump to the Cleveland Crusaders. Owner Nick Mileti had hoped to get an NHL franchise. When he was turned down, he simply joined the new league. The Rangers were in danger of losing their star defenseman and their 50-goal scorer. Rod Gilbert and Jean Ratelle, their other scoring heroes, also were in serious talks. Then came the break that ushered in the new era of players' salaries in hockey, and thrust the sport to the top salary levels, exceeded only by basketball. The Rangers agreed to the greatest raises in history. They gave Park $200,000 a year to stay. They tore up Hadfield's old contract and signed a new one giving him $175,000 a year. They gave Ratelle and Gilbert the same. They offered Walt Tkaczuk more than $125,000.

Many other NHL teams, though, didn't believe the WHA would even get off the ground. They scoffed as one player after another defected. The California Golden Seals and the Toronto Maple Leafs each lost 11 players. The WHA began play, and when the season started, more than 60 players who had seen NHL duty were playing for the new league. The NHL lost virtually every law suit. It couldn't stop Hull from playing. It couldn't halt Sanderson.

Luckily, the new NHL teams created a stir. In Atlanta instant success at the gate and on the ice greeted the team. In New York the Islanders became hockey's Mets—a lovable collection of losers who nevertheless played before near-capacity houses. The league also got some backlash benefits. Sanderson jumped back after taking an $800,000 cash settlement from the Blazers. When the season ended, Parent also jumped back. Further, the NHL awarded franchises for 1974 to Washington and Kansas City, where there would be new arenas and heightened interest. People speculated just how long the war would rage before the leagues reached an agreement that somehow would halt the rise of the instant millionaires, hockey players.

By the second season of 1973-74, the owners closed their wallets a little but not before taking care of Gordie Howe and his children. Howe, who had ended a magnificent 25-year career with Detroit, was a part of the Red Wings' front office but not too happy about it.

The Aeros made Howe an offer he couldn't refuse. They would take him and his two sons, Mark and Marty, for a $2-million, four-year package. All Gordie had to do was to play a year "and one game." That game was for a token appearance when Houston moved into its projected new arena. Howe was overwhelmed. "My boys will earn more from the interest on their money in one year than I got in salary after ten years in the NHL," he said. So at age 45 Howe returned to active participation, ready to add still another remarkable chapter to the sports' longest playing career.

Neither Howe nor many of his contemporaries could recognize the face of hockey in 1974 when another far-reaching change took place: further realignment of the NHL. The league split into four divisions as it swelled to 18 teams with the addition of Washington and Kansas City. Soon it would be going to 20 by bringing in more clubs in 1976. The new divisions would have two divisions of four clubs apiece (these would be added to by the 1976 clubs) and two of five clubs in each. In addition, the play-off structure would be changed. The first finisher in each division would draw a bye, while the second- and third-place clubs would play a best-of-three first-round series. Then the more serious work would begin—three more series, each best-of-seven, to determine the Cup champion.

Ironically, the NHL was to play a major role in helping Murphy decide that a rival league could succeed. Murphy learned that there was going to be an American Hockey League meeting in the Bahamas, not far from Miami. Disguised as a television newsman, Murphy attended the meetings. The hockey dignitaries, which included many executives from the NHL, were more than pleased to talk to this television announcer from Florida. After all, the American League was contemplating putting a franchise in Florida, and it certainly pays to be nice to broadcasters who could talk about your product.

"Everyone was so nice to me," says Murphy. "One of the nicest was Emile Francis, the general manager of the Rangers. I had long talks with him. He was very informative. He assured me there was enough talent for an American League team in Florida." Francis explained to Murphy that there were many good players in the minors who never had a chance to make it to the big leagues. He also explained how their contracts worked, that most players were only signed for a year.

Murphy was off, visiting 40 cities in North America, talking to civic organizations, mayors, marketing experts, TV people, newspapermen. Of the 100 groups he spoke to for potential franchises, most turned him down. They were afraid to buck the NHL. But Murphy knew "the progress the sport was making was unreal. Hockey was lucrative as hell. Heck, the cost of a franchise in three years went from two million to six million."

It would cost only about $250,000 to acquire a WHA team. It started with 12 franchises, including Miami and San Francisco (which was given to Davidson as a sort of finder's fee.) Miami was shifted to Philadelphia, and Davidson sold his franchise to people in Quebec for $250,000. While the meetings were held in an attempt to stabilize franchises, an ABA official called to ask if he could attend. He was interested in a WHA franchise for Atlanta, he told Murphy. "The guy took notes throughout the meeting," recalls Murphy. "But after he left, I got word he was a spy from the NHL. I called and asked him if it were true. The guy admitted it. He told me that everyone has to make a living."

Finally, the WHA did breathe life. The league opened with 12 clubs: the New York Raiders, the Philadelphia Blazers, the Chicago Cougars, the Houston Aeros, the Los Angeles Sharks, the New England Whalers, the Quebec Nordiques, the Ottawa Nationals, the Winnipeg Jets, the Alberta Oilers, the Cleveland Crusaders and the Minnesota Fighting Saints.

The Whalers drew by far the largest attendance. As a whole, the league averaged about 5,200 fans a game. That wasn't at all bad for a first-year league, and indeed was better than the American Basketball Association had drawn in its third season.

Luckily, its upheavals after the first year were minor. Ottawa shifted to Toronto, Philadelphia went to Vancouver and New York first changed its name to the Golden Blades, then moved to New Jersey and became the Knights. The WHA still had 12 teams and planned to increase by adding Cincinnati, Indianapolis and Phoenix. The new league was here to stay.

3

THE DYNASTY BUILDERS

teams

THE TORONTO MAPLE LEAFS

Conn Smythe, believer in God, country, free enterprise and abstinence, resurrected the Toronto franchise, gave it a new name, infused new blood into it. During his reign, the Maple Leafs became not only the symbol of Canada, but the symbol of hockey as well.

Under his powerful guidance—some said thumb—he built dynasty after dynasty, each known for its Spartan leadership (Smythe remained at the helm for 35 years), its aggressiveness, cold-bloodedness and—the ultimate yardstick—success.

Smythe came to the Maple Leafs through an incredible series of detours, broken promises and lucky bets. Driving him was consummate confidence, a strong will that permitted him to take chances and the belief that he listened to the right drummer.

It began for Smythe in 1926. He was 31 years old and already a veteran executive of amateur hockey. The New York Rangers were to enter the league that winter and the Rangers' president, Colonel John S. Hammond, on the recommendation of Charles Adams, the Boston Bruins' president, elected Smythe to bring hockey players to New York.

Smythe immediately picked Frank Selke, who had worked with him on the Marlboros, a Toronto amateur club, as his Canadian representative. It started a long, professional relationship that ended 20 years later when Selke transferred to the Montreal Canadiens and built his own dynasty, one that eventually challenged and beat out Smythe's as the symbol of hockey.

The kind of team Smythe selected was made up of men much like himself. "I wanted guys who loved to play the game, to whom money was secondary," he explained. Seeking "sportsmen," he convinced many amateurs to turn pro. But his stubbornness toward this ideal proved his undoing before the Rangers ever played a league game.

Colonel Hammond wanted Babe Dye for his new club. Smythe objected. "Dye was more like a union man than a sportsman," Smythe insisted. "He wanted to organize the players." They continued to argue about Dye. Smythe got as far as the Rangers' training camp in Ontario (training camp was a Smythe conception). A few days later he met the colonel at the local train station. Accompanying Hammond was Dye—and Lester Patrick. It was the first Smythe had heard that Patrick had been appointed the Rangers' coach and general manager, that Dye was staying—and that Smythe was not.

In later years Smythe said that the Chicago Black Hawks' coach, Pete Muldoon, had whispered bad things about Smythe, that Muldoon convinced Hammond that the Rangers needed a man with a professional background and one with a name to lure fans if they were to succeed in New York. Smythe, bitter over the setback, nevertheless accepted the Rangers' invitation to attend their opening game in Madison Square Garden. It was there that his fortunes changed.

At the game he ran across Tex Rickard, renowned boxing impresario and builder of Madison Square Garden. Rickard could hardly help noticing that Smythe was miffed. When asked why, Smythe told Rickard that his Rangers contract had called for $10,000 but that he had received only $7,500. Although Smythe hadn't actually fulfilled his contract, Rickard immediately gave him a check for $2,500.

One week later Smythe, cash in pocket, went to a football game between his alma

PRECEDING PAGES: Rangers' Gilles Villemure and Jim Neilson hit the ice to stop Boston's Don Marcotte. RIGHT: Leafs' alternate captain Norm Ullman leads charge against Rangers.

9
A
TORONTO MAPLE LEAFS

mater, the University of Toronto, and McGill University. He bet the whole $2,500 on Toronto—and won. Another week went by, bringing the Rangers to town to play the St. Pats. The bookmakers assumed the Rangers were pushovers. Smythe knew he had built a good club and he bet his winnings on the New Yorkers, receiving odds of 3-1. The Rangers won, parlaying Smythe's money to $15,000. By then he had to admit, "I was feeling pretty good toward the Rangers."

The obvious acceptance of the new teams in the National Hockey League, and his penchant and knack for making money, convinced Smythe that his future was in pro hockey and not in the amateur ranks. With the 1926-1927 season well under way, it became apparent that the St. Pats were having trouble. Selke learned that they were on the market. He told Smythe, who organized some business associates, getting them to put up a large share of the purchase price. Smythe himself invested most of his winnings, and for $135,000 the deal was made.

The patriotic Smythe, a World War I prisoner who once attempted to saw his way out of his cell with a harmonica, immediately changed the team's name to the symbol of his country, the Maple Leafs. He also took his old school colors, blue and white, for his new team.

Starting as it did in midseason, the new management could do little with the club and finished last. On the final game of the season, against the New York Americans in Madison

LEFT: *Never-say-die Syl Apps, prone to the side of the cage, manages to hook in the puck for a goal as Ranger goalie Dave Kerr falls out of position.* BELOW: *King Clancy, enshrined in Hockey Hall of Fame.*

Square Garden, the club lost again. The players were disconsolate, in fact, miserable. While they were changing after the game, trainer Tim Daly bought some newspapers in the lobby. He dashed back into the locker room and passed the papers to the players. The headlines told of the conviction of the infamous Ruth Snyder, who had murdered her husband and was sentenced to the electric chair.

"Read this," said Daly. "You'll see that there are people even worse off than you are." In the next 44 years, the Leafs missed the play-offs only eight times; they won 11 Stanley Cups and six regular-season titles.

Smythe, club president and general manager, also appointed himself the coach for the 1927-1928 season, the first full one under the new regime. The Leafs failed to make the play-offs and for the next two seasons continued to flounder. Smythe set about cleaning house. It was an expression he used and he followed it strictly.

The first casualty was Coach Smythe. General manager Smythe appointed Art Duncan to lead the club for the 1930-1931 season. The club finished second. But early the next season it was in trouble again, failing to win in its first six games. Smythe spirited dour, resourceful Dick Irvin away from the Chicago Black Hawks and installed him as coach. Hap Day, a serious, hard-working player, was the team's captain. Day, Irvin, Smythe and Selke immediately presented a no-non-sense front to the players and to the public. The quartet was a nonsmoking, nondrinking collection of pros who believed in making Jack a dull boy.

Irvin was a gaunt-looking man, a former great player who had suffered painful wounds in World War I, who could sleep only on one side because of the pain, but who led the Leafs through one of their finest periods. His arrival coincided with two other events, each of which reshaped the Canadian—and especially the Toronto—way of life. The first was the construction of Maple Leaf Gardens, a building lovingly put together at the height of the Depression. The second was the medium of radio and with it the broadcasting across the country of Leaf games by announcer Foster Hewitt.

Smythe never believed in depressions. "How can there be a depression," he asked, "if they're printing money all the time? There's more money around today than there was yesterday, isn't there?"

And so, early in 1931, Smythe and his partners made plans to build a fine new arena to house their team. But if Smythe wasn't aware of tight money, bankers were. Selke, though, had an ace up his sleeve. The mild crew-cut executive had once been treasurer of the International Brotherhood of Electrical Workers, and although out of the post for five years, he still was a card-carrying member. He hit upon an extraordinary scheme: he would ask the workers to take 80 percent of their wages in cash, the rest in stock in the Gardens. More than 300 members of the Brotherhood were out of work at the time, so the union leaders enthusiastically endorsed Selke's plan. It was summarily presented to the workers and they, too, agreed.

In the spring of 1931, work began. To Torontonians, the building quickly became a symbol of Canadian doggedness, rising in the midst of the Great Depression, and they took it to their hearts. Five months after groundbreaking, on November 12, 1931, the building opened. The workers who had put it together had the largest share of any outside group buying stock in the Gardens.

That first game, won by the Chicago Black Hawks, 2-1, saw an immediate social change. Women dressed up for the game, swathed in furs, while their escorts wore tuxedoes. The high style (although not always in formal wear) has continued to this day. But despite the handsome turnout, many people still did not believe the venture would succeed. A lull in the opening-night ceremonies was referred to by Ted Reeve of the *Evening Telegram* as "two-minutes' silence in respect for the shareholders."

If the building gave the Leafs nationwide exposure, the start of Hewitt's radio broadcasts brought them intimately into every Canadian home, from Nova Scotia to British Columbia.

Hewitt's greeting, "Hello, Canada," heralded the start of another night of hockey and his Saturday broadcasts signaled the start of what was to become a household expression, "hockey night in Canada." It made hundreds of thousands of listeners forget their often shabby existence. In a British Columbia settlement the neighbors would visit the only house that had a radio. In northern Alberta a local movie house lost its Saturday night audience, thanks to Hewitt's broadcasts. The theater installed a radio and suddenly Saturday nights were sellouts.

Despite the economic squeeze Canada and the rest of the world were going through, the Gardens made a profit every year during the Depression. A prime reason was Smythe's housecleaning. He traded great players who earned great salaries when he thought they were at the beginning of the end of their usefulness, although their skills were still high enough to bring quality players in return. He unloaded Charlie Conacher at the age of 29, two seasons after Conacher was the league scoring champion. Busher Jackson, another star, went when he was 28. The fabled King Clancy lasted until he was 33. "These were the toughest trades I ever had to make," said

Leaf coach Conn Smythe, right, restrains American coach Red Dutton from attacking referee who had assessed a twenty-minute high-sticking penalty against New York.

Smythe. But he made them and the arena prospered.

Irvin was a fine innovator. In his year and a half of coaching with the Hawks he changed the tempo of the game by putting together three fast forward lines and giving each of them shortened shifts on the ice. His players were sometimes as fresh at the end of the game as they were at the beginning. He brought his theory to Toronto, where Smythe and Selke kept him supplied with the bodies to put Irvin's ideas into action.

Among the Leafs' stars of the thirties were Clancy, Syl Apps, Joe Primeau, Red Horner, Conacher, Jackson and Babe Pratt. Although history rates Conacher and Jackson as two of the greats, it is typical of Smythe's Cup-directed thinking that he had reservations. "After all," he said, "as great as they were, we won only one Stanley Cup with them."

Ace Bailey was another who starred for Toronto, but *his* place in the folklore of the sport was assured because of a concussion he received. In a game during the 1933-1934 season at Boston, Bailey was cracked in the kidneys from behind by the Bruins' Eddie Shore, whom Selke had labeled modestly as a "brute." Bailey tumbled to the ice, hitting his head as he landed, where he lay in a coma as blood poured over the frozen surface. In retaliation, Red Horner charged Shore and with one punch knocked out the Boston strong boy.

The next day, after Bailey had undergone brain surgery, his father arrived in Boston. He went straight to the Bruins' executive offices where he brandished a pistol and threatened revenge. Finally placated and convinced by Boston executives that Shore had meant no malice and that his son's injuries weren't fatal, the old man allowed himself to

be escorted by police, placed aboard a Toronto-bound train and sent home.

What quickly became known as The Ace Bailey Incident shocked the hockey world and even made the players, generally a lethargic lot when their own interests weren't at stake, stir themselves to novel action. They decided to hold a benefit game for the stricken Bailey, a game in which all the league stars would appear.

The benefit turned out to be the league's first all-star game. It was staged on March 14, 1934, at Maple Leaf Gardens, and a capacity house was on hand. Before the game started, two figures walked out to center ice—Bailey and Shore—where they stood alone. Shore offered his hand to Bailey, who grasped it warmly and, it was noted, "to a rousing volume of sound."

King Clancy probably was the Leafs' most popular player. He played defense with a fervor that was unmatched in the sport until Canadien Maurice (Rocket) Richard came along in the 1940s to explode on the scene as hockey's great right wing. Clancy was a fast skater, some believed the fastest, and had a low, hard, accurate shot—70 percent of his career goals were either the first of the game, the tying goal or the winning goal. He was an expert at "laying on the wood," tripping opponents with deft stickhandling and knowing how to use an opponent's legs as a screen when taking a shot.

Clancy, as many great hockey players seem to be, was a character. In the dressing room before one game he suddenly bolted off the bench to tell Smythe that he had left his religious medals at home and was leaving to get them. Smythe told him to forget it, that a game was going to start in a few minutes.

"If you think I'm playing without my goddamn medals, you're crazy!" shouted Clancy, and left to get them.

Clancy also had the mark of a combatant—he was virtually toothless. He once complained, "I've got only one tooth in my head, and that's the one that's hurting me."

Joe Primeau teamed with Chuck Conacher and Busher Jackson to form the storied Kid Line. Primeau was the playmaker. He also was, according to Selke, " the cleanest player I ever saw. I cannot recall him ever breaking a rule of sportsmanship."

Conacher was one of the supreme shooters in the game. He made every play a picture and was one of the most aggressive shooters ever to play in the league. He led the scorers in goals for five seasons and in total points twice during his 13-year career.

With the rumbling of war in Europe, Smythe decided the war effort needed him, so he returned to the service. But that presented a problem back home, namely, who was to mind the store? Irvin was nearly 50 years old. "If something had happened to me," said Smythe, "I would have wanted a younger man to coach the club and make the decisions." So after the 1939-1940 season, despite the Leafs' third-place finish and semifinal victory in the play-offs, Smythe dismissed Irvin. In Irvin's nine seasons, he coached Toronto to four first-place finishes and one Cup victory.

Irvin, naturally, got back into hockey within a year. Babe Siebert, just named coach of the Montreal Canadiens for the 1939-1940 season, had died in a swimming accident. The Canadiens used Pit Lepine as an interim coach, then grabbed Irvin as soon as he became available. At Montreal, "overage" Irvin started a new and successful career.

It wasn't all seriousness at Maple Leaf Gardens during Irvin's tenure. In a game against the Hawks, for instance, a Toronto shot smacked Chicago goalie Charlie Gardiner in the head. He was replaced by goalie Wilfie Cude, but Cude got hurt, too. Gardiner returned, his head swathed in bandages. Someone threw a derby onto the ice. The beturbaned Gardiner nonchalantly picked it up, put it on and went back to playing goal, looking like an Oxford-educated Arab.

Irvin's successor at Toronto was the Leafs' former defensive stalwart, Clarence (Hap) Day. He played ten years at Toronto, leaving in 1937 to finish out his career with a final season with the New York Americans. The next two years he refereed. He was only 39 years old when Smythe brought him back to his old club which he was to coach through 1949-1950. During his stay the Leafs won five Cups, becoming the first club in league history to win three in a row, a string they started in 1947. In 1942, against the Detroit Red Wings, Toronto became the first team to capture a play-off series after dropping the first three games of the four-of-seven competition.

Day's coaching career spanned much of the playing career of Theodore (Teeder) Kennedy, who retired when he was 30 years old in 1955. Together, they enjoyed huge success. Kennedy played on five Cup winners and this fact alone prompted Smythe to choose him as the most valuable player ever to work for the Leafs. He was a winner who, in 13 seasons, was never named to the first all-star team. He was simply a dogged competitor who made few mistakes and never gave up. His talent received recognition from his teammates, however, who twice named him the club's most valuable player and named him captain for his last seven seasons. The Hart Trophy, for the league's most valuable player, went to him only once.

Replacing Day wasn't easy. Smythe, after much cajoling, finally got Joe Primeau to lead the club. Primeau never wanted the job, having become a highly successful businessman. In his first try at coaching, though, he led the Leafs to another Stanley Cup. "You can't quit now," Smythe insisted. Primeau stuck it out until the end of the 1952-1953 season, then won his way.

Another Leaf star was plucked out of the referees' ranks when Smythe got King Clancy to take over. The one thing connected with hockey that Clancy couldn't do, however, was coach. "He was the best in the world for everything but that," said Smythe. "He scored hockey by the number of fights. If you lost, 7 to 1, but won five fights, he figured you won the game."

Clancy was gently removed from the bench and made assistant manager. He was replaced as coach by Howie Meeker and then by Billy Reay, who led the 1957-1958 and 1958-1959 clubs. But the Leafs did not have much success. At the urging of Smythe's son, Stafford, Reay was replaced and George (Punch) Imlach brought in. Two years later, Stafford took over the generalship of the Maple Leaf operations and Conn Smythe's active career ended.

Imlach replaced Reay in midseason, taking over a club that had finished last the season before for the first time in 29 years. Imlach brought them back into the play-offs—nine straight times in fact, and won the Cup three straight years, starting with the 1962 series.

The Cup, Smythe often admitted, was the most important thing to a Toronto team. Not that he didn't like finishing first. But if it was a question, say, of playing a star when you were battling for first place, or saving him for the play-offs, you did the latter. Imlach was of the same mold. An expert manipulator of talent, he soon got the reputation as the most demanding coach in the game. To Imlach, no one man was bigger than the team. Even established stars found themselves sitting out games or being sent to the minors if they did not give their all or play the way Imlach wanted them to.

He insisted on calling Frank Mahovlich, a 48-goal scorer, "Maholovich," and Carl Brewer, an all-star defenseman, quit rather than play for him. But Punch, whose clubs played uninteresting clutch-and-grab hockey, still got his teams into the play-offs, wisely picking up older players, such as Andy Bathgate, who was able to give him a good series, or Terry Sawchuk. He had such classic players as Tim Horton and Dave Keon, and got the most of Johnny Bower in goal and Allan Stanley on defense and George Armstrong, the captain.

But not enough new men were coming up. After the Bower-Sawchuk combine had lifted the Leafs to the 1967 Stanley Cup, the team finished fifth the following season. It barely made the play-offs in the 1968-69 campaign, and was eliminated in four games by the Bruins. Shortly after the final buzzer, Stafford Smythe, who had hired Punch Imlach, fired him.

Housecleaning had begun again, and Smythe picked 34-year-old Jim Gregory to be the new G.M. and 41-year-old John McLellan as coach. They rebuilt in the 1969-70 campaign, working younger players around such stars as Norm Ullman (acquired in a deal for Mahovlich) and Keon. Horton was traded to the Rangers. The Leafs made the play-offs in 1971, combining age and youth, with Bob Baun back to lead the precocious defense.

Other deals brought them Jacques Plante (who went on to post the lowest goals-against average in the league) and Bernie Parent as the netminders. This protean collection of players extended the Rangers to six games in the first round of the 1971 play-offs, and observers were once again counting the Maple Leafs in future plans for success.

But the next two years virtually traumatized the team and its city. First came a blockbusting disclosure that the president of the club, Harold Ballard, and the former president, Stafford Smythe, were being investigated for fraud. The 1971-72 season was a traditional campaign in which the club took a long, hard look at promising newcomers such as Jim Harrison, Jim McKenny, Darryl Sittler, Garry Monahan, Rick Ley and Mike Pelyk.

Scoring fell off dramatically, though, with Ullman managing only 23 goals, Keon 18, and Ron Ellis 23.

The Leafs were being challenged for the final play-off spot by a resurgent Detroit team when Wilson became sick and Clancy came back to lead the team behind the bench. The club won for Clancy and managed, barely, to make the play-offs.

Parent was a proven goalie, even though he was relatively young. And with Plante still around, and the young defense gaining experience, the Leafs' future looked promising. Then the WHA came along. Parent's lawyer claimed that his client had never signed a valid NHL contract. The Miami Screaming Eagles of the WHA quickly signed Parent, the NHL's first jumper. The Leafs weren't sure what was happening, but they knew one thing: they didn't want to get into a bidding war.

Like many other clubs in the established league, the Leafs didn't believe the WHA would even get off the ground. And even if it did, the Leafs didn't want to set a precedent by negotiating with a player who was thinking of jumping. They thought that the other clubs in the NHL would stand firm beside them. They learned to their dismay that once other players began jumping, it was every club for itself. Thus, they lost Parent without even attempting to keep him, while other clubs—the Rangers, for example—kept their stars by paying them incredible salaries.

In all, the Leafs lost eleven players from their organization, including Selwood, Ley and Harrison. And of course, Parent. No other team in the NHL was hit as hard. On top of that, Ballard went to jail, convicted of fraud and misusing Maple Leaf Gardens funds. Gregory took over the hockey operations, and the team's lawyer, Bob Sedgwick, was named the team governor and represented the club at league meetings. Bill Ballard (Harold's son) took charge of overall operations of the Gardens.

Although he was in prison, Harold Ballard still had much influence in running the team. Indeed, he approved various deals the club frantically made in an attempt to right itself. But little went right. Henderson, one of the stars of the Team Canada series with the Russians, was injured and had a poor season. Ullman continued to slump. To help Plante in goal, the Leafs brought up a pair of goalies who had no previous big league experience—Ron Low and Gordon McRae. The team finished sixth in 1972-73 with its poorest record in 15 years.

Present Leaf team blends players of all ages— veteran Dave Keon (LEFT), and younger Jim McKenny (BELOW).

Dramatic changes took place in 1973. Red Kelly, who had been negotiating with Ballard while Ballard was in prison, returned to Toronto to coach. The club reorganized virtually overnight. It brought in three new goalies in Doug Favell (from Philadelphia, in exchange for the rights to Bernie Parent), Eddie Johnston (to complete a deal with Boston for Plante) and Dunc Wilson from Vancouver. Suddenly, the Leafs had three major league goalies.

In addition the Leafs brought over two members of the Swedish national team, Inge Hammarstrom and Borje Salming. Lanny McDonald, Ian Turnbull and Bob Neely made the jump from the juniors. The Leafs jumped out quickly and Toronto once again was a place for winning hockey.

THE MONTREAL CANADIENS

In the intimacy of the Forum, where 80 percent of the ticket holders are French-Canadian and everyone knows hockey, the first-time spectator immediately senses there is something special about the place and its famed tenants, the Canadiens.

And there is. It was here that Howie Morenz brought the Flying Frenchmen national fame when he was called the Babe Ruth of hockey. It was at the Forum where Maurice (Rocket) Richard brought wild-eyed fans to their feet screaming with his irresistible attack whenever he was near the goal mouth. It was here that fans pelted the league president, Clarence Campbell, with tomatoes and almost killed him with debris after Campbell had suspended Richard at the end of a season. And it was here where Toe Blake suddenly announced his retirement in 1968, after the Canadiens had won the Stanley Cup for the eighth time in his 13th season as coach.

The Canadiens grew out of the need of Montreal's French community to be represented in big-league sports. Before the start of the 1909-1910 season the National Hockey Association granted a franchise to Les Canadiens. Money was put up by a businessman from Cobalt with the understanding that French sportsmen would take over the club as soon as possible. In its first season the club finished last. The next year it finished second.

To insure the continued association between the team and its community, the NHA agreed that from then on the Canadiens would sign French players only, the other clubs not being permitted to contract for any French skaters. Before the 1911-1912 season was halfway over, the Canadiens had stirred up their volatile fans by promoting bitter feuds between themselves and the other local team, the English-speaking Wanderers. This began a tradition that rivaled the long-standing feuds between the mother countries and continued after the Wanderers left the league and the Maroons took their place. During the Maroons' tenure the Frenchmen and Maroon players rarely spoke to each other.

By 1916 the Canadiens were displaying the class that would lift them so often to the top of their league. They won their first title that year—and their first Stanley Cup. They also finished first during the 1916-1917 season, the National Hockey Association's last. The Frenchmen failed to win the National Hockey League title in the new league's first year as it should have, had fate been more history-minded. They lost it on the final day of the season to Toronto. But over the next 50 years they won it 16 times, an NHL record.

At the time the league consolidated, Leo Dandurand and Joe Cattaranich were the Canadiens' owners. They and Leo Letourneau had purchased the club in 1921 for $11,000, less than the hot dog and soft drink receipts at one Canadien game today. Dandurand coached the club as it entered its modern era and it was he who brought the great stars to Montreal.

One of his first deals elicited a resounding "non" from the French press and Canadien fans. He traded folk hero Newsy Lalonde to the Saskatoon Sheiks for Aurel Joliat, a slight (140 pounds), ulcer-ridden left wing. Joliat looked so sickly that many times throughout his 16-year career opposing players thought he had an incurable illness. In his first year he played on a line with Sprague Cleghorn and Billy Boucher. The next year Howie Morenz joined the club and suddenly hockey became big league in the

After only a year's absence from Stanley Cup competition, Montreal came back, beating Boston; then, led by fast-skating Yvan Cournoyer (shooting), taking Minnesota, 4-2.

minds of many Canadians and Americans.

Morenz was the catalyst. Known as the Babe Ruth of his sport, skating with Joliat and Boucher, he led the Canadiens to the Cup in his first season. Ruth was a power ballplayer. Morenz was a total hockey player. He was a dazzling skater, leading his line on rink-long thrusts. Some said he made a puck dance. If he did, he was its inseparable partner.

He became a Canadien after Dandurand visited his home in Stratford, Ontario, armed with a $2,500 contract. That didn't impress Morenz, but Dandurand then pulled out a stack of small bills totaling $850. The mountain of banknotes convinced Morenz to leave home. In his second season, 1924-1925, he put in goals at a one-a-game pace, scoring 30 in 30 games. In 1929-1930 he had 40 in 44 games, and during his career he tallied 270 times.

Before Morenz started scoring goals for Montreal the Canadiens were barely known outside of Quebec. His fame and that of the Canadiens spread simultaneously, given an impetus with the construction of the Forum, the first new building erected by a National Hockey League club. It was a departure from the skating-rink buildings which had housed most eastern hockey. The Forum was made specifically for hockey and built at a time when not all the clubs were making money. Within seven years, five more clubs had built all-purpose arenas.

Forum general manager William Northey wanted a place that could hold 13,000 spectators, but the owners believed that to be a utopian figure. They decided 9,500 to be more realistic. The Forum opened November 29, 1924, before a capacity crowd of 9,500 and turned away thousands. (The Canadiens beat the St. Pats, 7-1.) The fans included

Montreal's strength has been in skating and just plain great hockey players. The men on these pages are no exception. CLOCKWISE FROM LEFT: Aurel Joliat misses a goal; Joliat again; Howie Morenz, the best of them all; tough Butch Bouchard; Georges Vezina, perhaps the best goalie ever.

Maurice "Rocket" Richard scores on an assist from brother Henri, the Pocket Rocket (16). Henri later became known to some as the Rocket. Bill Gadsby and Gump Worsley are the Rangers.

those in the so-called "Millionaires' Section," where people stood for 50 cents.

To make sure the building was busy when the Canadiens weren't around, the heads of the Forum, James Strachan and Senator Donat Raymond, bought themselves another hockey club (the Maroons) and paid $15,000 to the league for the franchise. They appointed Dunc Munro to take charge of the Maroons and gave him a three-year contract–including the right to print and distribute programs for all Forum events. Munro made an extra $50,000 a year with his programs.

The Canadiens had an annoying habit of continuously coming up with an outstanding goalie. As they entered the modern era scholarly Georges Vezina was their netminder. Known as the Chicoutimi Cucumber (for his birthplace and his coolness under fire), he was in a sense the Lou Gehrig of hockey. Gehrig played in every Yankee game from his first appearance until he was finally forced out by terminal illness. Vezina first put on a Montreal uniform in 1910–and played in every Montreal game until 1925 when he was forced to retire because of tuberculosis. In most of the 367 games in which he appeared, goalies were still not allowed to get off their feet; yet Vezina was able to stand erect while catching most of the pucks that flew at him. Today the Vezina Trophy is awarded to the goalie on the club with the lowest goals-against average.

Sylvio Mantha was another member of the Canadien dynasty during the twenties and thirties. He epitomized the Canadien skater–colorful and fast. Camille Des Roches, long-time Canadien publicist, said of the Frenchmen, "All were wonderful skaters. They liked to play a wide-open game, and seemed to skate better than the English players. It was a natural talent. We're outgoing, like the Italians and Spanish, and I guess we play hockey the same way."

The Canadiens became the darlings of the French-speaking community. Much of the affection accorded the team was a sort of peer identification with success. Many Frenchmen were considered second-class citizens by a haughty English majority. A knowledge of English was essential in areas such as banking and civil service, but a high percentage of the French population grew up in insular communities where only French was spoken at home and in school. When they moved to the big cities in search of jobs, they found a barrier–nonfluency in English–standing between themselves and status. But the Canadiens–this was something different for the French. Here was a collection of Frenchmen who had risen above generally humble beginnings, who had made it big while retaining their identity.

Cecil Hart was the coach who benefited from these fine players. He replaced Dandurand for the 1925-1926 season and coached until the end of the 1931-1932 campaign. The Canadiens won two Cups for Hart. Lalonde, Dandurand again, Mantha, Hart again, Jules Dugal and Pit Lepine handled the Canadiens over the next nine seasons, the least successful in the club's history. It finished first just once during the span and won no Cups. Crowds dwindled to 3,000 a game during the Depression.

Bad management went hand in hand with bad coaching. There was little discipline in the clubhouse. Players drank wine, whiskey and beer beside their lockers. Local newspapermen had *carte blanche* in the dressing room and were most happy to hoist a few with the players.

The president of the Forum, Senator Raymond, finally bought out Dandurand and Cattaranich in 1936 as the club neared bankruptcy, transferring ownership of the Canadiens and the Maroons to the Forum. Management decided that one head was better than two. One club would be dropped and the choice was easy. Montreal was a predominantly French city, the Canadiens were predominantly French. In 1938, the Maroons ended their NHL career.

Dick Irvin, dismissed from Toronto be-

cause of his age, became the Canadiens' new coach for the 1940-1941 season. The strait-laced Irvin immediately banned reporters and hangers-on from the dressing room. He shored up the team's sagging spirits, watched curfew deadlines closely and frowned on liquor. His squad included Toe Blake, a skilled left wing who had won the scoring title two seasons before; Bill Durnan, who turned out to be the top goalie of his time, and Butch Bouchard, a giant of a defenseman who relied on finesse rather than brute strength.

In Irvin's first three seasons, the Canadiens remained a mediocre club, finishing sixth, sixth and fourth. But in that last season, 1942-1943, a pugnacious, beady-eyed forward who played the "wrong" side of the line joined the team. His name was Richard. From that year on the Canadiens built a seemingly endless series of seasons in which they put on the ice the most talented clubs in the history of the game.

Maurice the Rocket was everything to his fans. The most goal-directed player the sport had ever seen, he was irresistible from the blue line in, a bull who firmly believed that the man in the other uniform was his mortal enemy who should be dealt with accordingly. His remarkable career repeatedly was interrupted by ailments and ultimately was cut short by an injury that had already stopped one mythological hero—his Achilles tendon was severed. He retired in 1960, having scored 544 goals, nearly 200 more than anyone else had before. He became the first player to score 50 goals in a season, a season only 50 games long (1944-1945).

In later years, when Boom Boom Geoffrion and then Bobby Hull reached that figure in 70-game seasons, Richard's record was denigrated by some who claimed that he played against wartime athletes—rejects not good enough to be taken into the service. While it was true that many clubs were depleted—the Rangers lost 13 regulars—the Canadian army miraculously overlooked many other stars. There was talk that good players at home helped the war effort by helping morale, and the level of play in wartime was greater for hockey than it was for baseball in the U.S.

Richard's goal-scoring ability was all the more remarkable because of the position he played. He was a right wing with a left-handed shot. When the puck was shoveled to him, he generally had to switch hands to enable him to cradle the puck and carry it safely into an opponent's defensive zone. But he had a magnificent, accurate backhand, and some theorists maintain that because he could shoot so well both ways he had an advantage by playing on the wrong side.

Richard, Blake and Elmer Lach formed the Punch Line or, as one writer called them, "a trio of mad dogs in a savage quest for goals." They were joined by the great Durnan, who didn't play goal in the league until he was 28 years old. Durnan made the all-star team five times and won the Vezina Trophy six times. He once turned in four consecutive shutouts and held the opposition without a goal for 309 minutes 21 seconds, a modern record. Ken Reardon, a completely irritating player whom fans either loved or hated, was still another force on those great teams.

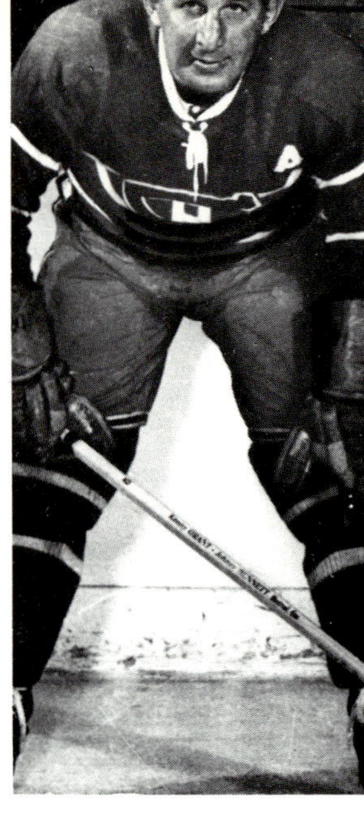

CLOCKWISE FROM RIGHT: Goalie Jacques Plante stops a Boston rush; Hall of Famers Ken Reardon, Toe Blake (in his playing days) and Elmer Lach; Gump Worsley, then a Ranger, now a North Star, makes a fantastic stop on a shot from the point. "Le Gros Bill," Jean Beliveau, tries for the tip-in.

These stars helped the Frenchmen finish first for four consecutive years, starting with the 1943-1944 season. In 1946 Frank Selke joined the team as managing director, following 20 years in a highly successful and profitable partnership with the Maple Leafs.

Selke's first year, he later recalled, "was crazy. It took me a long time to get to know the French players. They reacted to praise, not criticism. They would be up, they would be down." Selke, in charge of the entire operation, marveled at the wealth of talent. But he also realized that while the Canadiens had fielded the greatest team in hockey, there was a lack of depth on the parent squad and the farm system was failing to produce.

To insure a continuous flow of talent to Montreal, Selke organized clubs from Nova Scotia to British Columbia. At one time, six of the teams vying for the Memorial Cup (an amateur competition for players under 20) were Canadien farm teams. Selke's seedlings grew into a crop that included Jean Beliveau, Boom Boom Geoffrion and Dickie Moore.

Both Beliveau and Geoffrion joined the team in 1950, when Richard was at his zenith. Over the years, each suffered to some degree by playing in Richard's shadow. Geoffrion's first scoring championship, captured in the 1954-1955 season, was bittersweet. It came when he was in a close race with Richard who had led the league in goals many times but never in total points. Richard was suspended the last few games of the season (prompting the tomato-throwing incident at Clarence Campbell) while Geoffrion picked up points (often to boos) and won the title.

Beliveau was not as flamboyant as the Rocket or the Boomer, but he was a flawless skater, graceful and powerful. They named him Le Gros Bill, after a French-Canadian Bunyanesque folk hero. In later years Beliveau, who had become a Canadien only after two years of negotiation (he had been making $20,000 a year as an "amateur"), said that it was impossible to try to live up to Richard. "If I scored two goals, they wanted three. If I got 40, they wanted 50."

The Montreal power play was a marvel in those years. Geoffrion, married to Morenz' daughter, played the right point. Doug Harvey, the powerful, smooth defenseman who was able to slow the game down to his deliberate pace almost at will, played the left side. Up front were Richard, Beliveau and Bert Olmstead, a star in his own right. The power play was so strong that Dickie Moore, who set a league scoring record, wasn't even part of it.

Because the Canadien power play was so destructive, the rule was actually changed so that once a team with the man advantage scored, the power play ended. Before the change, in the final minutes of a game against Chicago, the Hawks had a 1-0 lead. Chicago drew a penalty, Richard scored twice within two minutes and Montreal won. In another game, Boston had a 2-0 lead when one of the Bruins was sent off. In the following two minutes, the Canadiens got three goals and won, 3-2. The rule was changed shortly after.

Irvin was dismissed by Selke after the 1954-55 season, and Toe Blake took over. Another new batch of stars was on the way, including Richard's younger brother Henri (the Pocket Rocket) and Jacques Plante, the masked goalie.

Harvey, Beliveau, Geoffrion and Moore were reaching their prime, and with this superb collection of talent led them to nine first-place finishes and eight Cups over the next 13 years. Blake never approved of Plante's hypochondria, however, and eventually dumped him to New York in a trade for Gump Worsley. Plante had been popular in Montreal, the first goalie ever to wear the mask.

A short box of a man, Claude Ruel, replaced Blake for the 1968-69 season. The Canadien's critics quickly hooted him down. But Ruel led the squad to a Cup victory.

The 1969-70 campaign signaled the end of an era. After 21 consecutive seasons of appearing in the play-offs, the Canadiens finished fifth, losing out on the final day to the Rangers.

Ruel was replaced shortly after the 1970-71 season began by Al MacNeil, a former Montreal defenseman. The club acquired Frank Mahovlich, and some of the younger players began to come through. The Canadiens again were Stanley Cup contenders.

The Canadiens didn't waste much time attempting to get back into contention. Shortly after the 1970-71 season began, Ruel was dismissed and Al MacNeil took his place. More changes were made; the big one was the acquisition of the great Frank Mahovlich from the Red Wings. Yvan Cournoyer became a big scorer and Pete Mahovlich, Frank's brother, turned into a star. The younger players, such as Jacques Lemaire and Marc Tardif also produced top seasons. Guy Lapointe was unveiled on defense.

Late in the season the Canadiens finished with a rush and brought up Ken Dryden, a Cornell University graduate, to man the goal. In a memorable play-off, the Canadiens ousted the Bruins, who had finished first with a record point total. The Canadiens reached the final round, though veteran center, Henri Richard, was complaining about being benched by MacNeil. But with a sense of history like his brother's Richard came off the bench in the last game of the finals and scored the winning goal against the Black Hawks. The Canadiens were world champions only a year after missing the play-offs.

Dryden received a unique distinction. He

won the Conn Smythe Trophy as the play-offs' most valuable performer—and still was eligible for the rookie of the year award the following campaign. This he captured in 1971-72 as the Frenchmen continued to improve. The great Beliveau had retired. MacNeil was replaced behind the bench by Scotty Bowman. Richard was the new captain, and Guy Lafleur the number-one draft choice, made it big as a regular. The club didn't win the play-offs in 1971-72, though. They were ousted in the first round by the Rangers.

The next season the club reached a peak. It set a record by losing only 10 games all season, even though J. C. Tremblay jumped to the WHA. Dryden won the Vezina Trophy. Young, strong defensemen and forwards helped the older players. The Canadiens' depth was the talk of the league. This time, the Habs sailed through the play-offs, capturing the Cup as Cournoyer set a play-off mark of 15 goals. In 1973, Dryden quit the club to become a law clerk after he failed to reach a contract agreement. Several other players jumped leagues. But the Frenchmen still had a nucleus of fine players, enough to insure a play-off berth for many years.

TOP: Montreal's Ken Dryden, widely considered hockey's finest goaltender when he was playing. Dryden quit hockey in 1973 but was expected to return with another team in 1975 for a fabulous salary. ABOVE: A typical Montreal Canadiens' fan—belligerent when called upon, knowledgeable to the highest degree.

THE NEW YORK RANGERS

Despite money, fans, the thrill of New York and their reputation, strangely enough the Rangers have been one of the least successful clubs over the long haul in the league's history. Whenever it appeared that they were on the verge of long success, they floundered. Yet their history is as colorful, their top players are as great, their leadership is as fine, as any in the league.

Tex Rickard built the Rangers in 1926 after having been duly impressed by the profits shown by other clubs in the league, as well as by the money made the year before by New York's first entrant in the NHL, the Americans. Colonel John S. Hammond, a proud Garden executive who knew nothing about hockey, hired Conn Smythe to run his club, then fired him, replacing him with Lester Patrick. Patrick led the Rangers through their most successful era.

New York was a night town in the 1920s. Hockey was a big night out. The rumrunners and their ladies of the evening mingled with society and the Rangers drew from a wide spectrum of New York's population for their following. A sense of haphazardness, of "flakiness," has always pervaded the Ranger operations. The publicists who churned out information on the new team did not always tell the truth, contributing to the legend.

The Rangers actually were named for Rickard's boyhood idols, the Texas Rangers. But to the fans, the players were described as real-life descendants of the western law enforcers, men who had traded their rifles for hockey sticks. To ensnare the city's Jewish population, it was said that goalie Lorne Chabot's name was really Chabotsky. Oliver Reinikka's name was altered to the Italian-sounding Rocco. Patrick finally put a stop to the publicity after hearing of the wildest plan yet—the kidnapping of star Bill Cook.

With such stars as Chabot, the baldish Ching Johnson, Frank Boucher and Bill and Bun Cook, the Rangers took off in their first season, finishing first in the American Division of the league. In their second season they didn't finish first but won the Cup in a memorable series, forced to enemy ice by the circus which kept Madison Square Garden booked during the finals, a routine that continued until 1967.

After finishing second that year (1927-1928), the Rangers eliminated Pittsburgh and Boston to move into the play-off finals against the Montreal Maroons. All the games were played in Montreal, at the Forum. The Maroons captured the first contest, 2-0. In the second period of the second game, with the score 0-0, goalie Chabot was seriously injured when a puck slammed into his left eye.

Now without a goalie, Patrick implored the Maroons to permit him to use a goaltender from another club, but Montreal refused. Patrick took his players into the dressing room for a conference. He was 45 years old, a former great player. His white hair and sharp features had earned him the nickname Silver Fox. "Boys," he told his men, "I'm going to play goal. Check as you've never checked before, fellows, and help protect an old man."

Patrick was protected as few goalies have ever been. The Rangers turned into fiends, crushing any Maroon who wandered into New York territory. The few shots that got off, Patrick managed to stop. Early in the third period Bill Cook scored to put the Rangers ahead. Nels Stewart, whose shot had sent Chabot to the hospital, tied the game with fewer than six minutes remaining. Patrick

Steve Vickers (8) exemplifies the determination of the Rangers' hustling "Bulldog Line." Teaming with Walt Tkaczuk and Billy Fairbairn, Vickers became a star.

Cooper
21
8

held up. At the end of 60 minutes, the clubs were tied, forcing the game into sudden-death overtime. After 7 minutes 5 seconds, Boucher scored for the Rangers who then went on, inspired, to win the Cup.

Patrick remained with the Rangers until 1946, serving as their coach-general manager until 1939 and as their general manager after he turned coaching duties over to Boucher. His teams were known as the Rollicking Rangers, the Boisterous Blues and the Broadway Blues. The original club stayed together for nearly ten years. Its success may have been due to the fact that the players stuck together on the ice and off.

Bill Cook was the leader. A big, strong right wing, he led the league in goals with 33 in 44 games in the Rangers' first season. His spirit set the tempo. One major battle in 1934 epitomized that spirit.

The New Yorkers were playing the Montreal Canadiens in the Garden and, as usual, an opposing player was selected to shadow Cook. Nels Crutchfield was the Frenchman chosen for the job. He did his job too well. Suddenly Cook lost his temper. Using his stick in the manner of an angry mother, Cook slapped the blond, handsome Crutchfield with a series of short raps. Crutchfield lifted his stick and brought it down full force on top of Cook's head, poleaxing him to the ice.

"You would have thought poor Bill was dead," recalled Muzz Patrick, Lester's son, who was at the game and who eventually became a Ranger himself. "Cook went down in a pool of blood. They brought him into the dressing room. I remember the blood was gushing and they had to get those large bath towels to soak it up." Cook insisted on returning after the blood stopped flowing. A helmet was found for him and he took tothe ice (most of the fans had never seen a helmet worn before) and received a standing ovation. He then scored the winning goal.

In the middle of the Rangers' turbulent style, like the eye of a hurricane, was the diminutive Boucher. An easygoing, nonflappable center, he played the game cleanly. The Lady Byng Trophy, awarded for clean play coupled with skill, was his seven times in eight years. After he had won it for the seventh time, the league decided to give him the trophy outright, replacing it with another one.

The only real glory that belonged to the Rangers in their first 40 years came under Boucher and Patrick. In Patrick's 14 seasons as coach-general manager the club finished first twice, won the play-offs twice and made the play-offs 13 times. In Boucher's first year of coaching, the club won the Cup again and in the 1941-1942 season it finished first. The Rangers' second era, with such players as Neil and Mac Colville, Alex Shibicky, Phil Watson, Bryan Hextall and Lynn Patrick, marked the beginning of the end of their fortunes. But before the Rangers went down they generated a few sparks.

The Rangers of the thirties were tough boys in the night league. Broadway was theirs. The fans didn't dash home for the suburbs after games then, and Times Square was crowded well past midnight. Into this fun atmosphere charged the Rangers. Most of the second-generation Rangers were young and unmarried. Most had a showgirl whom they'd meet after a game before melting into the show business crowd. They also felt at home in New York, an attitude that changed after the war when the Rangers' fortunes changed. "We could walk into any night club," said Muzz Patrick, "and the patrons would stand and cheer."

Thirteen Rangers served in World War II, virtually ruining the franchise. Starting with the 1942-1943 season, the Rangers finished last five times in seven years. At the end of the war Patrick left, his post as general manager taken over by Boucher. Nothing much happened under Boucher, who gave up coaching in 1948 and turned the reins over to Muzz's brother, Lynn. Boucher remained as general manager until 1955.

In the 13 seasons following the start of

ABOVE: The early days of Madison Square Garden were not exactly sellouts. 6,392 watched this game. FAR LEFT: Bill Cook and Lester Patrick. LEFT: Goalie Lorne Chabot saw his name changed by the Rangers to Chabotsky in order to attract the city's Jewish population to the games.

World War II, the Rangers made the play-offs just twice. After Boucher, Lynn Patrick, Neil Colville, Bill Cook and Muzz Patrick took turns coaching the team. Then another era began when Fiery Phil Watson became the coach for the 1955-1956 season. The Rangers failed to make the play-offs in their first try for Watson, but succeeded in three straight seasons afterward.

New Rangers included Andy Bathgate, Camille (The Eel) Henry, Harry Howell. Watson pushed and punished his men. He exploded after every defeat. Finally, midway through the 1959-1960 season, he left. Alf Pike took over, in turn being replaced by Doug Harvey, the Canadiens' great defenseman. Harvey, who lived high and spent well, dedicated himself (in his fashion) to reviving the Rangers. As player-coach he led the team to a fourth-place finish, good enough to make the play-offs, but not good enough to win. A hypnotist was hired. The Rangers promptly lost. Harvey left and was followed by Muzz Patrick, Red Sullivan and Emile Francis.

Francis had been an eminently forgettable goalie, briefly with the Rangers and with the Chicago Black Hawks. He had always been a hustler, though, and knew how to make a dollar. In his younger days he ran semiprofessional baseball teams (he played shortstop) and once imported a Cuban baseball team to face his own squad. A story came out about that game, how the Cubans, angry over the way the game went, had chased Francis through the Saskatchewan wheat fields. "What?" said Francis when he was asked about the incident. "It was me who was chasing them."

An aggressive player who had made a study of his craft, he was inserted by Muzz Patrick into the Ranger front office where he served as assistant general manager. From there he engineered the trade that sent Bathgate to the Toronto Maple Leafs in exchange for Bob Nevin, Arnie Brown and Rod Seiling, who were to become a part of the Rangers' new breed. Francis himself replaced Patrick as general manager in 1964. In the middle of the 1965-1966 season he dismissed Sullivan as coach and took on both duties.

The club was largely his at that point. He had developed Rod Gilbert and Jean Ratelle. He had traded for Brown, Nevin and Seiling. "The club wasn't going well," he explained. "Since it was my team, it was me who had to take the responsibility." The team finished last that season, but in 1966-1967 wound up fourth and made the play-offs for the first time in five years.

For most of the season the Rangers had been first or second. They were the only winning club in town. The Jets and Giants in football, the Mets and Yankees in baseball and the Knickerbockers in basketball had been disappointments. People became interested in hockey again. At one late-season game, with nothing particular at stake, fans were offering $30 for a $5 seat.

In the 1967-1968 season the New Yorkers finished second in the East Division, four points behind the Canadiens. It was their best finish in ten years and coincided with their move into the new Garden atop Penn Station. They sold out every game played in the new $44-million building; 17,250 fans paid for each game. About 2,000 of those paid $750 for one season ticket as part of a package deal. As they had been in pro football and baseball, corporations for the first time were heavy buyers.

The Rangers' sudden emergence as a factor in the league had been demanded by the Garden management. The Rangers are a subsidiary of the Garden and the officers of the parent corporation wanted, no matter the cost, a winning team for their new arena—both for prestige and gate receipts. Francis had the money to work with, but money doesn't buy much in the National Hockey League. The East Division clubs are all wealthy. Players are more important.

If Francis, before he became a coach, was a behind-the-scenes man, he became a public figure one night in 1965 during a game against the Detroit Red Wings. The Wings had just scored a lightning-quick goal—it went in and out of the cage before most of the fans and players could see it. But the goal judge spotted it and flipped a switch that put on the red light to signal goal. As though the switch had sent a charge through his seat on the promenade, Francis leaped up and ran over to goal judge Arthur Reichert to argue the call. Reichert insisted the goal was in; Francis insisted it wasn't. While Francis was protesting, two fans told him to keep quiet. Words were exchanged and seconds later fists were flying, Francis being the prime target.

Then followed one of the strangest sights ever seen in the Garden. The Ranger players had watched the argument from the rink, behind the ten-foot-high protective Herculite glass. Suddenly Vic Hadfield, skates and all, climbed the wall. In seconds he reached the top and dived over it into the melee. Other Rangers followed. At one time six of them were climbing the wall, laboring like Sisyphus straining for an impossible foothold.

After the game Francis sported a black eye. Bill Jennings, the Rangers' president, threatened to bar Reichert from the building. Reichert, who in more than 20 years of major league judging had been overruled just twice by a referee (and one of those times, Reichert insisted, he was right), reiterated that the shot went in. The next day films confirmed Reichert's judgment.

Francis' rapport with his players, combined with a juggler's hand, helped bring the team out of the wilderness during the 1966-1967 season, but the players lacked the total confidence so necessary to success in the NHL. So Francis made another move before the season's start that had an incalculable effect on the future of the team. The Cat lured Boom Boom Geoffrion out of retirement. At the age of 35, the bombastic Geoffrion, who spoke of himself in the third person ("The Boomer is pleased"), worked on the Rangers' collective psyche. He had learned his lessons with the Canadiens well. "The team that thinks it's a winner is a winner," he told the young players. "Don't go around with those long Ranger faces."

In the dressing room he was the team scold, constantly peppering good-natured abuse on the young Turks he thought should be producing more. Although he did not play a full season, he scored 17 goals—and the first one in the play-offs against his old team—in a remarkable comeback. The next season he suffered a bleeding ulcer, but still played part-time, on the power play. After the campaign, with a year to run on his playing contract, he was appointed the Rangers' coach by Francis, who felt that he had done his job by leading the team back to respectability. Francis remained in his post as general manager.

It appeared to be a new era under Francis. But Ranger fans could look back to a history filled with weird happenings. Indeed, for years the Rangers were like the old Brooklyn Dodgers—crazy things just seemed to follow them around. A game against the Americans is a case in point.

It was March 27, 1938. The clubs were tied in a best-of-three series to see who would advance to the semifinals of the Cup play-offs. The Rangers had the younger team—the Patrick boys, Watson, Hextall, goalie Davey Kerr and Babe Pratt. The Maroons had old Ranger Ching Johnson and Nels Stewart, who had scored most of his 324 career goals with the Montreal Maroons. The Americans' coach was Red Dutton, who admitted that the Rangers had the better club. "But we'll be there," he cautioned.

There was no score in the opening period although the red light had flashed. A woman fan sitting next to goal judge Charles Porteous reached into Porteous' booth and flipped the goal switch during a Ranger attack. "I nearly fell off the bench," said Dutton. The 16,340 fans stood, not understanding. The referee finally straightened it out.

The Americans failed to score in the second period and were trailing 2-0 in the final 20-minute session. Lorne Carr beat Kerr early in the period and midway through the period, with Dutton using five forwards, Stewart rapped in the tying goal. The goalies —Kerr and the Americans' Earl Robertson— were on the spot. The teams went through one scoreless 20-minute overtime. Then another. In the third extra period it almost ended quickly.

Ott Heller, a Ranger defenseman, grabbed a rebound with his glove while trying to protect his goalie. An automatic penalty shot was called. The Rangers convinced the officials that Heller was more than ten feet from the cage and the call was changed.

Then the Rangers threatened. Cecil Dillon had a breakaway and swooped in alone on Robertson. The goalie didn't budge, the shot bounced off his pads, the third overtime ended. The clubs had completed the equivalent of two full games. It was past one A.M. The vendors had run out of hot dogs and coffee. Finally Carr put the disk in after 40 seconds of the fourth overtime and the Americans were in the finals. It was 1:25 in the morning, four hours and 40 minutes after the opening face-off.

For the 1968-69 season, Francis appointed Geoffrion the coach. The job had lasted half a season when Geoffrion's ulcer acted up. Francis returned as coach, and to many it appeared the start of a new era for the Rangers. It was the final game of the 1969-70 season. Because of the close race and the league rules, the Rangers had to beat Detroit, scoring at least five goals, while the Montreal Canadiens had to lose at night to Chicago.

The Rangers had led the league for more than half a season, then suffered crippling injuries. Brad Park, their leader, was injured. So was Jim Neilson. Walt Tkaczuk, a brilliant young center, had been brutally checked continuously and had a poor second half.

But a strange sight unfolded at the Garden. The New Yorkers were unstoppable. They began pouring in goals faster than they had all year. At the end, they had won, 9-5, after taking 65 shots. That night, the Canadiens were routed by the Black Hawks.

Francis, who always boasted about his young players on the farm, nevertheless traded several away to make deals to fill gaps when it was apparent his farm crop wouldn't produce as he hoped. Finally, he rested Ed Giacomin, alternating him with Gilles Villemure, and for the first time since 1940, the Rangers captured the Vezina.

Giacomin, an intense, salt-and-pepper-haired goalie, was perhaps the most important of the Rangers in their new era. Three times in five years he led the league in shutouts, and became the most exciting netminder in the game with his quick reflexes and quick stick.

As popular as Giacomin was Rod Gilbert, a handsome Frenchman with lightning moves and a bristling slap shot. His center was Jean Ratelle, who many believed was the club's finest forward, a lithe, graceful player who never got rattled. They were complemented by Hadfield, a wing who loved corners.

The 1971-72 season was going to be the year, everyone was convinced. The line of Ratelle-Hadfield-Gilbert was coming into its own. Soon, it became the most feared line in the league. It went on a record scoring binge. It became history's first line to produce three 40-goal men. But Ratelle was injured while in the midst of the battle for the league scoring honors with the Bruins' Phil Esposito. The rest of the team slumped. The Rangers barely held second place in the East Division. Hadfield got a pair of goals on the final day of the season to become the club's first 50-goal man. Ratelle went over the 100-point mark. It was a solid team. Still, it had to face the Canadiens in the first round of the 1972 play-offs.

The Rangers upset the favored Canadiens. Then they shocked everyone by disposing of the Black Hawks in four straight. The Rangers were in the final round of Stanley Cup play for the first time since 1950. But they were no match for the Bruins and dropped the Cup in a six-game series.

There were no dramatic changes on the

Jean Ratelle misses fine chance to score against Boston. Ratelle, Rod Gilbert, and Vic Hadfield formed the "Gag Line," the highest scoring trio in Ranger history.

club in the 1972-73 campaign except for the addition of Steve Vickers. Vickers accounted for 30 goals and was named rookie of the year. Another failure in the play-offs prompted Francis to give up the coaching again. This time he selected Larry Popein to lead the team for the 1973-74 season, one which began badly with a slump. In midseason Emile Francis once again took the helm as the Rangers sought the Cup, which they hadn't claimed in 34 years.

Thanks to a millionaire groceryman impressed by a Stanley Cup hockey game, Boston had the honor of becoming the first United States city to put a team in the National Hockey League.

By 1924, Charles F. Adams, president of the First National stores, had been a longtime hockey buff. He had seen the game played among amateurs in the Boston area, but that year he went to Montreal to see a Stanley Cup game. He returned, convinced that professional hockey could succeed in Massachusetts.

Skaters were scarce, though. When Adams heard that the Patricks were having trouble out west, he was able to engineer the purchase of the Patricks' entire league. He then sold the players to the rest of the NHL, keeping the players he wanted for himself. The Bruins, then, cost Adams only $15,000.

It was one way to get Eddie Shore, a rushing defenseman whose reputation was building in Canada. But Adams wasn't happy with many of the other choices. He needed more players. He hired Art Ross, whose playing career had ended six years before, as his general manager and coach. Ross went traveling—thousands of miles across Canada. He scouted anyone he thought he could get. Since many professionals were tied up by other NHL clubs, Ross looked at amateurs, many of whom he persuaded to turn pro.

The Bruins dropped 11 straight games early their first season, but Ross hung on and his teams bounced back. He coached them from their first year until 1934, then from 1936 to 1939, and finally from 1941 to 1945. Over the years the Bruins built several strong teams, but in their first 40 years captured only three Stanley Cups.

The wildest Bruin and, some say, the greatest player ever, was Shore. He started his big-league career in 1926 at the age of 24. A big man—he could grasp a basketball with either hand—he was involved in more unusual happenings, more fights, more hockey lore, than any other single player.

Perhaps the most frequently told story is the Christmas week fight in Boston, when Shore's ear was nearly severed. The club doctor told him it would have to come off. Shore stormed out of Boston Garden and trudged through the windswept, snow-covered streets in search of a doctor's shingle. He went to two doctors, both of whom told him the ear would be lost. Finally he found a physician who said he would try to save it. The doctor wanted to give Shore an anesthetic.

"Just give me a mirror, Doc," said Shore. "I want to make sure you sew it on right."

Shore was born in Saskatchewan, the son of a farmer. In later years he told of his life as a youngster, of the beatings his father gave him when chores weren't done right, of operations he performed on farm animals, of Herculean field tasks. His early days toughened him—he played 14 seasons in the NHL. Six times he was an all-star, four times the league's most valuable player. A stone wall on defense, he could also carry the puck and score.

He missed a train to Montreal one night when his cab broke down in a snowstorm. After several phone calls, he reached a wealthy friend who offered the use of his car and chauffeur. Fine, said Shore. He would drive to Montreal. After a few hours of night driving on icy roads, the windshield wipers failed. The chauffeur, petrified, refused to go on. Shore took the wheel, driving with one hand while his other hand reached around to the

Derek "Turk" Sanderson, mod and popular Bruin, leads a rush against Montreal. Sanderson, Esposito, Orr and Company produced the highest-scoring team in the history of hockey.

windshield and scraped it. The car skidded off the road and the two men were unable to push it back. Shore, using a tire jack for an ax, broke off some nearby branches, put them under the wheels and got them moving.

Nearly 24 hours later the car arrived in Montreal. The game already in progress, Shore rushed to Ross, announced his arrival and insisted on playing. Ross, as he told the story in later years, said, "Eddie tried so hard to get there that I thought I'd let him dress. But I had no intention of playing him." Shore was adamant. He played and scored. Boston won, 1-0.

The Bruins had two great lines during the Shore years, Boston's best era. Into the Bruins' fifth season came the Dynamite Trio—Dit Clapper, Cooney Weiland and Dutch Gainor—as the team captured its first Cup. Then came the Kraut Line—Milt Schmidt, Woody Dumart and Bobby Bauer, each of them from Kitchener, Ontario (which, in pre-World War I days, was known as Berlin). They finished 1, 2, 3 in scoring in 1940, but despite their presence, the Bruins took a turn for the worse after the war. In 1960 the club reached its low point. For five straight seasons it finished last. Yet, while the Bruins were foundering, the fans continued to turn out, not capacity, perhaps, but almost.

The Boston area has always been one of the best hockey grounds in the United States, with most of the colleges and prep schools in the area fielding excellent teams. Furthermore, there are thousands of ex-Canadiens (mostly from the maritime provinces) in Boston loyal to the game. In fact, while the Bruins were finishing last, they outdrew the Celtics, even as the basketball team was winning the NBA championship eight straight years.

During this dormant period, the Bruins waited impatiently for a boy in Parry Sound, Ontario, to grow up. His name was Bobby Orr. Weston Adams, who had assumed the presidency from his father, and some of his friends went to see a midget game in Ganonoque, Ontario. It was a night off for them and they had heard about a player—not Orr—who might bear watching. But their eyes soon riveted on a blond, crew-cut 13-year-old. "He was very small," said Adams. "But he just looked like a hockey player." The Bruins spoke to Orr's parents and managed to get the youngster committed to Boston.

When he was ready for the major leagues, Orr hired a lawyer, the redoubtable Alan Eagleson, Players Association attorney as well as ex-member of the Ontario parliament. Orr thus ushered in a new era in hockey's employer-employee relationship as well as a new era for the Bruins. He got the contract he wanted—believed to be worth a quarter of a million dollars—and made Boston a contender. By the end of his first season, 1966-1967, he was being called the greatest defenseman in the game. Harry Howell of the Rangers won the Norris Trophy as the league's best defender that season and said gratefully, "I'm glad I won it now. No one else but Orr will win it for the next 20 years."

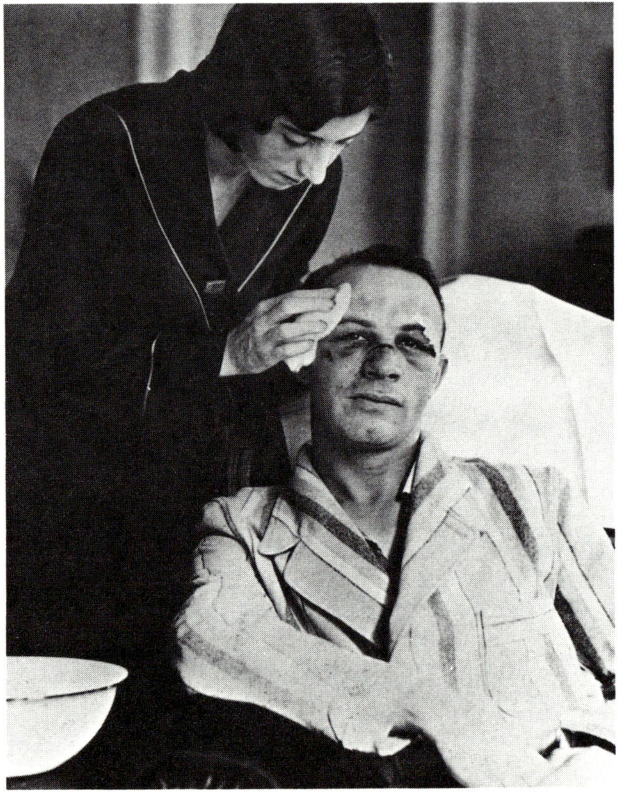

FACING: Meanest of them all, Eddie Shore, is treated by his wife following a typical game. LEFT: Milt Schmidt. BELOW: The '38 Bruins. From left are Portland, Pettinger, Clapper, Hollett, Dumart, Goldsworthy, Schmidt, Getliffe, Sands, Shore, Cowley, Thompson, Jackson, Weiland and Bauer. Schmidt, Dumart and Bauer, all from Kitchener, Ontario, finished 1, 2 and 3 in scoring in 1940. This was the last great Boston team before 1968–1969.

BELOW: Milt Schmidt, eventual general manager of Boston, is decked in a rough game by Dean Prentice. FACING: Bobby Orr, perhaps the finest ever, challenges Los Angeles King

In the 20 years following the departure of Ross as coach, the Bruins' luck paralleled the Rangers'. Coaches came and went as the postwar years proved disastrous. Clapper, Buck Boucher (a member of the large Boucher family), Schmidt, Phil Watson, Schmidt again and finally Harry Sinden, in 1966, had the club. Sinden took over a team that had finished last in five of the previous seven seasons —and next to last the other two years. In his first chance with Boston, the club slipped to last again. During the 1967-1968 season his team arrived. It ended in third place, the highest finish by a Bruins' squad in ten years.

Orr was the backbone of the team, but he also had Phil Esposito, who had played on Bobby Hull's line (and in his shadow) at Chicago, and Terrible Teddy Green, the rough, expert defenseman. Both were superlative players, especially Esposito, who in 1969, smashed the single-season scoring record by almost thirty points. He got a fine effort out of John (The Chief) Bucyk as Sinden built one of the roughest aggregates the league had seen in years. Their style was adored by the loud and bloodthirsty Boston fans.

Some of their attitude may have been honed by frustration. The last time they had seen a Bruin team in first place was 1941, when they also saw their last Cup champions.

Orr had what may have been the finest season in history for the 1969-70 campaign. The Bruins won the Cup for the first time since 1941 (fittingly, the winning goal was scored in overtime against St. Louis by Orr, on an assist from Derek Sanderson). Orr not only became the first defenseman to lead the league in scoring, he shattered all defensemen's marks with 33 goals, 87 assists and 120 points. He captured the Hart, Norris, Ross and Smythe trophies.

The collection, known as the Big Bad Bruins, reached its peak in the 1970-71 season. Finishing first for the first time in 30 years, they averaged 5 goals a game with the most massive scoring ever produced. Esposito accounted for 152 points, scoring 76 goals to bust Hull's mark by 18. Orr garnered more than 100 assists.

The Bruins didn't appear to miss Sinden, who had quit after the Stanley Cup victory. Tom Johnson, his replacement, led the Bruins to a better regular-season record, but was unable to take them to the Cup.

The Bruins were merely continuing a tradition that marked all their good clubs—pugnaciousness. It started with Shore, continued with Schmidt and was inherited by Orr & Company. Shore believed that every player should try as hard as he did, but never took into account that most had lesser skills. His idea of how the game should be played—his way—carried over into his business ventures, where he became successful as the one-man boss of the Springfield Indians of the AHL.

Shore remembered starting the hard way. He expected his players to earn their living the same way. When they couldn't suit up for a game, they were supposed to sell popcorn before the game or get to work painting the arena. Others blew up balloons or sold programs. And when a player was in a slump, he often got this advice: "Stay away from your wife."

Don Johns, who played for Shore in the early 1960s, remembers being called into Shore's office one day during a slump. "You're not combing your hair right," said Shore, deadly serious. "Part it on the other side." To make sure a player followed his advice to keep his legs closer, Shore tied the player's legs together. Another time he chained a goalie to the cage so he wouldn't wander.

During Shore's early years, the Bruins underwent so many changes under Ross that it was said Boston had three clubs—one coming, one going, one staying. Eventually Shore, Clapper and Harry Oliver made the Hall of Fame. Clapper was the league's first 20-year man. He played nine years as a forward and 11 as a defenseman and was the first defenseman ever to reach the 200-goal plateau.

The Dynamite Trio sparked the Bruins to four straight first-place finishes, starting with the 1927-1928 season, a feat that was matched, beginning in 1937-1938, with the Kraut Line Bruins. Oliver was a 155-pounder, "smooth as silk," who never spent more than 24 minutes in the penalty box in any of his 11 major league seasons.

Schmidt, who anchored the Kraut Line, was the kind of player executives call a "throwback." He didn't believe in injuries. The team doctor once said he didn't believe a man could play, as Schmidt did, with the assorted injuries he had received. He scored 229 goals in his career (and added 346 assists), was a three-time all-star and was named the most valuable player once.

The Kraut Line was broken up, ironically, by World War II. Schmidt, Bauer and Dumart entered the Royal Canadian Air Force as a unit in 1942. One great Bruin remained, Bill Cowley. An extraordinary playmaker, he was able to spot his man anywhere on the ice. He won the most valuable award twice and made the all-star team four times.

There didn't appear to be any drive behind the Bruins after the war. The club eventually rebuilt its scouting staff (as the Rangers did) and went after young, aggressive players. The front office was realigned, with Schmidt taking over the general manager's duties. It seemed only fitting that as the Bruins entered a new phase, led on the ice by Orr, they were directed from the executive suite by the man who had been a symbol of previous great Boston clubs.

The Bruins powered their way to the top of the East Division in 1971-72, as Esposito and Orr turned in further remarkable seasons. It was an overpowering team, with players such as Derek Sanderson, Ken Hodge, Wayne Cashman and Fred Stanfield abetting the proven heroes. In addition, Gerry Cheevers set a record in goal by playing 33 games without a loss. It was little wonder, then, that the club captured the Cup for the second time in three years. The word "dynasty" was bandied about, with good reason. On defense there was Dallas Smith, expert and heady, complementing Orr. There were proven goalies in Cheevers and Ed Johnston.

The Bruins had a reputation for doing crazy things at their height. And this club was no exception. Cashman was once arrested for reckless driving. When told at the police station that he could make one phone call, he casually dialed not his lawyer but a Chinese take-out restaurant and ordered supper.

The head of this collection was Johnson, a pipe-smoking bow tie wearing, soft-spoken leader. He said often, only half joking, "I send them over the boards and hope they listen to what I told them."

One of the keys to the Bruins' success was the club's tremendous penalty-killers—Eddie Westfall and Sanderson. The club led the league with 18 shorthanded goals in the 1971-72 campaign. But when the 1972-73 season began, the team found itself radically altered. It did not believe Cheevers would jump to the WHA and so didn't bother protecting another goalie, Dan Bouchard. But Cheevers jumped. So did John McKenzie and Sanderson. Westfall was taken in the expansion draft.

In a strange twist, Sinden came back to the team as managing director. Schmidt kept the title of general manager, but Sinden called the shots. The Bruins he took over went nowhere. Johnston was poor in goal and the other goalies—Ross Brooks and John Adams—were only fair. So Sinden shook up the club again. He dropped Johnson as coach, even though Johnson had compiled the finest won-lost record of any coach in recent years. Armand (Bep) Guidolin, who had once been the youngest player to see NHL action (he was 16) took the coaching reins. And for a goalie Sinden acquired Jacques Plante, who was 44 years old.

Under Guidolin the team reeled off 10 straight victories. Sanderson returned. Orr and Esposito were picking up points at a tremendous pace. A young rookie center, Greg Sheppard, played well. The club's country-

club life stopped under Guidolin's reign. Boston finished with a rush and grabbed second place from the Rangers.

Housecleaning was needed for 1973 because Johnston went to the Maple Leafs for Plante, who quit the Bruins to jump to the WHA. The Bostonians acquired Gilles Gilbert for goal from Minnesota in exchange for Stanfield. Younger players got their chance, Orr and Esposito were as effective as ever and the Bruins were fighting Montreal for first place.

LEFT: Bobby Orr, who has won the best defenseman award for six straight years. The last man before Orr to win it, Harry Howell, remarked at the time, "I'm glad I won it now. No one else but Orr will win it for the next 20 years." BELOW: *Phil Esposito scores the record-breaking point in his first record-breaking season, 1969.*

THE DETROIT RED WINGS

The Red Wings began life as the Cougars, then were known as the Falcons after many fans complained that they had never seen a cougar. Finally, they received their lasting nickname in 1933 from James D. Norris, Sr., who bought the team.

But any history of the Wings must immediately start with Jack Adams. Adams bounced through life known as Jolly Jack, a big, smiling, red-faced hulk of a man with a superb knowledge of hockey and people. In his 35-year career as the Red Wings' general manager he brought Detroit 12 regular-season championships—including a record seven straight, starting with the 1948-1949 season—and seven Stanley Cups.

Detroit's first year in the National Hockey League, which is true of many clubs, was a disaster. The syndicate of local businessmen who bought the club wanted profit and a contender immediately. They got neither. They lost $84,000, although the Cougars played their home games in Canada in Windsor's Border City Arena.

Enter Jack Adams, 32 years old, finished with his Ottawa playing career. Aware that Detroit was in trouble as it prepared to start its second year of hockey in 1926, he asked league president Frank Calder to act as his agent and see if perhaps the Cougars' owners would be interested in giving him a job. They were interested enough to make him coach and general manager. He coached for 20 seasons.

In his first season with Detroit, the Cougars moved to their new home, the Olympia, where the club showed a profit of $175,000. Adams was a natural promoter who talked hockey constantly. He would walk over to strange people at parties, pull out a roll of tickets and hawk them. When the Depression hit, though, fans did not come out as they did in Toronto.

Norris, meanwhile, had been amassing one of the country's great personal fortunes with the Norris Grain Company in Chicago. In slightly more than 20 years, having come to the United States in 1911 after his grain business in Montreal had gone bankrupt, he had built a shipping and grain empire that totally dominated business in the Great Lakes area.

Looking around for leisure activity, he decided to buy a hockey team. The logical club was the Black Hawks who played in his own city, Chicago. He could not, however, get Major Frederic McLaughlin to part with the Hawks, even though Norris had gone to the extreme of buying Chicago Stadium, the Hawks' home. A man named Arthur M. Wirtz owned a sizable piece of the Olympia, though, so in 1933 Norris and Wirtz traded. Norris wound up with the presidency of the Detroit team, Wirtz with the cavernous stadium in Chicago.

Norris' first act was to change the Falcons' name to the Red Wings, after a club he had played on in his youth, called the Winged Wheelers. The Winged Wheelers' insignia was a wheel with red wings. It fit Motor City perfectly.

Norris' second act was to summon Adams. "I'll give you a year on probation." Adams stayed, and stayed, and became proud of claiming that he and Norris never had a signed contract between them. Any doubts that Norris may have had about Adams' ability vanished after one year, a year in which the team finished first. In the third year of Norris' rule, the Red Wings won their first Stanley Cup. Through the thirties and forties they continued to be contenders and during a stretch that started in 1939 the Wings set a

After bad seasons, the Red Wings reorganized the heart of their club. Andy Brown, Bill Collins (22), and Thommie Bergman (4) protect the goal. Brown and Collins have left, for Pittsburgh and St. Louis respectively.

record by making the play-offs 20 straight years.

The Wings' first great player was Ebenezer (Ebbie) Goodfellow. "He was," said a Wings official, "Gordie Howe, before Howe came along." His career, which spanned the 1930s and early 1940s, was somewhat protean. In the 1930-1931 season he led the American Division in scoring with 25 goals. But the Wings still hadn't won a Stanley Cup.

For the 1934-1935 season, then, Adams stunned the sports world by shifting his great star to defense. The move paid off the very next season when the club won the Cup and Goodfellow was named a second-team all-star defenseman. He made the first team for the 1936-1937 season, again as a defenseman as the Wings again won the Cup. Despite Detroit's fifth-place finish in the 1939-1940 campaign, Goodfellow had the rare honor of being named the league's most valuable player as well as an all-star defenseman.

After winning the Cup in 1937, the Wings failed to make the play-offs the next season. Adams realized he had made a mistake by sticking with the same club, a mistake he vowed not to make again.

Although known as Jolly Jack, Adams

LEFT: Detroit's Ebbie Goodfellow hustles after a rebound while American goalie Worters hustles after his stick. BOTTOM: Ted Lindsay is smashed to the ice by the Rangers' Eddolls. Lindsay, in only 17 years, accumulated 1,808 minutes of penalties, a National Hockey League record. Even Howe won't be able to catch that one. BELOW: "Black" Jack Stewart, another of Detroit's infamous badmen, slips and falls during a game in 1947 against the Rangers in New York. Ed Laprade skates after the puck.

was a disciplinarian, his temper never very well concealed. He often chewed out his players, even after he had given up coaching to remain as general manager. His dressing-room harangues were feared. He also liked to needle. When he was displeased with Gordie Howe he would go into the dressing room between periods, rip the rind off an orange and flip the pieces at Howe.

Conditioning was important to Adams. During the war he had one player who got under his skin by refusing to get into shape. Adams brought an exercise bicycle into the locker room and made the player ride it. First, though, he tossed a heavy flannel army blanket over the player to make sure he sweated off the extra pounds.

One day Adams walked into the room and there was a figure, covered with a blanket, pumping furiously on the bike. Smoke was billowing from under the blanket. "See, you guys," said Adams to the other players. "There's a fellow who's really putting out. Why, the blanket's steaming." It wasn't until Adams moved closer that he noticed the strange odor. Tearing away the blanket, he discovered the player—smoking a cigar.

The great postwar Wings' teams astonished the hockey world with a collection of great, steady players. Black Jack Stewart was a rock on defense. Ted Lindsay, on the left side of the Production Line, was one of the league's top players. A rabble-rouser, Lindsay also was a team leader. He played with the Wings for 16 seasons before retiring in 1960. Four years later he returned to play one last season.

Sid Abel was the Production Line's center. Team captain when he was 24, he was named an all-star at two different positions in his career and was also a recipient of the most-valuable-player award.

FACING: A young Gordie Howe flips the puck over a fallen Glenn Hall. LEFT: New Detroit superstar Mickey Redmond launches attack.

The goalie during the Wings' seven straight titles was Terry Sawchuk, according to Adams the best netminder in the history of the league. For five straight seasons Sawchuk produced a goals-against average under 2. With today's longer schedules, split goaltending and tiring travel, Sawchuk's record appears to be safe.

There also was Red Kelly, leading the defense, a calm man in a hostile sea whose worst expletive was "hang." Syd Howe (unrelated to Gordie) became one of the most famous war-year Wings because of one feat. He scored six goals in one game, the first player in modern history to accomplish the double-hat trick.

Still, there would never have been a Production Line, seven straight titles, 20 straight years in the play-offs—perhaps even a great history—were it not for Gordie Howe. Slope-shouldered, magnificently muscled Howe caused Adams to change his whole theory on hockey. Adams didn't like to see his players shooting too much. He thought they should be patient and wait for the good chance. He also believed in trading players once they got on in years. He could apply neither theory to Howe.

Young Gordie, 18 years old, joined the Red Wings for the start of the 1946-1947 season. As a boy, he practiced his shots in Saskatoon, Saskatchewan, by drilling a tennis ball against the side of his house, "shaking the roof," as his mother remembered. He had come to Adams' attention when he was 16, attending a tryout camp. After Gordie had split the defense, shifted the stick to his left side and scored, Adams took him aside and told him, "You'll make the big club one day, son."

Gordie, a shy, polite six-footer who weighed 200 pounds, sat on the bench for most of his first season, which also was Adams' last in the dual role of coach and general manager. Adams turned over the coaching to Tommy Ivan the next season. Howe was put on a line with Abel and Lindsay. With Howe on right wing, the trio soon became known as the Production Line, named for its output because it functioned like the factory production lines that turned out America's cars.

With each victory Howe's legend grew. He became acknowledged as the greatest all-around performer in the game, probably the greatest ever to skate. He moved, it appeared, leisurely, and when he turned on the steam it looked as though he was barely straining. He was quicker than most, bigger than most, rougher and dirtier than most. His hard, accurate wrist shot, his great backhand shot, coupled with strength that allowed him to shoot while players were draped over his legs or arms, produced goals and more goals.

He not only eclipsed Maurice (Rocket) Richard's league career record of 544 goals, but became the first player to score 600 goals. In his 22nd season, the 1968-1969 campaign, he reached the 700-goal plateau. The Art Ross Trophy, for the league's leading scorer, was his six times; and the Hart Trophy, for the most valuable player, was also won by Howe six times.

Howe earned the nickname "Power" from his teammates. Besides lasting for more than a quarter-century, he survived palace revolts, along with his long-time center, Alex Delvecchio. The pair, however, couldn't prevent the club's falling on hard times, beginning in 1967, when it finished last in the East.

Abel, who had been Howe's coach most of his career, stepped down in 1968, following 11 seasons as coach, the previous six as general manager. Bill Gadsby came on in 1968 as the field leader. His tenure didn't last long and Abel was back behind the bench, following reports that Bruce Norris, the Wings' president, wanted a phone connection direct to the players' bench so that he could coach Gadsby play by play.

Abel went back to the general manager's office again for the start of the 1970-71 cam-

paign as the Wings plucked Ned Harkness from the ivy-covered walls of Cornell University to make the big jump to the pros. An early player revolt (it appeared Harkness and many of the players didn't get along) was aborted. In a strange denouement, Abel—and not Harkness—left. Harkness became general manager, and Doug Barkley, another ex-Wing, took over. The team, ripped by confusion, finished last in the East, beaten out by two first-year teams. Harkness had a massive rebuilding job in front of him.

That season also marked the end of an era—Howe retired. As the 1971-72 season started, Harkness had changed virtually the entire roster. Six of the team's leading players —Howe, Frank Mahovlich, Garry Unger, Bruce MacGregor, Pete Stemkowski and Wayne Connelly—were gone, as were the goalies. Harkness wanted his own team. One of the new players was a sensational rookie, Marcel Dionne. The fleet little center set a record for points by a rookie. But there wasn't much depth on the club and the goaltending was erratic. Before the season was over, Barkley was replaced by Johnny Wilson.

Harkness's radical ideas produced a winning team in the 1972-73 season. Dionne reached superstardom and Mickey Redmond set a club mark with 52 goals. Goalie Roy Edwards tied for the lead in shutouts with six. The Buffalo Sabres held on despite intense pressure from the Wings at the end of the campaign and beat out Detroit for fourth place and the play-offs.

For the 1973-74 season, Harkness was replaced by the excitable Ted Garvin. Delvecchio remained, though, for his twenty-third season. After the club started poorly, Garvin left, and Delvecchio became coach. His retirement as a player marked the end of Detroit's great era.

Detroit's problems are graphically illustrated by Billy Dea's attempt at penetrating Chicago defense, never an easy accomplishment.

The Muldoon Curse hung over the Black Hawks for the first 40 years of their existence and even in big, hulking, tough Chicago there were moaning fans who wondered if indeed their beloved Hawks were doomed to the life of an also-ran.

Pete Muldoon was the very first coach of the Hawks, a position at least as tenuous as the presidency of a banana republic. Until the Hawks finally finished first during the 1966-1967 season, there were 26 coaching changes. Muldoon was luckier than many of his successors. He lasted one full season as the Hawks finished third the first year. The club had been brought to Chicago by Major Frederic McLaughlin, who formed his team with many players from Portland of the defunct Western League. The major, who sported a semi-walrus mustache, was an international polo star. He named his club for the Blackhawk Field Gun Battalion, which he had headed during World War I.

When Muldoon was fired after his year, he cried angrily, "The Black Hawks never will finish in first place." Over the next eight seasons the club finished second five times. Twice, it missed the top rung by one point, the frustration finally ending with its great 1966 team which included five all-stars.

Yet, there were all-stars in the early years. The first Hawks' teams, in fact, had such players as Charlie Gardiner, Dick Irvin, Hugh Lehman and George Hay, each of whom made the Hall of Fame. Irvin came to the Hawks with an established reputation. He had been a star of the Western League (in one game he scored nine goals) and was the league's leading scorer its last season. The Hawks had high hopes for Irvin who, like many of their other acquisitions, was well past 30. But in the ninth game of the season, he suffered a fractured skull that ended his playing career.

Lehman was a top goalie, but was 40 years old when he joined the club. Hay, a 150-pounder, was overlooked by the Hawks once they had him. He scored 14 goals in his first season and was named by the coaches to an all-star line with Howie Morenz and Bill Cook. Hay was traded to Detroit the next season, where he became the leading scorer.

The only top player who remained for any length of time was Gardiner. He lasted seven years, posting a 2.13 goals-a-game average while racking up 42 shutouts. In the play-offs he was superb, allowing an average of 1.66 goals in 21 games. He won the Vezina Trophy twice and made the all-star team twice. But in 1934, three months after he was named an all-star for the second time, he died.

Gardiner's last season marked the first time the Hawks won the Cup. Tommy Gorman had the honor of leading the club from the bench that season. By then, eight years after the team's start, he was the tenth coach. Irvin had coached for one and a half seasons and had instituted a new concept, that of three forward lines. He believed in depth, hoping that numbers alone would prove enough. It was a theory close to the heart of the old soldier, Major McLaughlin, who thought in military terms—outnumber the opposition and you will win. But Irvin's tactics failed simply because there weren't enough good players to pull it off. A fresh third-string player still couldn't play as well as the opposition's somewhat-tired first-stringer.

The Hawks won their first Cup on a shot by the smallest player on the ice, Harold (Mush) March, a 150-pounder who tallied in

Tony Esposito, perhaps the most frustrating goalie one on one, thwarts Vancouver's Bobby Schmautz in the annual All-Star game. Tony is the stalwart backstop on Chicago's stingy defense.

SCHMAUTZ
9
35
NORTHLAND
9

the second overtime against Detroit. There were 16,500 fans in the cavelike intimidating Chicago Stadium on April 10, 1934, 16 months after a snowstorm had forced the National Football League championship into the huge arena. When March put in his goal, he was hugged for ten minutes by teammate Lionel Conacher. The fans refused to leave until they saw March. The diminutive right wing was pulled away to skate around the ice in a victory lap to five more minutes of applause. And only a few weeks earlier, Chicago sports writers had wondered whether March was up to play-offs since he hadn't scored consistently during the regular season.

In 1935, the Hawks acquired Earl Seibert, an all-star defenseman with the New York Rangers. He played ten years for the Hawks, making the second all-star team six straight seasons, then the first team three straight times.

Elwin (Doc) Romnes was another stalwart who helped the Hawks to the play-offs. Two seasons before he had won the Lady Byng Trophy for gentlemanly conduct. But in the play-offs he successfully saddled Toronto star Red Horner by chopping the Leaf down with semilegal maneuvers.

The Hawks still were contenders in the years immediately preceding World War II. They brought up John Mariucci, a brawny defenseman who had played football for the University of Minnesota. Mariucci, whose role was that of a policeman on the ice, was involved in one of the longest battles in the league's often-violent history, a 15-minute fight with Black Jack Stewart of the Detroit Red Wings.

The Hawks were on their way to a last-place finish as the postwar player depression that had hit Boston and New York also struck Chicago. For the Hawks, it was the start of a downward spiral that saw them finish last nine times in 11 seasons. Major McLaughlin had died in 1944, and there was little direction of the club. It was December 4, 1946, and the Hawks were being shut out for the second time in four games. There were signs of trouble in the second period, when Syd Howe boarded Doug Bentley, whose brother, Max, dashed over and fought with Howe and Sid Abel. Referee Frank Clancy did not see the Hawks' Alex Kaleta get slashed early in the contest and he failed to see Stewart cut Mariucci in the final period. Incredibly, Mariucci was told to go to the penalty box when he retaliated, blood streaming down his face. He was sent off, said one writer ironically, "apparently for spilling gore on the ice."

Mariucci and Stewart fought on the ice, were separated and chased into their respective penalty boxes. They fought some more, blood all over Mariucci's uniform. Finally each was ejected from the game. The man hardest hit, though, was the Hawk coach Bill Tobin. He had gone to the dressing room to complain to Clancy, for which he was given a $100 fine.

James D. Norris, the son of the Wings' owner, saved the Hawks' foundering franchise when he bought it in partnership with Arthur M. Wirtz, whose wealth was nearly as great as Norris'. Wirtz' money came from banking, real estate and hotel interests. The club they took over had trouble meeting bills and for a time the league ran the Hawks. Norris was a man about New York, the head of the International Boxing Club and a major owner of Madison Square Garden.

An enigmatic man who enjoyed the company of Broadway characters and persons living on the fringe of the law, he was court-ordered to break up his boxing club since it was in violation of federal antitrust statutes. Of his close relationship with notorious criminals Norris said simply, "If you want to do business in boxing you have to deal with the people who can supply the fighters."

FACING: The Black Hawk policeman in the 1940s was Johnny Mariucci. Here he gives Canadien Murdo McKay a verbal hammering. ABOVE: Pierre Pilote pushes Montreal out of range.

Norris poured all his energies into the Hawks, probably spending a million dollars acquiring players. "I know of $100 million I can put my hands on," he once said. "For sure, there's $200 million around, and I'm probably worth $300 million." During the 1965 play-offs against the Montreal Canadiens, Norris dispatched a check for a million dollars to the Toronto Maple Leafs, offering to buy Frank Mahovlich. He was playing cards with some Chicago newspapermen when he told them about his offer. Just as he finished talking about the million dollars, one of the card players told him, "I'll raise you a dollar." Norris looked at his hand and said, "I'll pass."

The 1957-1958 season was the last year of Chicago's longest drought. It failed to make the play-offs, but there were signs of better things to come. An 18-year-old left wing named Bobby Hull, a blond, muscular skater, joined the club. That same season, Glenn Hall was acquired from the Wings to play goal. The next year Stan Mikita joined the club, as did Ken Wharram. The club was ready to move.

Led by Hull and Mikita, the Hawks made the play-offs ten straight seasons, starting with the 1958-1959 campaign. In 1961 they captured their first Cup since 1938. Hull was the draw. Dubbed The Golden Jet, Hull shattered records early. On skates, he was a presence. The action centered around him, action of which he always seemed to be the core. He introduced the slap shot, the ultimate weapon in his hands. With it he could score from 70 feet out. It zeroed in on goaltenders at 118 miles an hour, faster by 15 percent than anyone else's shot. He also was the fastest skater in the league and, along with the Red Wings' Gordie Howe, the most powerful.

By his third season he led the league in goals and total points. In his fifth season,

LEFT: Hull usually carried a "shadow," sometimes three. BELOW: The result of a stiff check was a split lip and broken jaw. Hull stayed in.

1961-1962, he became the third man to score 50 goals in a campaign as he tied the mark set by the Canadiens' Richard and equaled by Geoffrion. They only reached that magic figure once. Hull did it again in 1965-1966, scoring 54 goals. The following season he notched 52, and in the 1968-69 campaign he broke his own record again when he scored 58 goals and 107 points.

The season before he got his 54, he had won the Lady Byng Trophy. But in the play-offs against the Canadiens he changed. Claude Provost who said, "I like Bobby," was assigned to hound Hull, to pester him, to stop him. Frustration was piling up (Hull scored in only one of the seven play-off games) and Hull finally started to hit back. In the next few years other shadows were assigned to him: the Wings' Bryan Watson, the Rangers' Ron Stewart, the Canadiens' John Ferguson (who broke Hull's jaw in a fight in 1968, then swung at it again a few weeks later while Hull was playing with it wired).

Glenn Hall was a marvel in goal for ten straight seasons, setting a league mark by playing in 490 consecutive games. He came to the Hawks after being named the all-star goalie the previous two years with the Wings. An unlikely-looking hockey player, he threw up before virtually every contest. Often he would leave the ice in the middle of a game when he suddenly became violently sick to his stomach. Despite his troubles, he led the league in shutouts four times while he was with Chicago and was a first-team or second-team all-star choice eight times. His remarkable career took another turn in 1967 when he was drafted by the St. Louis Blues, for whom he continued to star.

In many ways Mikita was the most remarkable of the trio of great Chicagoans. Born in Czechoslovakia, he spoke often of the taunts and insults he suffered as a boy in Canada. At five foot nine and 165 pounds, he was fragile but wiry. He was also pugnacious ("If you had a face like mine, you'd fight, too.") and was at first disliked by the opposition for his devious ways. After getting hit, he'd lie on the ice, in seeming agony. But if the referee didn't blow a whistle, he'd quickly get up and get back in the play.

Mikita started using the curved stick, a scythelike weapon that soon spread throughout the club and was finally adopted by most of the league's great shooters. He discovered the curved stick during a practice session in which his blade was bent. Trying a shot with it, he liked the effect. Then he and Hull bent a few sticks under a door. The curve in the middle of the blade gave it a whipping action. The puck "did tricks." On a 40-foot slap shot, it might travel straight for 35 feet, then, to the total anguish of the goaltender, suddenly dip.

Despite the impressive array of stars, the Hawks lacked depth, especially on defense. The 1967 trade that sent Phil Esposito, Ken Hodge and Fred Stanfield to Boston didn't help. The Chicagoans plummeted to last place in the East during the 1968-69 campaign.

But good deals followed the bad ones, and they acquired a baldish defenseman, Bill White, from Los Angeles, got a goalie named Tony Esposito (Phil's brother) from Montreal and turned a red-haired college kid named Keith Magnuson into a pro. And so, the Hawks, in 1970, playing with a strong defensive style, became the first club ever to leap from last to first in consecutive seasons. Esposito was runaway rookie of the year.

Esposito, in 1970-71, with back-up help from Gerry Desjardins, also acquired from Los Angeles, had another fine season. Hull, his brother Dennis, Pat Stapleton and Magnuson, who set a league mark of 291 minutes in penalties, were too much for the West Division—the Hawks finished first by 20 points over St. Louis.

For the first time since the initial expansion in 1967, the West had a truly powerful representative as well as a sensational drawing card in Bobby Hull. If St. Louis was the first West team to make its division respectable, the Hawks became the first to make the division feared. In the Hawks' 1971 semifinal series against the Rangers, they picked up a shutout in the second game, breaking the streak of West ineffectiveness against the East.

The Hawks appeared ready to take over the dominance of the West, abetted by boisterous crowds packed into Chicago Stadium for every game.

The mature players were joined by Dennis Hull, who vaulted to stardom with a 40-goal career season in 1970-71. Cliff Koroll, who had played with Magnuson at Denver University, also made it big.

The team had an even better year during the 1971-72 season, capturing the division trophy by 21 points over Minnesota. Hull reached 50 goals for the fifth time, and Esposito turned in an extraordinary season in the nets. He shared the Vezina Trophy with Gary Smith. In 48 games, Esposito recorded nine shutouts, posted a goals-against average of 1.76, and had a won-lost-tied record of 31-10-6.

With such players as the two Hulls, Pit Martin, Mikita, Jim Pappin and Koroll for the scoring, and with one of the best defensive squads around, the Hawks appeared to have a lock on the West Division. But the newer clubs improved dramatically in the 1972-73 season, particularly the Flyers and a solid Minnesota team. More importantly, although the Hawks never figured it would happen, Bobby Hull jumped to Winnipeg of the WHA, ending his 15-year reign as king of the NHL forwards. A supreme effort was needed from Mikita, who had been bothered the previous two seasons by back problems. He rose to the occasion this time and spoke of his drive to keep the club going "without Bobby." Mikita, in fact, was one of the league's leading scorers until he got hurt again late in the campaign.

The club traded for Ralph Backstrom, and it got clutch goals from the experienced center late in the season. From the juniors it brought up defenseman Phil Russell, who broke in successfully, as few rookie backliners do in the NHL.

The Hawks again finished first—for the fourth straight time—and easily handled their first-round Stanley Cup foe, St. Louis. Next came the Rangers, who were heavily favored to stop the Hawks. The Rangers won the first game, but the Hawks came back, led by Dennis Hull and Stapleton, to win the next four.

The final series, against the Canadiens, produced the highest scoring play-off series in history. The Frenchmen took the first two games, but the Hawks came back with two victories in the next three. Then the Canadiens won the series in the sixth game. In all the Canadiens scored 33 goals in the six games while the Hawks picked up 23.

Although the Hawks had bowed out in the finals for the second time in three years, they looked forward to the 1973-74 campaign. They had uncovered some promising youngsters in John Marks, Dave Kryskow and Len Frig. Smith was traded to Vancouver for Dale Tallon who the Hawks hoped would replace

Bobby Hull. In fact, they offered him Hull's old number 9, which he promptly rejected. The Hawks had to start the season without Stapleton and Backstrom, both of whom jumped to the Chicago Cougars of the WHA, but Chicago had successfully faced such adversity before.

Complementing a rock-hard defense, Chicago has for years had one man who sometimes single-handedly controls the pace of a game—Stan Mikita, here leading a foray over the blue line.

THE LOS ANGELES KINGS

The day after the great expansion draft Jack Kent Cooke took an unbelieving reporter aside and placed his left hand gently but firmly on the newsman's shoulder. As though taking an oath on a bible, he raised his right hand and said, "Remember, as God is my witness, I'm telling you today that the Los Angeles Kings will win the West Division championship. You look at the standings next April 1 and you remember who told you."

From any other man the statement would appear ludicrous. But with Cooke, talk that at first seems wild becomes fact. One of three-quarters of a million ex-Canadians to settle in the Golden West, Cooke was a successful soap salesman in Canada. Eventually he made friends with communications king Lord Thomson (now Lord Thomson of Fleet). Together they ran various newspapers and radio and television stations while Cooke also managed to operate the Toronto Maple Leafs baseball team. With William A. Shea of New York, he became a prime force in the formation of the Continental League.

When the Continental League gave up, coming close to, but failing, equality with the American and National Leagues, Cooke retired to Pebble Beach, California. Bored with retirement at age 50, he started to collect sports franchises. Within a few dynamic years he had acquired a 25 percent interest in the Washington Redskins, bought the Los Angeles Lakers basketball team and, in a bitter fight with Los Angeles Rams owner Dan Reeves, won the franchise for a hockey team. Cooke placed on his board of directors a fellow Canadian, Lorne Greene, star of the television show "Bonanza." Lord Thomson also was placed on the board, along with Shea and Edward Bennett Williams, one of the most famous trial lawyers in the country.

The man Cooke selected as his general manager for the hockey club was Larry Regan, whose background, in its way, was as unusual as Cooke's. NHL rookie of the year in 1956-1957, he played only four more seasons. He became player-coach of the Pittsburgh team of the American League before going to Austria where he organized hockey leagues in major cities and coached the national team for three years. Then he returned to the United States in 1965 as a player with Baltimore of the American League. Cooke hired him the following season to begin preparations for the Kings. Cooke, the old baseball man who believed in the Branch Rickey theory of dynasties, and Regan went for youth in the draft. They also had a fine back-up in the Springfield team.

Before the season was a month old, it was apparent that Cooke knew exactly what he was doing. The Kings were beating everyone and were the West's dominant club. They started their season at an arena in Long Beach. Their permanent home, The Forum, was not scheduled to open until December 30, 1967, some three months after the season's start. Though called the Forum, the facade actually was Greek-inspired. The inside was bathed in pastel. But no matter. At the start of the new year it was there, open in Inglewood, only 12 miles west of Los Angeles City Hall. A crowd of 14,366 that included movie and television personalities turned out for the opening game, won by the Flyers, 2-0.

That game proved critical. On April 1, the Kings finished second—only one point behind the Flyers. Coach Red Kelly had molded a surprising club, which included two good defensemen, Bill White and Dale Rolfe, both

Vic Venasky hounds the Rangers' Billy Fairbairn. In their short history, the Kings have had mixed success, sometimes displaying strength even against obviously superior teams.

10

rescued from Springfield. The goalie was Terry Sawchuk, who delivered in many clutch games, and they received a 26-goal output from Cowboy Bill Flett, a calf roper from Alberta.

Los Angeles was a far cry from Canada, and the players often spoke of the difficulty of leaving the swimming pool to put on equipment and play a hockey game. Visiting teams —especially those from the East—also had their problems in adjusting to the time difference.

This was a phenomenon for hockey players—living in year-round sunshine. But it was a help in winning games at home. Teams traveling to Los Angeles had to adjust first to a different time zone, then to the weather. It was not easy to loaf in the sun, swim in the hotel pool and then suddenly don hockey gear and throw body checks.

Is it any wonder, then, that the Kings had the best home record of any expansion team their first season? In fact, they did better at home than the established Red Wings did and posted the same home mark as the Black Hawks. If the Kings had a problem, it was, strangely, attendance. That hard core of ex-Canadians who Cooke had figured would support his team simply hadn't appeared. Finally he was moved to say, "Now I know why so many Canadians moved down here. They hate hockey."

Some of the Kings' players didn't like L.A. Many found they couldn't adjust to this

LEFT: Larry Mickey is held illegally by Boston's Cheevers. TOP: Joyal is stick-checked by Gary Sabourin (11). ABOVE: Scotty Lemieux duels for the puck with Star Bob McCord.

different way of life, in which they had to get their minds thinking cold while their bodies soaked up the sun. And though they had the time-zone advantage at home, they had to contend with jet lag on their road trips.

Eventually, Eastern clubs began finding ways to combat the shock of playing on the West Coast. "I've told my players to set their watches to Eastern time," one coach explained. "I want them to act and sleep and eat as if they're back home. That's the only way we'll overcome the three-hour time difference."

The Bruins' Phil Esposito had another idea. "As soon as I get to L.A. I go in my room and turn on the air conditioning. I don't go near the pool and I don't walk around. Then I feel just as if I'm in any other city."

By the second year, the Kings began to feel the toll of travel. They won only five road games, the poorest mark in the league. Their scoring slumped. But they brought up a rookie goalie named Gerry Desjardins, who appeared in 60 games. Only Cesare Maniago of the North Stars saw more duty. The Kings managed to make the play-offs again, winding up fourth, and even got past the first round of Cup play.

Kelly quit after the season, a result of intense arguments with Cooke. He had led the squad to the play-offs their first two seasons. They were to be the only two play-off berths for the Kings in the team's first six seasons.

Hal Laycoe replaced Kelly for the start of the 1969-70 season, following a remarkable coaching career in the Western League where he took seven titles in nine seasons. But the Kings' team he inherited was filled with dissension. Desjardins complained, "It's like being in a shooting gallery. I wish they'd trade me." Rolfe, White and Ted Irvine also didn't see eye-to-eye with management. These players, and some others, got their wish. In wholesale deals they were traded. Cooke explained, "When you've got some rotten apples, they can make a whole barrel get bad. So you get rid of the apples." Whatever the Kings' problems, they remained unsolved that season.

The arrival of Eddie (the Entertainer) Shack failed to generate victories. Shack, a big, brawny, hustling wing, came with his reputation as a flake intact. When he was traded to the Kings he arrived by helicopter, wearing Bermuda shorts. The club floundered, and Laycoe didn't last the season. He was replaced by Johnny Wilson, who could do no better. The team finished last.

Regan himself took over for the 1970-71 season, becoming the club's fourth coach in 18 months. The team now had some better players. Juha Widing, Finnish-born, became a regular and turned into a 20-goal scorer. Hollywood nicknamed him Whitey. The experienced Bob Pulford was added from Toronto, and Harry Howell and Gilles Marotte beefed up the defense. The team's scoring had improved, but its goaltending was suspect. The Kings were in danger of again finishing at the bottom, to the displeasure of the Montreal Canadiens, who had a vested interest in having the Seals finish last. The Canadiens had the right to the Seals' first draft choice in 1971, and if the Seals finished with the poorest mark, the Canadiens would pick first of all the teams. The Frenchmen had their eye on Guy Lafleur, touted as the best amateur in Canada. Some people suspect that what happened next was a deliberate ploy on the part of the Canadiens to make sure the Kings finished ahead of the Seals. The Canadiens traded the experienced and still good Ralph Backstrom to Los Angeles for two unknown players. In 33 games Backstrom delivered 14 goals and added 13 assists for 27 points. The Kings halted their slump and finished fifth. The Seals were last.

Regan turned over the coaching for 1971-72 to Fred Glover, and another poor season followed. At the end of the campaign, the Kings chose Pulford to man the bench and the club's fortunes changed dramatically. Pulford, a quiet sort, nevertheless had definite ideas on how hockey was to be played—espe-

One of the most important requirements for any hockey club is a sound goaltender, and the Kings have one in Rogatien Vachon. Here, "Rogie" stops a point-blank shot by Rangers' Vickers.

cially with the material at hand. He believed in organization, conditioning, and defense. He attended practice and skull sessions of the Rams' football team, asking questions, looking for ways to relate football success to hockey. At last, he had a proven goalie in the small but nimble Rogatien Vachon. To supplement Marotte on defense, he picked up the experienced Terry Harper, and for scoring he had Mike Corrigan and Bob Berry in addition to Widing.

The club was one of the turnaround surprises. It stressed tight play. In fact, it turned in the best penalty-killing record in the league, killing 86.5 percent of its penalties and allowing a league low of only 31 power-play goals. In the previous campaign, it had the worst mark in the NHL, killing only 76.2 percent of its penalties. The Kings yielded 60 fewer goals during 1972-73. Despite this dramatic change, the club missed the play-offs, but only by three points. Two youngsters, Vic Venasky and Don Kozak played impressively in their first pro seasons.

The Kings, with Pulford back, faced the 1973-74 season with even greater hopes. Their defense had proven itself, and the goaltending with Vachon was exceptional. Improved scheduling would end the grueling cross-country trips. Perhaps the Kings would again be one of the strongest new teams.

THE MINNESOTA NORTH STARS

People in the United States think of Minneapolis and St. Paul as the Twin Cities, but it is St. Paul that feels the sibling rivalry. When great cities are mentioned, you hear of Minneapolis, not St. Paul or even Minneapolis-St. Paul. As a result, St. Paul tends to snub its neighbor, a reaction people in Minneapolis tend to resent. That is why Bloomington, an area southwest of, and equidistant from, the cities, is the home of the Minnesota Vikings football team, the Minnesota Twins baseball team and the North Stars hockey team.

When expansion was announced, Walter Bush, an attorney; Gordon Ritz, a construction executive, and Bob McNulty, communications magnate, worked together toward getting the franchise. Former college hockey players, they had been partners in running the Minneapolis Bruins of the Central League and had a long hockey background. They got five other businessmen interested in the project, for a total of eight men—four from St. Paul, four from Minneapolis. Their big problem was a place to play. They discussed, among other places, the State Fair Grounds midway between the Twin Cities, and the St. Paul Auditorium. The Fair Grounds turned out inadequate. They then went before the league's board of governors—at this point no other group from the area had expressed interest—and were told that the St. Paul arena would have to be renovated. Fearing the voters would not approve, the group turned to a third site, an area adjacent to Metropolitan Stadium in Bloomington. A deal was worked out with the Stadium commission to build a sports center there.

Suddenly a rival group cropped up to bid for the franchise. The NHL, now familiar with Bush, awarded the team to his group with the condition that it build its sports center. Six million dollars was raised by playing on an inter-city rivalry between a group of successful, civic-minded citizens known as the Minutemen. The Minutemen of St. Paul tried to outdo the Minutemen of Minneapolis, and vice versa. Each city's boosters went at it with relish. Enough money was raised for the arena and 5,800 season tickets were sold in the process.

Management selected as the team's general manager-coach Wren Blair, an easygoing leader with a history of success, most recently with the Boston Bruins. Blair generally is credited with discovering Bobby Orr.

At the draft Blair tried to get the best defense. As it worked out, the North Stars wound up with better forwards when, during the first season, their defensive choices ran into difficulties. The Stars made the play-offs their first year, but Blair expressed puzzlement during the season at the way the fans reacted. They didn't cheer enough, he said. They were almost blasé. Ten minutes before the game the stands would be deserted. At the opening face-off, the place was filled. The area had one of the best traditions of hockey in the United States, perhaps the best. The fans knew and appreciated the game. They cheered a good play by an opponent as evenly as they applauded a North Star maneuver. The trouble was, Blair contended, they didn't cheer loud enough. Minnesota's average attendance the first year, however, was the best of all expansion teams—11,800.

Its first draft choice had been Cesare Maniago, a lean, friendly netminder who had had a brief fling at stardom with the Rangers. Some nights Madison Square Garden had echoed to the shouts of "Hail, Cesare!" In fact,

Minnesota's brilliant new star, Jude Drouin, battles Montreal's Jacques Laperriere near the boards. Drouin led his team to two upset victories in the 1971 Cup games.

BELOW: Barry Gibbs (2) is stopped by teammates and refs.
FACING BOTTOM: Cesare Maniago helplessly watches puck roll off his glove and into the cage. RIGHT: Cesare stops one.

Maniago for a while was in favor over Ed Giacomin. But in one game Maniago got hit in the mouth with a puck. Between periods coach Emile Francis asked Maniago how he felt. "I don't think I can make it for the next period." Francis, an ex-goalie who had once played goal with his dislocated shoulder strapped to the iron crossbar, stared at him as the room fell silent. Exit Maniago.

The 6-3 netminder quickly became a favorite of Minnesotans and he had an outstanding first season, playing 48 games in a year when the two-goalie system became widely accepted. He turned in six shutouts (topped only by Giacomin's eight) and allowed only 2.77 goals a game. There were other outstanding players in the North Stars' drive to fourth place, four points behind the leading Flyers in the tightest race in NHL history. Ray Cullen and André Boudrias, who finished with 53 points, tied for fourth as the division's leading scorers. Dave Balon and Mike McMahon tied for eighth with 47 points each.

The team sagged during the second half. It was never quite the same following the death of Bill Masterton, one of the squad's most popular players, the first player in professional hockey to die as a result of a game injury. It happened on January 13, 1968, at

the Center in a game against Oakland and had repercussions that tore into the very nature of hockey's image. Masterton, a 29-year-old center who had come out of a four-year retirement, collided with Billy Harris and spun off into Larry Cahan. It appeared to Blair that Masterton was unconscious as he fell. He landed hard on the ice, hitting his head. Thirty hours later he died.

On January 16, the league played its all-star game at Toronto. Every official was present. Masterton's death became the prime topic as a pro-helmet faction grew strong, asking that helmets be made mandatory equipment. A controversy raged: would Masterton have died if he had worn one?

"Helmets?" said one coach with a sneer. "Show me one good player that wears them." Another coach picked up a newspaper. The headline said Masterton was the first player to die from a game injury. "There's your answer to helmets," he said. "All these years, and only one death."

Among the players the question remained in dispute. Stan Mikita said he would start wearing one, and did. Ken Schinkel of Pittsburgh admitted that "you're an outsider if you wear one. Let's face it." The Canadiens' Bobby Rousseau had started the season with a helmet, but discarded it. He said it dulled his sense of awareness.

Campbell expressed amazement and, at the same time, sorrow. "There's the sticks, the skates, the puck and the boards, and when you think that it never happened before. . ." He was not about to press for a rule that required helmets, for over the years in hockey a tradition had grown that you take the bruises, cuts and imminent danger as part of the game.

Despite the Stars' second-half letdown, most polls for the 1968-1969 season picked them to win the West Division title. Blair had chosen John Muckler, Ranger coordinator of player personnel, as his successor on the bench. Muckler had been groomed in the Minnesota organization for a year, serving as general manager and coach of Memphis in the Central League.

The North Star club Muckler took over did not approach its first-season skills. Cullen remained consistent, but Wayne Connelly, McMahon and Boudrias suffered scoring letdowns which were not compensated for by the fine play of Claude Larose, obtained from Montreal. The team went through a nonwinning streak of 14 games and Blair replaced Muckler. Blair told his coach to go to Florida for a few weeks, and then the pair would take a fresh look at the situation. Blair took over as interim coach, but he was shopping around for another field general. Even though the North Stars failed to make the play-offs, the outlook was promising. Young players were gaining polish, especially Danny Grant who was awarded the Rookie-of-the-Year Trophy and scored 34 goals.

Again, the North Stars were to be reckoned with, and when the realigned West Division opened play for the 1970-71 season, more than a few observers thought Minnesota could finish second, behind Chicago. They had a new coach in Jackie Gordon, a moon-faced man of few words who had left the Rangers.

Defense was on Gordon's mind—how to cut down the goals-against. Minnesota drastically cut its goals-against, scored less, but still shaved the goals-against by 34. He employed a three-goalie rotating system, with Maniago, old Gump Worsley and Gilles Gilbert filling the nets. Although the Stars' scoring fell off by 33 goals, the club made the play-offs, finishing fourth. The best was yet to come. The first three years, St. Louis had won every round of play in its own division, and was the only West club ever to play in the final round.

Helped by Doug Mohns, a 37-year-old defenseman, the North Stars toppled the Blues in the first round. The victory seemed symbolic. The North Stars, playing well against Montreal in the second round of Cup play, felt ready to take over as leader of the expansion teams.

Bill Goldsworthy (8) appears to be the main concern of Rangers. Goldsworthy has been a consistent scorer on a team that depends heavily on defense.

This they did in the 1972-73 season, the first in which they posted a winning mark. Gordon was a maestro behind the bench, orchestrating his lines so that old and young players blended together. The heroes on attack were Bill Goldsworthy and Jude Drouin, who had set a record the season before for assists by a rookie. But goal scoring was not the Stars' forte. It was defense and goaltending. Ted Harris, acquired from Montreal, showed his class with steady play that kept the North Stars in all their games. Harris, the captain, was also the policeman. And behind him in the nets he had the ageless Worsley and the solid Maniago. Worsley still refused to wear a mask, one of the last holdouts. But it didn't seem to affect him. He sported a 2.12 goals-against mark.

Some people thought the North Stars had stayed with some of their older players a bit too long as the 1972-73 season began. But the North Stars were right in the battle for the West Division title, this time inching even closer to Chicago. Dennis Hextall turned in a top scoring season, and Lou Nanne and J. P. Parise were clutch performers. In addition the Stars unveiled rookie Buster Harvey. When Worsley decided to retire, Blair and Gordon reluctantly acquiesced. Gilbert did not do as well as his replacement, but Maniago had another solid season. The Stars wound up tied for second with Philadelphia, but the Flyers finished second because they had scored more goals.

The North Stars' power play had been one of the poorest in the league. In an attempt to pick up more goals, they traded Gilbert to the Bruins for Fred Stanfield, who had been one of the key operatives on the Bostonians' famed power plays. They also convinced Worsley, at the age of 44, to come back. Early in the 1973-74 campaign after a poor start, Gordon resigned, blaming the agonies of pressure. He was replaced by Parker MacDonald.

THE CALIFORNIA GOLDEN SEALS

The San Francisco Bay area was a natural for big league hockey—everyone believed. Sports prospered there—the Oakland Raiders and San Francisco 49ers of football, the San Francisco Giants in baseball, professional and college basketball. There was a huge population, a point for national television. The area also had a hockey team, the San Francisco Seals of the Western League. They were owned by the Shasta Corporation, the company that controlled the Ice Follies.

Barry van Gerbig, 27, former Princeton hockey player, back-up goalie on the 1960 Olympic team and a man of means, brought his business associates to California, joined forces with Shasta and bought into the San Francisco team. Van Gerbig's contingent applied for, and was granted, the franchise for the Bay area and bought out Shasta. It elected to move the franchise to Oakland's new Coliseum, rather than playing in the Cow Palace in San Francisco. Their new team was called the California Seals. Van Gerbig and his partners put up $450,000 to indemnify the Western League for the loss of its San Francisco team, which disbanded. It was only one of many payments.

Had they known that fewer than 10 percent of the fans who had seen the San Francisco team play came from Oakland their approach might have been different. But they called their club the California Seals, hoping not to localize it and to give it a broader image than the name "Oakland" would have lent.

Despite handsome facilities, there were immediate attendance problems. For one thing, San Franciscans were not inclined to make the trip to Oakland. It wasn't only the distance (the trip could take well over an hour). It also involved San Francisco's insularity where Oakland is concerned. There is great inter-city rivalry. Secondly, the Seals' management didn't make a strong enough pitch to Oakland residents. Oakland people would have preferred a team in their city to go by the city's name.

The club's backers never imagined financial problems of the kind encountered in Oakland. They had just put up $2 million for the franchise, had to pay for operating expenses and salaries, almost half a million went for indemnification, and now suddenly they were called upon for even more funds when gate receipts failed to cover day-to-day operations. While warring over funds, they at least agreed to change the team's name from the California Seals to the Oakland Seals.

"I think we realize," said president Frank Selke, Jr., "that our future is in Oakland's fans, and not in San Francisco." Business and civic groups in the area were pressed into service to help sell tickets. Benefit nights were staged. Ticket prices were cut. But on the ice the players, feeling the effects of internal wrangling, played poorly. Almost from the first weeks they trailed, finishing last with only 15 victories in 74 games.

It was understandable, of course. The fans who did turn out were spirited, but it was impossible to make enough noise to compensate for the usual 8,000 empty seats in the 12,500-seat Oakland-Alameda Coliseum Arena. Furthermore, there had been too many changes even before a team was fielded. Rudy Pilous, the club's original general manager, was dismissed before the first face-off and replaced by Bert Olmstead, a former player who became the coach as well.

The league loaned the team more than $250,000 to keep going and Labatt's Brew-

Dick Mattiussi (6) of the Seals cross-bodies Sabres' Gerry Meenan and successfully stops the play. Mattiussi's hard play could not keep the Seals out of last place in 1971.

TORIAVILLE
NORTH
15
9
15

eries loaned it more than $600,000. In exchange, Labatt's got the option to purchase the club and move it to Vancouver if the franchise were ready to give up. Labatt's, an aggressive company, desperately wanted the Seals. One of its chief rivals, Molson's, had owned the Canadiens and the product—beer—had been established with the Montreal team. But another group bought into the Seals, relieving some of the disenchanted partners of their obligations. This new faction was led by Potter Palmer, whose group owned the Harlem Globetrotters basketball team.

By its second season the Seals' management had been restructured. Olmstead resigned, replaced as general manager by Selke, the son of the highly successful Toronto and Montreal executive. Fred Glover, the highest scoring player in the history of the American League, took over as coach.

Except for goalies Charlie Hodge and Gary Smith, only three players of those originally drafted remained with the team. The Seals started out the 1968-1969 season well. They were second during the first half, trailing only the runaway St. Louis Blues. Their standing was a remarkable accomplishment considering what had gone before, and the fact that attendance was still poor. Such players as Billy Hicke, perhaps the most popular of the Seals, Gary Jarrett, Ted Hampson and Carol Vadnais had brought the Seals back

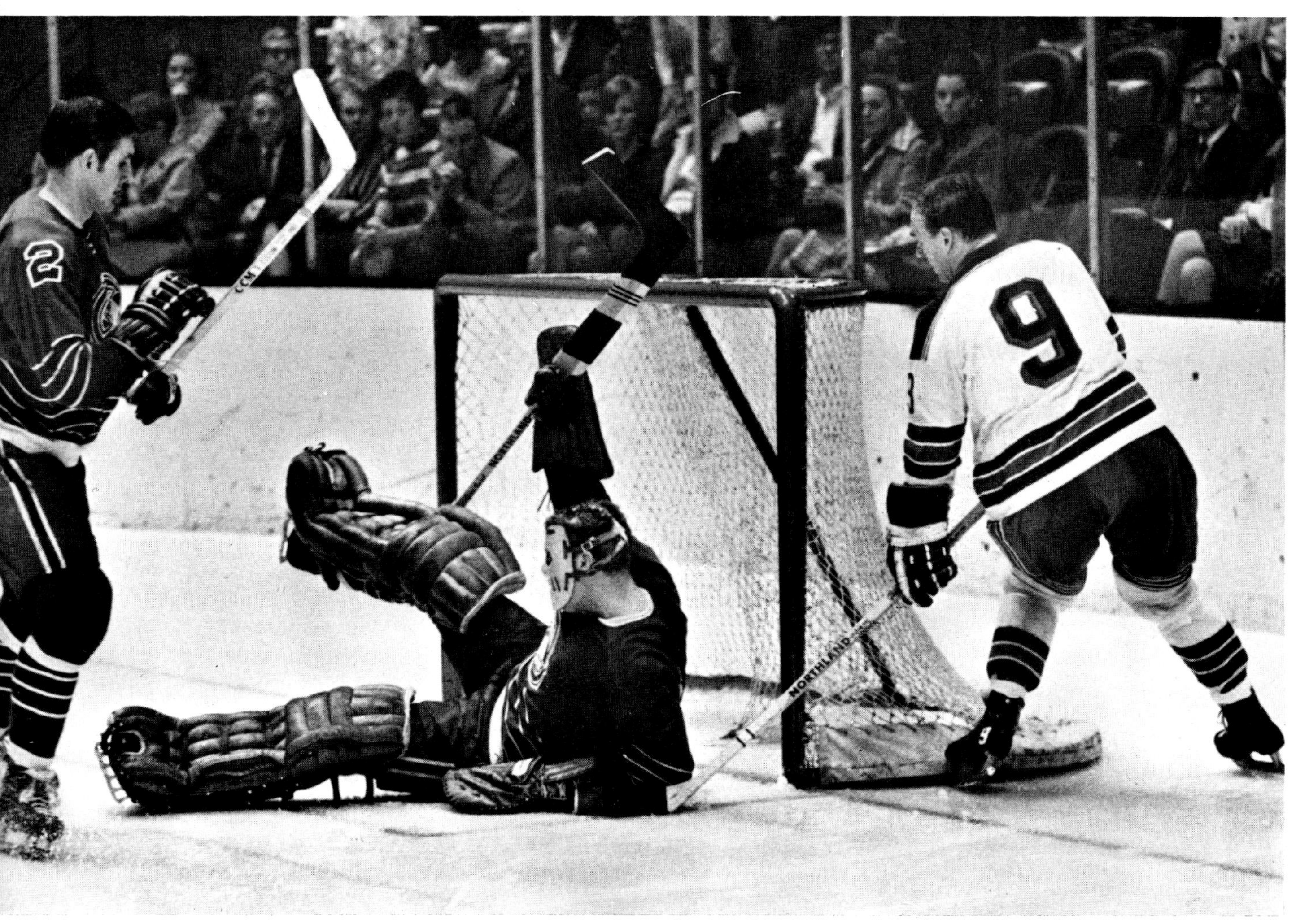

ABOVE: Doug Roberts watches with relief as teammate Gary Smith smothers a shot by Ranger Reggie Fleming. FACING: Bert Marshall (19) jaws with Chico Maki of the Hawks.

16
22
19

to contention. Still, there remained unrest.

In midseason, a Buffalo contingent led by the Knox Brothers invested in the Seals, hoping to move the club to Buffalo. League President Campbell said no. The Seals finished a remarkable second.

With Vadnais turning into a one-man team—he played forward and defense—and Smith playing virtually the entire campaign—the Seals, losing money, running up debts, finished fourth their third season. A bitter power struggle was under way between—of all people—Charles O. Finley, the storm-tossed baseball owner famed for firing a manager a year, and an overextended company called Trans-National Communications. TNC had taken control of the Seals, but the league was unhappy with it. It had tired of advancing money, and had worried about the NHL image as reports repeatedly cropped up that the Seals were bankrupt.

The league also was worried about Smith, the Seals' goalie. He brought wandering to its ultimate, once nearly crossing the center red line in an attempt to score an empty-net goal. Because of Smith, the league now forbids goaltenders from crossing center ice.

The season was no sooner over than Jerry Seltzer, whose father had founded the roller derby in the Bay Area, put in a bid for the club. It was between Seltzer and Finley. The price was about $4.5 million—the total of the Seals' debts.

Finley's powerful friends on the NHL's board of governors made his selection virtually a certainty. Finley got the club. Before long, he dismissed Selke, with Glover taking on the dual role of coach-general manager. There was also a new name for the 1970-71 season: the California Golden Seals.

But the Seals were to be burdened for several years by their lack of a top draft choice. To acquire players, they mortgaged the future for the present. Because of their repeated low finishes in the standings, they could have acquired high draft picks. Instead, in the six seasons after their birth, they chose far down the list: thirteenth in 1968, seventh in 1969, tenth in 1970, eleventh in 1971, twenty-second in 1972, and thirty-fourth in 1973.

After four seasons only four original Seals remained. That fourth campaign, 1970-71, was further disaster for the Californians. They not only missed the play-offs but sank to the bottom of the West Division and yielded a record total of 320 goals. Smith appeared in an astonishing total of 71 games; he was by far the most overworked goalie in the big leagues.

For 1971-72, the Seals finally appeared to be headed in the right direction. The new general manager was the youthful Garry Young, with Glover coaching. Young played his young players at the beginning of the season and stayed with them. As a result, the team, whose average age was only about 23 years a man, suddenly started to deliver, or at least to establish a reputation for trying. The goalie was the 21-year-old Gilles Meloche, but even with an improved club, he had some difficult games. There was a night in New York, for example, when the Rangers shelled him for eight goals in a period and sent him to the bench in tears.

Under Vic Stasiuk, who succeeded Glover, the Seals were in contention for the play-offs most of the season. Finally, they showed their youth and wilted in the pressure of the final weeks. Still, there was cautious optimism until the WHA stole their touted Tom Webster and other proven goal scorers such as Norm Ferguson and Bobby Sheehan.

In some bizarre moves, Finley fired Young (who had become coach in addition to G.M.) after claiming that "Young almost ruined the franchise" by signing players to exorbitant salaries to keep them in Oakland. Finley said that Young had signed "secret" contracts with these players and had told Finley they were getting paid less than they actually were. Glover came back as coach, after briefly jumping to Cleveland. Without the core of their promising youth, the Seals fell to last again in 1972-73, and it appeared they would have to start all over again.

Goaltender Gilles Meloche, though occasionally bombarded by superior teams, has matured into a steady performer for the desperate Seals.

Considering the Flyers' first-year problems, which included losing the roof over their head, the Philadelphia entrant had a remarkable season in establishing itself as one of the more solid of the new teams.

The Flyers' origin was shrouded in secrecy. When word reached Philadelphia that the National Hockey League was expanding, a group of businessmen silently went to work. They did not make their plans for the franchise known, lest some other syndicate jump on the bandwagon. In fact, local sports writers did not even know about the franchise application until they saw reports coming in over the wires, and had trouble believing the reports anyway. For one thing, Philadelphia had no acceptable rink.

Jerry Wolman, despite his financial troubles, laid the plans and raised the money for both undertakings. His executive vice president of the Eagles, Ed Snider, was put in charge of the hockey club. Wolman could not extricate himself from his difficulties and eventually sold out to Snider, who bought 60 percent of the team. Snider had had previous dealings with a New York banker, Bill Putnam (experienced in arranging loans for new sports franchises), and brought in Putnam as president of the club with a 25 percent interest. Joe Scott, the team's vice president, owned the remaining 15 percent. The group also owned the new arena, which they called The Spectrum.

Bud Poile, a former player who had a highly successful career as a coach and general manager in the Western League, was named general manager. Keith Allen, who also had a successful coast history, was named coach.

The trolley-shaped arena opened on October 24, 1967, and the Flyers, who that season played the first game in the new Forum in Los Angeles, the new Madison Square Garden in New York and the Coliseum in Oakland, scored a 1-0 victory over the Penguins.

The Flyers had been the first new team to acquire a minor-league club—they paid $800,000 for the Quebec Aces of the American League. Their young players, after a halting start, regrouped around the league's two youngest regular goalies, Doug Favell and Bernie Parent. Twenty-two-year-olds born two days apart, the pair shared netminding duties and helped the Flyers post the lowest goals-against record in the new division, third lowest in the league.

By February the Flyers had established themselves as the most solid of the new teams. They averaged better than 9,500 spectators a game. Of their remaining seven home games in March, five were assured of capacity crowds of 14,558. Then the roof fell in. A roaring windstorm tore a huge section off the top of the Spectrum, located on the outskirts of the city in an open, unprotected area. It set up one of the most intriguing situations in league history.

The Flyers were on the road, at Madison Square Garden for a Saturday afternoon contest, when they learned they could not play in the Spectrum until repairs were made. They had a home game scheduled against Oakland for the next day. The game also was to be the CBS Game of the Week. The television network was as frantic as the Flyers. No game in the league's history ever had been canceled. But there was a very real possibility that the Oakland-Philadelphia game would be called off. That would leave CBS without a telecast since no other clubs were scheduled to play

In 1973-74, the Flyers were the first legitimate Stanley Cup contender the expansion clubs have ever had. Ross Lonsberry, a key member of that team, screens Dryden.

an afternoon game that Sunday.

After extensive talks, however, the Rangers allowed the teams to use the Garden Sunday afternoon. The Garden sold no tickets for the game—it allowed everyone who had a ticket for that night's Ranger game in for free. More than 12,000 fans showed up, on a first-come, first-serve seating basis.

The Garden was the first neutral "home" site the Flyers used. They also played a home game in Toronto against the Boston Bruins, in a contest that saw an ugly stick-wielding fight between the Flyers' Larry Zeidel and Eddie Shack. Zeidel, the only Jewish player in the league, claimed that he had been continually abused by racial slurs hurled from the Boston bench. Campbell investigated, but no action was taken except for an admonishment that racism had no place in hockey.

Loss of their home ice affected the Flyers' performance and their big lead over the Kings dwindled. They played their last five home games in Quebec, and held on to capture the division title by one point—winning the Clarence S. Campbell Bowl as West Division champions.

In their second year, Allen was elevated to general manager. After the season, Vic Stasiuk, a hard-nosed former player, took over. The Flyers' third campaign began brightly, with a rookie named Bobby Clarke leading the offense. Clarke, a diabetic (who wore contact lenses on the ice), had to take daily insulin shots. The team began to wield strange power over the stronger (on paper) Rangers—all six games ended in ties. But in the Philadelphians' final eight games they earned only two points and missed the playoffs.

Their mastery over the Rangers amused the rest of the league and stunned the Rangers as they continued into their fourth season. A Flyer victory extended the New Yorkers' nonwinning record against Philadelphia to 10

ABOVE: Philadelphia's most exciting new player, Bobby Clarke, starts up on a backcheck. RIGHT: Philadelphia ruggedness goes unappreciated in a nearly empty Los Angeles Forum.

games. Late in the year, Parent was traded to Toronto in a complicated three-way deal involving Boston. The Rangers finally won against Philadelphia. But the Flyers got into the play-offs, winding up third. Clarke became an all-star with 27 goals and 63 points, and luckily Favell returned to his rookie form.

Even the most optimistic Philadelphia partisans must have had their doubts after the incredibly disheartening wind-up to the 1971-72 campaign, in which the Flyers missed the play-offs with only four seconds left in the season. The Flyers were tied with the Buffalo Sabres, 2-2. A tie, worth one point, would have given the Philadelphians 67 points, good enough for fourth place over the Pittsburgh Penguins, who were being defeated by St. Louis. It would have meant that the Flyers' new coach, Fred Shero had produced a play-off team in his first try. But as the seconds ticked away, the Sabres' Gerry Meehan took a desperation shot that sailed into the net. The Flyers had lost the game and the season. Though the Flyers were tied in points with the Penguins, the light-scoring team totaled only 200 goals, and it missed the play-offs on the basis of goals scored.

Despite the disappointing finish, there were some promising signs. With a team-leading 35 goals, Bobby Clarke had reached stardom, and a late-season deal had brought in Cowboy Bill Flett, who contributed 11 goals in just 31 appearances. For 1972-73, the Flyers were expected to improve but not to the shocking extent that they did.

The team from the City of Brotherly Love established itself as the "baddest" club in NHL history. Earning the nickname "the Broad Street Bullies," the Flyers simultaneously became one of the highest scoring and most pugnacious teams in the NHL. And they helped Philadelphia rid itself of its image as home for big-league sport's biggest losers.

Led by Clarke, who became the first player on an expansion team to amass 100 points and the first in his division to become the most valuable player, the Flyers finished second, only eight points behind the Hawks. Rick MacLeish arrived from the minors and notched 50 goals, and Flett, wearing a Buffalo Bill goatee got 43 goals in only 69 games. Bill Barber, a rookie, got 30 goals, and a player fresh from the juniors, Tom Bladon, starred on defense.

Favell anchored the team in goal and didn't worry about being protected. Andre (Moose) Dupont joined the club from St.

FACING: Barry Ashbee, a veteran hitter, waits for the face-off at his defensive position. LEFT: Bobby Clarke faces off against Chicago. BELOW: Captain Bobby Clarke fights Flames' Noel Price.

Louis and averaged almost two penalties a game. Dave Schultz, who led the league with 259 minutes in penalties, set a record as the most penalized left wing. Don Saleski, with 205 minutes in the penalty box, achieved similar renown among right wings.

It shouldn't have been surprising, then, that for the first time Philadelphia captured a Stanley Cup round. They advanced past Minnesota but bowed to Montreal, the eventual champions, in a hard-fought series.

The man who kept the club happy was Shero, who came to Philadelphia opposed to long hair and beards. ("It takes too long after a game to dry your hair," he said. "And anyway, wet hair makes the players catch colds.") But when the Flyers won, hair length didn't matter.

The Flyers continued to show they were for real in 1973-74, when with Parent back they started remarkably. Still Toronto property in the NHL, the goalie was traded to the Flyers in exchange for Favell. In the team's first 12 games, Parent turned in five shutouts.

The Bullies were proving to be as good as they were tough.

THE PITTSBURGH PENGUINS

The Penguins made a fatal mistake in the draft. They aimed almost exclusively for experience, for players who might give them one last season of good play. The idea was to attract fans and make the club's name respectable. It was the same type of thinking that created the New York Mets and which took the Mets nearly ten years to overcome. The people who made the moves at Pittsburgh wanted to put out a representative team immediately.

The city had an excellent hockey tradition, and the year before expansion the Hornets, Pittsburgh's American League entry, had won its regular-season division title and the play-offs. Pittsburgh fans, thought the Penguins, would be unhappy with anything but a winner. Jack Riley, past president of the American League, was made the Penguins' general manager. Red Sullivan, who played in the National League for nine years and coached the Rangers and Ranger farm teams, was named the Penguins' first coach.

The average age of players drafted was 31 years, the oldest roster of any professional team. The Penguins' first two picks after the goaltenders were Sullivan's old Ranger teammates Earl Ingarfield and Al MacNeil. Their 19th choice was the highest scorer in Ranger history, Andy Bathgate, no longer around.

Bathgate, for years one of the top players in the game, was the 101st player taken in the draft. His attitude was lackadaisical. On the first day of training camp, Sullivan took Bathgate aside and told him, "Andy, if you want to work, you can make it here. But the first time I catch you reading *The Wall Street Journal*, you're out."

The place where Bathgate and Company were going to bring Pittsburgh major league hockey was the Civic Arena, a handsome building seating 12,508. The arena had the only retractable dome in the world for a building its size (in the summer the roof opens for concerts). It took the Penguins a while to get moving their first season—too long, thought many who were close to the situation. Within a matter of weeks they rutted around fourth place and failed to generate momentum among potential fans. Worse, they had a poor record at home. Their first season they won only 15 of 37 home games—only Oakland won fewer games at home.

Originally, 20 Pittsburghers, led by State Senator Jack McGregor and a law school classmate, Peter H. Block, owned the team. They had successfully fought off a bid by a syndicate from Washington to establish a franchise. But by December there was word that the Penguins were up for sale. An Atlanta group led by the owners of the Atlanta Braves baseball team made a bold pitch for the team. In the back of their minds was the possibility of moving the club to Atlanta, which in recent years had built a new stadium for football and baseball as well as a new arena for basketball which could be used for hockey.

The deal fell through when Atlanta failed to meet the price. In addition to the $2 million for the franchise, the Penguins' owners also had paid the American Hockey League $300,000 for the loss of the Hornets. They weren't about to lose money.

The Penguins didn't start to become a factor in the standings until late in the season. In the meantime, Bathgate was the surprise of the league. He wound up the division's leading scorer with 59 points on 20 goals and 39 assists. Ingarfield had been one of the top scor-

Defenseman Darryl Edestrand (later sent to Boston) sails past goalie Andy Brown after Brown's save. The Penguins, always on the verge of success, have been rebuilding.

25
VICTORIA

ers earlier in the season, but had been injured.

The Penguins' regular goalie was Les Binkley, a 31-year-old rookie. Binkley, a shoulder-shrugger, wore contact lenses. His twitch seemed to get worse when pressure was greatest. When he caught the puck his mouth curled upward in a half smile. One of the Penguins' bright spots as he saw action in 52 games, he recorded six shutouts. Late in the season the Penguins started to pick up points on the four clubs ahead of them. They needed to change places with just one to make the play-offs. Winning their last four games of the season, they missed fourth place by only two points. The club that took fourth, the Minnesota North Stars, had beaten the Penguins once and tied them once on the weekend before the Penguins started their final streak.

After its first season, a syndicate headed by a 39-year-old Detroit financier, Donald H. Parsons, took over. Parsons collected banks like Cooke collected teams, but a tight-money market forced Parsons to turn over control of the operation to the league within two years.

While the front-office movement was going on, the Penguins started their second season without their only 20-goal scorers. Bathgate was gone and Ab McDonald had been traded to St. Louis as the Penguins began a youth movement. The team finished fifth again.

For the 1969-70 campaign, Riley lured Red Kelly to Pittsburgh, where he replaced Sullivan. A swift center, Michel Briere, joined the club and had a fine rookie season. Al Smith took over as the team's No. 1 goalie, and Dean Prentice, well-traveled and approaching 40, snared 26 goals. Kelly got the team into the play-offs—in fact, it finished second.

Already, Kelly was making plans for the

ABOVE: Another brawl, this one with the Canadiens, saw both benches clear and 15 separate fights take place. RIGHT: McCallum dumps Pete Mahovlich.

1970-71 season. The backbone would be Briere —and what better player for a nucleus than a good 21-year-old center? But Briere was in a devastating car crash shortly after the playoffs. He lay in a coma for months, and as the season began he was near death. Kelly, who took over as general manager when Riley became acting president, couldn't fill the gap. The Penguins finished sixth.

Kelly and Riley had to find themselves some defensemen, as well as a leader. The team didn't lack for bidders, however, as half a dozen groups expressed interest in taking the club. Fans would turn out when it was doing well. That was something peculiar to Pittsburgh sports-followers—they didn't support losers. Riley again faced a rebuilding job. Even the club's symbol had a bad ending. In its first year the club had acquired a real penguin and spent two months teaching it to ice skate. He was ready to make his debut when he contracted pneumonia and died.

Perhaps hope was on the way. Late in the 1970-71 season, the Penguins acquired the Princeton-educated Syl Apps, Jr., son of the former great player for Toronto. Briere had died and now Pittsburgh again had to look for young leaders. They found them in Apps and Greg Polis both of whom matured in the 1971-72 campaign, as Kelly again led the team into the play-offs. Polis got 30 goals and Apps led all Penguin scorers with 59 points, including 25 in one 31-game stretch. The ageless Tim Horton joined the club, lured from retirement with a $100,000 contract (and a chance for his wife to be near her parents).

Still, it was not a very strong club, lacking depth and enough big guns. The scoring strengthened in 1972-73, in which season, strangely, the Penguins posted their best record yet failed to make the play-offs. They were floundering early in the year when Kelly was abruptly dismissed and Ken Schinkel turned from playing for the club to coaching it.

Perhaps the most remarkable player on the squad was Lowell MacDonald. He had sat out the entire 1971-72 season following knee surgery and was attempting to come back at the age of 31. With 34 goals and 75 points, he won the Bill Masterton Trophy, donated by the Professional Hockey Writers Association for "perseverance, sportsmanship and dedication." MacDonald set club records for a left wing. In addition, he had the best "plus" mark of any forward in the West Division. He was plus 41, which meant that with MacDonald on the ice and both clubs at equal strength, the Penguins outscored the opposition by 41 goals.

Al McDonough, a newcomer, got 35 goals, and with an 85-point campaign, established himself as one of the league's top centers. Dave Burrows, a rookie, had the unusual distinction of breaking into a club on defense.

More youngsters joined the club for the 1973-74 season, including a surprise center fresh from Harvard, Bob McManama. The team's number-one draft choice was Blaine Stoughton and another closely watched rookie was Denis Herron in goal.

A young and aggressive management that had saved the franchise in 1971 was apparently looking to young and aggressive players to make the Penguins a consistent contender. One thing was sure: old age wasn't about to creep up on the club any more. It might take time, but the club was going to be heard from as its young players blossomed.

LEFT: Greg Polis, a budding star, was traded in 1974 to St. Louis, a move that was questioned by some. ABOVE: Al McDonough takes puck from the Rangers.

THE ST. LOUIS BLUES

Rhythmic clapping, loud madrigal singing and unbridled enthusiasm greet the Blues when they charge onto the ice of the St. Louis Arena. Perhaps the warmest, most loyal fans in the National Hockey League consistently fill the building, built in 1929, for the club that made expansion teams respectable. The crowd sings, "When the Blues Go Marching In," before the first period, before the second period, and before the final period. Goals for St. Louis are greeted by standing ovations, but enforced silence is the response for an opposition score. Mickey Mouse, say most. Effective, grant all.

It didn't appear it ever would be this way when the city was tapped for an expansion franchise. In fact, few people in St. Louis had the inclination to field a major league hockey team. Sidney Salomon 3d, known as "Sonny," a long-time hockey enthusiast, liked the idea. But his father, Sidney Salomon, Jr., one of St. Louis's most important citizens and head of a vast insurance empire, did not want to start a new venture.

The Salomons had many projects under way, including a huge motel in Florida. Sidney Jr. had had sports interests in the past and was involved at different times with baseball's Cardinals and Browns. He was a former treasurer of the Democratic National Committee and had been one of the country's largest fund raisers for John F. Kennedy's successful 1960 presidential campaign. The only way he thought he might be interested in his son's venture would be if "Sonny" could convince other groups in St. Louis to come along and help share the operation. No one came forward. The league, meanwhile, announced it had given five franchises to five cities and was holding the sixth for St. Louis.

The league made it clear, however, that a suitable place was needed to play. And Chicago owned the St. Louis Arena—the suitable place to play. Anyone wanting a franchise for St. Louis had to play in the Arena or build a new one. However, the league did not favor the idea that one team would be paying rent to another and stipulated that the Arena had to be purchased from the Hawks.

The Salomons, with Robert Wolfson, a local businessman, finally decided to apply for a franchise. They agreed to purchase the Arena for $4 million (which also included indemnification for the St. Louis Braves, Chicago's Central League team). The deal hinged on the Salomons' receiving the franchise. Naturally, Chicago would not stand in the way.

When the Salomons visited with the league's board of governors they brought something extra along with their presentation—the club's name. It would be called the Blues and became the first expansion club to be christened. They estimated it would take $350,000 to modernize the Arena. By the end of the second year they had spent more than $2 million, and had an arena that offered the finest sightlines in the sport.

Lynn Patrick was the Salomons' choice as coach and general manager for their new team. He brought 27 years of NHL experience with him, the last 17 as an administrator or coach. The Salomons wanted a man of Patrick's caliber and standing, one with wide knowledge and intimacy with the Establishment (with whom deals would have to be made) to help get the team off the ground. Scotty Bowman, 34 years old, was named assistant coach and assistant general manager. Bowman's promising playing career had been cut short by a head injury when he was 18.

Garry Unger, Blues' bona fide superstar, leads the West on a charge during the All-Star game. Traded from Detroit, Unger led the Blues in the 1970s.

SHER-WOOD
SHER-WOOD

At 21 he was coaching in the Canadiens' farm system. Eventually, he became a chief scout and troubleshooter for the Canadiens.

Patrick and Bowman merely sought the best players available, regardless of experience or age. First, of course, was goaltending and defense, and the only consideration was who could do the best job. Their first choice was the Hawks' goalie, Glenn Hall, despite the fact that Hall claimed he would not leave Chicago. The Leafs' Terry Sawchuk had said the same thing. So did a remarkably large number of other players, who hoped to use the threat of retirement as leverage in contract negotiations. Hall, as expected, signed with the Blues.

The season started slowly for St. Louis. After two months they were near the bottom of the division. The defense and goaltending were holding up. In fact, the club's goals-against record was second only to the Flyers among the new clubs. But there was little scoring, with the club averaging just over two goals a game. According to plan, Bowman replaced Patrick on November 22, 1967, as coach and general manager and Patrick became managing director. Patrick had done his job and now it would be up to Bowman to see how far he could take the club. One week after he took office he made the trade that St. Louis fans will always be grateful for—he acquired Red Berenson from the Rangers in exchange for Ron Stewart, the Blues' leading scorer.

In New York the deal was viewed with curiosity. Berenson had two goals in 19 games with the Rangers. The season before he hadn't scored in 30 contests. Berenson, though, was one of those players who could not perform well if he rarely saw action. An injury the season before, after he had been off to a strong start, kept him out of the starting lineup and he never was able to get back in.

He withdrew, giving a picture to New York reporters of a loner, sitting by himself reading a book. In an angry moment his coach, Emile Francis, once told a reporter, "If I see him reading a book on the bus one more time I'm going to throw him off." Bowman and Patrick knew of Berenson's talent. In short order, Berenson became the Blues' Mr. Everything. He killed penalties, he played on the power play, he took regular turns. A few weeks after the deal, Patrick predicted that Berenson would be the West's first superstar.

With Berenson scoring, the Blues moved. Dickie Moore, the 37-year-old former Canadien star, was acquired in midseason. Retired for two years, he was nevertheless on Toronto's player list (the Leafs had been his last club). The Blues talked him back, giving Toronto Pat Quinn in exchange. Doug Harvey, 43, was also signed by the Blues, thanks to Bowman's rapport with ex-Canadiens.

Although the Blues had momentum, they weren't exactly destroying the opposition. Then came what may have been the turning point in the Blues' fortunes. Certainly neither they nor their fans were ever the same again. The Blues had the largest crowd in their short history on January 27, 1968—13,873. The Rangers led by 3-0 going into the final period.

Slowly the Blues came alive. They started to score and the crowd responded. They applauded wildly, sang and chanted. For each St. Louis goal the organist played "When The Saints Go Marching In" (replacing "Saints" with "Blues") and nothing could stop the team then. They tied the game, then won it, 4-3. The crowd gave them a standing ovation, and two traditions were born. One was the total involvement of the fans for their club, the second the belief that the Blues could always come back.

The club wound up third its first season, suffering fewer losses than any other West club. But if the fans thought they had seen something in the regular season, they were more than surprised in the play-offs. In the first round of the post-season tournament the Blues turned back the division-champion Flyers, 4 games to 3, playing two overtime contests. They met the Minnesota North Stars in the West Division final, with the winner to meet the finalist from the East Division. The

Blues-North Stars series also went to the limit of seven games, and four of them were forced into overtime. The deciding contest was played at St. Louis.

The Blues trailed, 1-0, with fewer than three minutes to play when Moore tied the score. When the Blues skated onto the ice for the overtime session, the Arena was in a frenzy. Neither team scored in the first overtime period. The second overtime started with deafening noise. It took 2 minutes and 50 seconds before Ron Schock, who hadn't scored in the play-offs, put in the goal that gave the Blues the victory. One observer at the game said the fans sang and cheered for hours afterward. Although that report is exaggerated, thousands did wait outside long after the game, talking wildly about their team, the first West Division club to have a chance to win the Stanley Cup.

The chance never materialized, but the Blues came close with a memorable effort. The Canadiens swept the four-game series, but the Blues extended them to two overtimes. Every game in the series was decided by one goal.

For the start of their second season the Blues unveiled another goalie to share duties with Glenn Hall—Jacques Plante, out of hockey since 1965. Plante was yet another former Montreal great. He was New York's property, taken by the Blues during the 1968 draft. Bowman had heard that Plante was in shape (he was 39 years old) and had looked good in a brief appearance in training camp with the Oakland Seals the season before when he was an assistant coach with Oakland.

Plante was anything but humble upon his return. "At last," he said, of Hall, "I have a good back-up goalie." The pair combined to win the Vezina Trophy as the Blues made a runaway of the West Division, which they were to do again in the 1969-70 season. Crowds became standing-room-only and their hero was Berenson. He became a 35-goal scorer in his first full season with the team. But the frenzied St. Louis fans were denied an in-person view of one of the great performances in the history of hockey by Berenson.

It occurred at Philadelphia—Berenson's six-goal night. They came on November 7, 1968, as he became the second man in modern history to accomplish the feat. The Red Baron scored his team's first five goals, a record, including four in the second period, a record for one session. His sixth goal in the club's 8-0 victory brought him a standing ovation.

He was well rewarded when he returned home. The Salomons gave a $750 watch to any Blue who got the hat trick. Berenson got not only his watch, but also received a station wagon with a canoe perched on top and a shotgun inside.

In the 1969-70 season St. Louis acquired Phil Goyette who, at the age of 36, turned in his finest season. He totaled 78 points and captured the Lady Byng Trophy. For the third straight year, the Blues were the West Division representatives in the Stanley Cup finals —and for the third straight year went down.

It was obvious that the organization was going to undergo some radical changes in the 1970-71 season. The Hawks were coming into the division, ending the Blues' dominance. Al Arbour, the defensive anchor, became the coach, with Bowman remaining as general manager. Although the Blues again were the only expansion team to post a winning record, the other teams were making up ground. And, of course, they wanted to catch Chicago.

In late season the Blues made a drastic change—Berenson was traded to Detroit for Garry Unger, a younger player. Berenson charged that his activity as president of the Players' Association was the reason. Bowman denied it, but the first signs of a rift in the harmonious club were appearing and, for the first time, the Blues were ousted from the play-offs after one round. Immediately, reports that Bowman was unhappy with his position came out, and it was believed he wanted to be fired so that he could collect on the remainder of his contract. Finally, he left. Harmony did not reign in the castle of the first West Division kings.

The Blues were the only expansion team to make the play-offs each of the first six years. Still, there were signs of slippage. Despite Unger's surge to stardom, the team produced only one 20-goal man in 1970-71—Chris Bordeleau. Changes were in order, and they came in breathtaking succession. Bowman left to become coach of the Canadiens. Sid Abel took over as coach. Hall finally quit, and to replace him during the 1971-72 campaign, five goalies were employed. Only Jacques Caron among them could stop the puck with any regularity. The Blues were somewhat bumptious with the three Plager brothers around, but the scoring fell off, and suddenly the Blues were just another club.

While the Blues shuffled personnel, one key member of the team remained securely at his post—behind the organ. The man at the keyboard was Norm Kramer, and it was said that he was worth a goal a game to his team. At first the opposition—especially the older clubs—complained about his pounding to inspire the Blues when they needed a goal. However, their complaints were ignored, so the protesters began retaliating in their rinks. Soon every organist in the league was copying Kramer. He reached the height of his notoriety at the 1970 All-Star Game, in St. Louis, when the Chicago Black Hawks demanded equal time on the organ for the East Division. It was an unheard-of situation—a fight over which organist would perform. Eventually, it was agreed that Kramer would play for part of the game, and the Hawks' organist, Al Melgard, would play for the remainder.

Despite Kramer's best efforts, the Blues floundered. Abel left the coaching ranks to become general manager, and Bill McCreary took over behind the bench. Abel then began a series of deals with the Rangers that would lead some people to say that the Blues were simply the New Yorkers' western farm team. It appeared that the Rangers were loaning players to St. Louis for seasoning, only to reclaim them once they had matured. Abel's first deal was to send Gene Carr, the club's number-one draft choice, left-winger Jim Lorentz and veteran Wayne Connelly to the Rangers for Jack Egers, Mike Murphy and Moose Dupont. Egers and Murphy, who would later return to New York, teamed with Unger, and the three youngsters became known as "the Whiz Kids." Each cracked the 20-goal barrier. Dupont, meanwhile, became the team policeman.

Still, it wasn't enough. The other clubs in the division were stronger, and McCreary couldn't get a winning effort from his men. He was dismissed, and for the second time, Arbour became coach. He got the Blues into the playoffs.

Brawny Barclay Plager mashes wiry Bobby Rousseau into the boards as Garry Unger hunts for the loose puck.

Their opponent, the North Stars started as though they were going to blow past the Blues. They scored victories in the first two games before the Blues came back to win the next two. Minnesota won the fifth game, and St. Louis tied the series with a sixth-game decision. The teams, predictably, went into one overtime, then a second, in the deciding game. Finally, Kevin O'Shea, a Minnesota reject, scored the winning goal for St. Louis on a slap shot. Improbably, the Blues were past the first round, but they were eliminated in the next one.

Further changes marked the Blues in 1972-73 as they fought their way back to respectability. The club started shakily, and not surprisingly Arbour was fired. Jean-Guy Talbot replaced him, and the club moved into the play-offs. In 1973-74, with Chuck Catto replacing Abel as G.M., Murphy and Egers found their way back to the Rangers, and the Blues again began looking for goal scorers to supplement Unger, the red-haired flash whom everyone expected would lead the team through the 1970's.

THE BUFFALO SABRES

When the Buffalo Sabres' first season ended in the spring of '71, only eight NHL teams had better won-lost records.

People from Buffalo had long since tired of jokes about their city, once described by a Broadway columnist as "a good place to be *from*." When the suggestion was once made to bring Buffalo into the big leagues, an owner sneered, "I don't want a town named Buffalo playing in my building."

The march to respectability began one day in 1965 when one of the world's wealthiest squash racquets players, Seymour Knox III, was playing golf with Freddie Hunt, the general manager of the American League's Buffalo Bisons. "Say, Seymour, what about big league hockey in Buffalo?" asked Hunt. The idea was all Knox needed. He discussed it with his brother Northrup, who happens to be one of the world's top polo players. Together the brothers formed Buffalo's first family, with interests in banking and Woolworth's. Still the hockey Establishment wasn't impressed. Buffalo still didn't have the big league image. Moreover, Buffalo, with almost a million people, was only a 90-minute drive from Toronto. The Maple Leaf games were seen regularly in Buffalo. If this huge United States market suddenly gained its own hockey team, it wouldn't be interested in watching the Maple Leafs.

That was the major reason the Knoxes were denied in their bid to join the great expansion of 1967. Luckily for Buffalo—and hockey, as it turned out—there was agitation for another Canadian team to join the league. Parliament was putting pressure on the NHL, which finally consented to bring in Vancouver for the 1970-71 season. However, Vancouver alone would swell the league to 13 teams, an unacceptable number. It had to have an even number of clubs. And so Buffalo was added.

The choice of the man to lead the club was easy. Punch Imlach was available. A year before he had been fired from Toronto when his club bowed out of Stanley Cup play and the Maple Leafs' president, Stafford Smythe, had announced, "Gentlemen, the Punch Imlach era is over." Smythe never envisioned what would happen next. The Imlach era indeed was over at Toronto. But it started again at Buffalo.

Imlach needed a bit of luck to get players who could score goals. And he had the luck. The right to the first choice in the amateur draft would be dramatically decided on a spin of a wheel of fortune between the Sabres and the Canucks. Imlach won. Immediately, he chose Gil Perreault, the most acclaimed junior in Canada. Now Imlach had his goal scorer, a center pegged for stardom. Then came the draft to stock the new teams. There was a toss of a coin, and Imlach won again. He immediately chose Tom Webster from Boston, then just as quickly traded him to Detroit for Roger Crozier, one of the game's top goalies. With two lucky moves, Imlach had the start of a hockey team—a scorer and a goalie.

In time, he added such proven old-timers as Don Marshall from the Rangers, Phil Goyette from St. Louis, Reg Fleming, the belter from Philadelphia, and Eddie Shack.

By the time the season was ready to open in the 10,429-seat Memorial Auditorium, 4,500 season tickets had been sold. The first few weeks went along unspectacularly as Goyette and Marshall held out. The Sabres had dropped their home debut on October 15, to the Canadiens by 3-0. Perreault looked very promising, but Imlach couldn't get a pair of wings to go along with the rookie.

Rookie-of-the-year Gil Perreault stays close to superstar Bobby Orr. Perreault was one reason Buffalo played to consistently full houses.

The club did all right in its first campaign, which started with the optimistic Imlach prediction that "Buffalo will be the first expansion team to win the Stanley Cup." He didn't mean right away, of course. When the first year was over, only 8 teams in the 14-team league posted better records. Perreault quickly established himself as a star, setting a record for most goals and most points by a rookie with 38 and 72 respectively. Of course, he was named rookie of the year.

Within a week after the season ended, the Sabres sold 6,000 more season's tickets for their Memorial Auditorium, which had to be expanded to accommodate the fans. The Sabres created more interest their first season in Buffalo than did the football Bills.

Perhaps Imlach's key moment that first season was his long-awaited return to Toronto. Everyone on the Sabres knew what this game meant to him. He sent his team onto the ice but delayed his own appearance. Finally, just as the game was about to begin he appeared, and the crowd applauded him wildly. The Sabres routed the Leafs, 7-2, and in the final minute the fans stood and chanted, "We want Punch! We want Punch!"

Before the second season, the incredible Imlach pulled off two more coups. First, he chose Richard Martin in the amateur draft as he continued to look for scoring power. Then he created a hockey controversy in what became known as the "funny draft." He took advantage of a loophole and plucked six players from other teams in the intraleague draft while he lost none.

In Martin, Imlach had a player overlooked by much of the public. Martin was chosen fifth—after Guy Lafleur and Marcel Dionne. They were supposed to be the top players available. But by the end of the season Martin became the greatest goal-scoring rookie ever, with 44 goals. He might have had 50 if a late-season injury hadn't sidelined him.

Imlach stepped down after suffering a heart attack in mid-season and turned over the coaching and general manager's job to Joe Crozier. By the third season—the 1972-73 campaign—Imlach was well enough to take over again as G.M. Now Imlach knew he had to go for defense to complement his goal scorers. He coaxed his old Toronto star, Tim Horton, out of retirement to play defense again. In the draft he took young defensemen, such as Jim Schoenfeld and Larry Carriere, and a goalie. Meanwhile, in the draft to stock the new New York and Atlanta franchises, the Sabres lost no one important. The three players Imlach did lose were all products of the "funny draft."

Under Crozier's dynamic leadership and with Imlach directing the deals and forming the club, the Sabres were the surprise story of 1972. Perreault, Martin and Rene Robert formed the formidable French Connection line. The team was in superb shape. Crozier had the players running all the time, even on the road.

"You should see people look at us in a Holiday Inn when we come down in the elevator at seven in the morning in our sweat suits," said Mike Robitaille. The team jumped off to an outstanding start. It went through 21 games at home without a defeat. Crozier was joined in goal by Dave Dryden, Ken's older brother. In addition, Don Luce and Jim Lorentz played hard-nosed hockey. Perhaps it was the professional wrestler-turned trainer who helped them get tough, perhaps it was a combination of things; the Sabres wound up winning, and making the play-offs. In Stanley Cup play, they extended the Canadiens to six games, after the Frenchmen won the first three.

With such a bright future, Imlach's boast about winning the Cup may prove valid. Imlach likes to say, "Hockey needs a Cinderella team."

Dave Dryden, Ken's older brother, bends to cover a loose puck. Dryden has become the Sabres' number-one goalie, succeeding Roger Crozier.

THE VANCOUVER CANUCKS

Before the NHL thought of expansion, the people of Vancouver, which is Canada's San Francisco, hotly desired a big-league franchise.

Their hopes were dashed in the expansion of 1967, but the league promised that the next time around, Vancouver would get first consideration.

The people were impatient. The Labatt beer people loaned the floundering Oakland Seals $600,000 on the condition that if the league permitted the Seals to move, they'd come to Vancouver. That didn't work out.

Meanwhile, the Vancouver Canucks of the Western Hockey League had been taken over by the Medicor Investment Corporation. It was believed that Punch Imlach, who owned a piece of the Western League team, would become the new franchise's general manager and coach.

The plot was only beginning to thicken. Medicor and Joe Crozier and Imlach disagreed on how much the latters' shares were worth. Toward the end of the Canucks' 1969-70 season, Crozier was fired as general manager, and with him went Punch Imlach's chance to take over.

Barely aware of what was going on in Canada's far west, Bud Poile was collecting money from the Philadelphia Flyers, the club he had launched as general manager only a few years before. But in December, 1969, he and the Flyers' top management disagreed on key terms, and he left.

In February of 1970, Medicor called on Poile. The next month, he signed on to be the new team's general manager. Poile hired Hal Laycoe as his coach for the new team, which would retain the Western League team's name.

Poile needed a leader. He chose Orland Kurtenbach, who had finished a disastrous season with the Rangers, following a spinal-fusion operation.

In the draft of junior players, after losing out to Imlach on the first choice, Poile took Dale Tallon, who could play forward or defense. It didn't matter to Poile how many centers or wings or defensemen were available—he went for the best players he could get. He took Pat Quinn from Toronto and Gary Doak from Boston; Wayne Maki from St. Louis; Rosaire Paiement from Philadelphia, and Kurtenbach.

Before the Canucks were even ready to play in their Pacific Coliseum, 12,000 of the 15,564 seats were sold on a season's basis. When the campaign began, the fans were pleasantly surprised. The Canucks actually played at .500 for more than a month.

Tallon was coming along, en route to a 56-point season; Andre Boudrias and Maki and Paiement were scoring goals at a heady clip. Then, two days before Christmas, Kurt was lost to the club. He stayed out for 26 games. The Canucks began to fall. They were also stuck with three goalies—George Gardner had been added—and they couldn't move one of them down for fear of losing him on waivers.

Still, the fans turned out. The club achieved a remarkable 98.7 percent of capacity as the Canucks became the fifth biggest drawing card in the league.

At season's end, the Canucks could look over several positive facts. They had finished sixth in the East, ahead of Detroit, and posted a better record than the Seals in the other division. They had a 34-goal scorer in Paiement. And all seats had been sold for the next season.

Vancouver's Barry Wilkens, face twisted in pain, lies stretched out on the ice with apparent back injury suffered in game with Rangers at Madison Square Garden.

14
14

Bryan McSheffrey assaults fallen Rangers Giacomin and Neilson. Vancouver's remote location helped cause Canucks' poor won-lost road record.

But something happened to the club in its second year. Laycoe said the players had been too busy reading their press clippings. Goal scoring fell sharply, even though the Canucks had drafted the talented Jocelyn Guevremont as their number-one amateur. Guevremont's 38 assists set a record for rookie defensemen. From six men who scored more than 21 goals, the Canucks fell to only three. Once after they were routed 6-0 by an established power, Laycoe had to soothe his players by telling them they had played as well as could be expected. "Isn't it a heck of a note on expansion," complained Laycoe, "that you have to tell your boys they played well while losing 6-0?" Then Laycoe added ominously, "You know who the victim will be for all these losses, don't you? It's the coach. He's always the one who gets fired." Sure enough, Laycoe was dismissed after the club's second season and replaced by Vic Stasiuk for 1972-73.

The club Stasiuk took over was one of the smallest in league history. It included 5-foot 9-inch, 155-pound Bobby Schmautz (who turned out to be the scoring leader), 5-foot 8-inch Andre Boudrias and 5-foot 6-inch Bobby Lalonde. The problems the Canucks had are indicated by the fact that these three finished among the top four on the club in scoring. The team also suffered in goal. For the second straight year, Dunc Wilson carried the major share of the goaltending in a three-goalie rotation. But the defensemen were young and inexperienced. Lack of backchecking by the forwards, mistakes on defense and overworked goalies resulted in the second worst goals-against record in league annals—339.

Attendance remained remarkable despite this poor record. It was obvious, though, that eventually the Canucks would have to remake the team to continue drawing crowds. Radical changes hit the club for 1973-74. Bill McCreary took over as coach, and Laycoe became general manager. In the Canucks' first big deal, Tallon was traded to the Black Hawks for Gary Smith, and the Canucks finally had their first proven big league goalie. Wilson jumped to the WHA, but Smith had been accustomed to carrying the load by himself. He had played for the Seals for four campaigns.

The Canucks had their best training camp, winning their first six games. They started out strongly, too. Their fans hoped that they had discovered some key players in youngsters Don Lever, Bryan McSheffrey,

Gerry O'Flaherty and Dennis Ververgaert.

Laycoe was attempting to combine the new players with the proven older ones—a stratagem that marked the more successful good clubs but one that isn't always easy to implement. He finally had a team with some size, and he lowered the average age of the club to under 25. Perhaps as important, he decided to go with his youngsters, testing them under fire. Any youngster who came to the Canucks knew at least that he'd get a chance. Tallon, Guevremont, Lever and Ververgaert were all first-round draft choices, and all became important cogs in the club machinery.

THE ATLANTA FLAMES

Logic said that hockey would be doomed to failure in Atlanta. The Deep South, after all, had never had major league hockey before. And Atlanta? Why, it didn't even have a regulation-size ice rink. The closest one was in Macon, 50 miles away.

But suddenly in early 1972, signs sprouted up on Atlanta street corners proclaiming "The Ice Age Is Coming to the South." The location was to be the Omni, a spanking-new arena. The Flames—perhaps the first team ever named to commemorate the burning of a city—wound up with a remarkably solid organization. The general manager was Cliff Fletcher, a Canadiens and St. Louis Blues product, who knew something about starting a hockey team. But the surprise was the coach—Boom Boom Geoffrion.

The bombastic Boomer became an instant folk hero in Atlanta, which had rarely heard a thick French-Canadian accent before. But the Boomer delighted Southerners when he told them, "Y'all come down to see us, ya hear?" He was a strange choice, it appeared at first. After all, he had coached a big league team—the Rangers—for only half a season. He had to quit because of a nervous stomach. How could he possibly handle a first-year team that was sure to lose more often than it won?

The Flames drafted very well. They came out with two of the more promising young goalies in hockey—Dan Bouchard and Phil Myre. Then they staffed the club with experienced players. In some respects, it was similar to what Fletcher's old team, the St. Louis Blues, had done to establish itself early. Noel Price, Pat Quinn, Ron Harris, Bill Plager—all had proven themselves as big league defensemen. The scoring, management hoped, might come from Jacques Richard, the Flames' first pick from the amateurs. Bob Leiter, Rey Comeau and Keith McCreary were also on the forward line.

This combination provided some of the more startling surprises hockey had seen. The Flames were a play-off contender immediately. They won five of their first ten games. The fans turned out, too, producing near-capacity crowds for every game. For more than half the season, Atlanta played over .500 and was the talk of hockey.

Of course, without goal-scoring it couldn't and didn't continue. Richard was a disappointment. He had come to Atlanta barely speaking a word of English. Now he had to learn it with a drawl. He became temperamental, seemingly a victim of rookie nervousness. The club finally folded down the stretch but not before solidly establishing itself. Four other teams finished with worse records. Only six other clubs had a lower goals-against average.

It was apparent that the team needed scoring punch for the 1973-74 season. The players had had a taste of winning, even dreams of making the play-offs. Now it was time to make the dream a reality. The Flames chose Tom Lysiak as their top draft choice. He had scored 58 goals with the Medicine Hat Tigers and was touted as the best potential scorer in junior hockey. In addition the Flames had Curt Bennett, who came to the team in a deal with the Rangers after the first season had started. Bennett was probably the Flames' first hero, a long-striding center who often started—and finished—end-to-end rushes.

This interesting collection of players got the Flames hovering around first place in the West Division through the early stages of the 1973-74 campaign; people were convinced the Ice Age had come to stay in the South.

Goalie Phil Myre and defenseman Noel Price collaborate in foiling Ratelle scoring attempt. Since they entered the NHL, the Flames have been a contending team.

19

THE NEW YORK ISLANDERS

The most expensive team in history—it cost about $11 million, including almost $5 million indemnity to the Rangers for moving into their territory—had a difficult birth. The pain began even before the club took the ice, in 1972. It was months before the owners, a group headed by Roy Boe, found a general manager. They got one finally in Bill Torrey, who had learned about trouble working for Charles O. Finley in Oakland. Torrey in turn had to get a coach; he found Phil Goyette, who had never been behind the bench before.

The team's nucleus, of course, was to come from the expansion draft—some 19 forwards and defensemen. Then the WHA sprang suddenly to life, and when the dust had settled, 7 of the 19 players on the Islanders' draft list had signed with the WHA. Fortunately, the New Yorkers chose first in the amateur draft, and they picked out a plum—Billy Harris, the juniors' top star. There was pretty good strength in goal, with the experienced Gerry Desjardins and a promising youngster, Billy Smith.

Once the season began at the new Nassau Coliseum in Long Island, hope almost vanished. The team tied a modern record for fewest victories—only 12 over the 78-game season. It yielded more goals (347), lost more games (60), and scored fewer points (30) than any team in NHL history. "I can't score for these guys," Goyette would say. Before the season had ended, Goyette had been ousted, and Earl Ingarfield, his one-time Ranger teammate had replaced him behind the bench.

The year had, though, unveiled a star in Harris. Though Billy had no experienced center to feed him the puck and often did all the work himself from his right wing spot, he managed to produce 28 goals and 50 points. Many observers felt that had he played for a more respectable squad he might have been named the top rookie.

The team's captain was Eddie Westfall, who had never been called on as a primary goal producer in Boston, which had been stocked with powerful players.

The Islanders did play at least one game their fans like to remember. The New Yorkers had won only once on the road by the middle of January. Then, having lost 12 straight games, they went to Boston to play the second-place Bruins. They had scored only six goals in their previous 8 contests. No one had beaten the Bruins at home in 13 games. Yet, incredibly, the Islanders jumped to a 5-0 lead. It grew to 6-1. Then the Bruins went to work, cutting into the edge. By the final buzzer, no one could quite believe that the Islanders had salvaged a victory, 9-7. The frenzied action moved Goyette to say, "I had a stiff neck watching the puck go back and forth."

Late in the season the Islanders acquired Jean Potvin, whose brother, Denis Potvin, happened to be the top young defenseman in Canada. Denis was shattering every one of Bobby Orr's scoring records for a defenseman in the juniors. The Islanders knew they'd wind up with the worst record and would therefore choose first in the junior draft. The Islanders' brass realized that drafting Denis might be easier than signing him. Having Denis's brother on the team might, they thought, convince Denis to play with the Islanders instead of with the WHA. The strategy worked. When the 1973 draft came, he was chosen first and signed by the Islanders. Suddenly, things were looking up. Al Arbour was the new coach. Denis soon became the talk of the league, and the New Yorkers appeared to have shaken off their first year's disaster.

Alternate captain Bert Marshall guards the palace door. The Islanders played well their second year; some predicted they would win the Cup before the New York Rangers.

THE NEW ENGLAND WHALERS

The New England Whalers hockey club won the first WHA championship without placing one player on the league's first all-star team.

The club's strength was its solid depth. Rather than going for the single superstar, the coach and general manager, Jack Kelley, opted for the proven performer in building his squad.

He acquired two good goaltenders, Al Smith and Bruce Landon. Former Bruin Tom Webster had 53 goals and 103 total points. Terry Caffery became rookie of the year and was the second Whaler to score 100 or more points.

For defense, Kelley obtained Ted Green of the Boston Bruins and made him team captain. Ted had the young, tough Jim Dorey with him and a third good defensive performer, Rick Ley.

The Whalers' founders were a young Boston businessman, Howard Baldwin, and his partner, a Harvard man, John Coburn. Baldwin chose his former college coach, Jack Kelley, to be the Whalers' coach and general manager. Kelley had become the most successful collegiate coach in the United States with his Boston University team that had won the national championship two years in a row.

In short order Kelley snared ten players from the NHL, including Green and Webster. He also shrewdly picked up five players who had either been born in New England or had played hockey there.

The Whalers' first season ended on a bizarre note, more comic than significant. The high-scoring team had won the Eastern Division title and, having advanced to the final round in the play-offs, was playing the Winnipeg Jets at Winnipeg.

The Whalers were trailing in the final moments of the game, and Ted Green, the prize NHL jumper, was in the corner trying desperately to dig out the puck and feed it to a wing. Suddenly a fan who had enjoyed a few too many reached over the boards and grabbed Green in a headlock. Freeing himself, Green swung at the fan but missed. The fan returned the compliment but also missed. Then the game ended and quiet was momentarily restored. But there was more to come.

This was to have been a special award night. A crippled boy was wheeled onto the ice in his wheelchair at the game's conclusion to make presentations to the most outstanding players. This ceremony would have proceeded without incident had not some official in charge of the festivities forgotten to tell Rick Ley that he had been chosen as the second star to be honored. Ley's name was announced, but there was no Ley. He had gone to the dressing room, disrobed and was in the shower.

When he failed to appear to accept his award, outraged fans swooped down to the Whalers' dressing room. Storming in, they ran into coach Kelley. Once again that night blows were exchanged. Whalers came charging out of the showers in defense of their coach. Shouting and shoving, the Whalers succeeded in clearing the fans from the room. Most of the crowd had left the arena, missing as zany a scene as hockey could provide: eight naked players giving the bum's rush to some unwanted visitors.

When they weren't chasing fans from their dressing room, the Whalers were playing winning hockey, despite the fact that they had no permanent home rink. They played half their home games in the Boston Garden and half of them on a nearby college rink. In its second year; the club played only in the Garden, sufficient proof that winning the WHA's equivalent of the Stanley Cup had made the Whalers major league.

Ted Green, captain and moving spirit of the Whalers, anchored a solid defense that combined with a hard-working offense and kept the New England team in first place.

THE WINNIPEG JETS

No matter what tricks Fate plays on Winnipeg, the club will always be remembered for its most dramatic moment—the signing of Bobby Hull. With a few strokes of a fountain pen, Hull and the Jets' owner, Ben Hatskin, gave credibility to the new World Hockey Association.

The deal that Hull agreed to has become one of the most famous financial arrangements in the history of sports. But it came about only after long and bitter disputes between Hull and the Chicago Black Hawks' management. When Hull accepted the Hatskin offer, he received from the league a million dollars in cash. He took the money in the United States so that he wouldn't have to pay the higher Canadian income tax. A million was, of course, more money than any one owner in the WHA could afford. So each team in the league was assessed $100,000 to convince Hull to leap. The cash drew about $1,000 a week in bank interest, part of a deal worth $1.75 million to Hull. In return he signed for 10 years as a player-coach.

The Jets soon found that signing other players was going to be nearly as difficult. The Jets became the target of players with more outrageous salary demands than anyone else in the new league, simply because they had been the first team to make a player a millionaire. "We can laugh about it now," said the general manager, Annis Stukus, when the season finally ended. "But some of the player demands were ridiculous."

One player, for example, who had been earning $22,000 a year in the NHL, asked the Jets for $60,000 and a $40,000 bonus for jumping. Another marginal player told Stukus, "I played twenty-two games in the NHL —I'm worth fifty-five thousand."

But Hull was the one everyone was interested in. He drove himself to make the league go. In the beginning he couldn't even play. He had to sit on the sidelines from the time camp started until September 30 because he was still under NHL contract, as was everyone else who had jumped. Even when October rolled around, with the opening of the regular season less than two weeks away, he couldn't play. Legal maneuvering restrained Hull from suiting up. He was preparing court cases, but he still was in demand. In every city that the Winnipeg team visited, Hull was the center of attention at mammoth press conferences. His time wasn't his own. He would be called at all hours of the day and night to appear almost any place in North America.

Bobby's weight fell from 197 pounds to 182. But he had a remarkable, single-minded determination to make this new league go. His pride and his career were wrapped up in the venture. With 604 goals he was, after all, the NHL's leader among active players. He was quitting the Establishment while still at his peak.

When the season did begin, Hull found himself still relegated to the sidelines. He was the player-coach, though, and drilled the club during scrimmages. Finally, he was permitted to play. When he went on the ice he yielded the decisions behind the bench to Nick Mickoski, the assistant coach.

The Jets weren't simply a one-dimensional team. Most of the players they had signed were above the journeyman class. Norm Beaudin and Christian Bordeleau were both to score more than 100 points. Larry Hornung was an expert on defense, and Ernie Wakely anchored the goaltending. The Jets easily won the Western Division title.

Winning was satisfying, but the Jets' expenses outran their income. The first 1,000 tickets sold for every Winnipeg home game went to pay Hull's salary. Still, there was a saving grace. As one executive explained, "Bobby made us major league. He would have been cheap for five million. We got a bargain. I would say it was the biggest bargain in the history of sports."

Bobby Hull flies down center ice. Hull was paid almost two million dollars to jump to the Jets. When he arrived, the new league suddenly became respectable.

THE CHICAGO COUGARS

Playing in one of the world's great hockey centers, in a city with an outstanding tradition of supporting the game, the Cougars barely made it off the ground in their first year. By the time the Cougars took the ice for the first time, they had had three different sets of owners. Small wonder there was confusion. The general manager that was to assemble a team was Ed Short, who had no hockey background although he was willing to learn. He had been a baseball man most of his life as road secretary, publicist, and general manager of the Chicago White Sox.

By early August, just a few weeks before the Cougars were to start training camp, Short had signed only one player, a pugnacious youngster from the Flyers named Bob Kelly, and by then Short was out of money. When his guarantees never appeared, Kelly quickly jumped back to the NHL. Now the Cougars had no players.

By the time the Kaiser brothers, successful real estate men, had taken over the club there were only days left before the season was to start. Short still was the G.M. The Kaisers kept him, since he was under contract from the previous owners. Short hurriedly signed "bodies" just to fill a roster. In camp only one player, Rosaire Paiement, had played a full campaign in the NHL. Only two others, Rod Zaine and Larry Mavety, had even been in the NHL the previous year.

The coach was the emotional Marcel Pronovost, a man who detested losing. Pronovost had appeared in 1,206 NHL games—at the time only 11 players had appeared in more. Pronovost, in fact, had seen virtually as much big-league action as all the Cougar players combined. Pronovost suffered through the Cougars' first season. By Christmas it was obvious the team would finish last in the Western Division. It gained the dubious distinction of finishing with the poorest overall mark in the first season of the WHA and with the fewest goals.

Bobby Sicinski, who amassed 88 points, led what scoring there was. Paiement, who led the club in goals with 33, added 69 points, and old Reg Fleming came through with 68. The defense was led by the ageless Larry Cahan, who was playing for his eleventh team in his twentieth season as a pro. Ron Anderson and Butch Barber also were part of the rear guard.

Midway through the season, when it was apparent that the club would have to start all over again, Short was dismissed. He was replaced by Jacques Demers, the personnel director who had previously been with a junior team outside Montreal. It was obvious that changes had to be made as soon as the season ended—and they were.

The breakthrough came when long negotiations with the Hawks' Pat Stapleton finally ended with Stapleton jumping across town and league. A perennial all-star for the Hawks, Stapleton signed a long-term deal worth more than $150,000 a season to become the Cougars' player-coach. Finally, the club had a proven major leaguer who wasn't collecting Social Security. Stapleton was a good choice, especially for a league that put such a premium on scoring and constant attacking. One of the best rushing defensemen in the sport, he could be counted on to carry the puck out of trouble.

Another good and experienced Hawk, Ralph Backstrom, the center, also jumped to the Cougars. Now the Cougars had two quality players. They changed goalies, too, acquiring Cam Newton from Pittsburgh. With these few moves, the Cougars became more competitive.

New goalie Cam Newton helps bolster a sagging Chicago defense. Acquisition of Newton, defenseman Pat Stapleton and Ralph Backstrom made the Cougars contenders.

1
7

THE MINNESOTA FIGHTING SAINTS

The Saints may have been the most brainy team on ice. They were led by a college-trained coach and general manager. Partly to appeal to the hockey-playing natives, they featured a sizable American contingent—nine players, many of them college educated. The last time that many Americans had played for a major league hockey team was more than 30 years before, when the Black Hawks hoped to bolster their attendance.

Coach-general manager Glen Sonmor had two degrees and had coached at Ohio State and at the University of Minnesota. He had had two flings with the New York Rangers in the mid-1950s, but his career was cut short when he lost an eye in an accident.

Sonmor knew exactly the type of team he wanted—one that could skate and could move the puck around, as the good college hockey teams did. He wanted to transfer that style to the pros. There were snickers in the league as he assembled his team, but that was before the Russians, with a similar style, embarrassed the NHL stars.

Sonmor learned all the intricacies of dealing with professionals after his years of taking care of young collegians. He even learned how to "babysit," the art of constantly attending on an athlete you want so that no one else can approach him. The player he sheltered was Billy Klatt, a natural for St. Paul, where the Saints played. Klatt had been born in Minneapolis. He had scored 34 goals for the Bruins' top farm club. Sonmor knew that Milt Schmidt, the Bruins' G.M., was after Klatt for Boston and was making some enticing offers. Sonmor had to get Klatt away from Schmidt and the NHL. First, Sonmor took the youngster to a golf tournament in Niagara Falls. The tourney was named for Tom Webster, one of the NHL stars about to jump. Sonmor knew that Webster would be at the tournament, as would Rick Ley and Brad Selwood—all young, promising NHL players about to switch leagues. As Sonmor explained, "I wanted Billy in the sort of atmosphere that would be conducive to making him jump." While Klatt was in the proper frame of mind, Sonmor suggested he call Schmidt to tell him he had decided to go with the Fighting Saints. Sonmor stayed at Klatt's side during the phone call.

In year one Sonmor found that the opposition took advantage of his players' lack of size. In some games his team was almost run out of the rink. His players weren't afraid of the fans, at least. After a game at Ottawa some observers were jeering the Saints. One of the spectators grabbed the flashily dressed Sonmor by his velvet jacket and said, "Yoo hoo, Liberace!" The players jumped to their coach's defense, fought off the belligerent fans and got safely to the dressing room.

The Saints made some changes for their second season. Sonmor relinquished the coaching duties to his assistant, Harry Neale. Like Sonmor, Neale had coached at Ohio State and also had been a member of the Canadian national team. To get more scoring, the Saints got a prize jumper in Mike Walton of the Bruins. Walton for years had been regarded as one of the NHL's better forwards. He was a consistent 20-goal man. The Saints also landed Walton's brother, Bob, who had led the Western League in scoring, and, on defense, another jumper, Rick Smith. The Saints had some proven players, such as Wayne Connelly (who led the team the first season with 40 goals and 70 points), Ted Hampson, and Klatt. The young Klatt had not disappointed, picking up 36 goals in his first campaign. Mike Curran and Jack McCartan anchored the team in goal.

Popular Saints Hampson (10) and Antonovich whirl up ice together. Like many WHA teams, the Fighting Saints are a blend of NHL jumpers and young, unproven Americans.

THE CLEVELAND CRUSADERS

The Crusaders and their flamboyant owner, Nick Mileti, were involved in some of the most significant aspects of the WHA's creation. Many of the strange events that took place in Cleveland had far-reaching effects in the NHL. It is likely that the wholesale salary raises that suddenly became the rule in the NHL would never have taken place had Mileti not attempted to buy the heart of the Rangers by offering million-dollar deals to Rod Gilbert, Brad Park and Vic Hadfield. These superstars stayed put, but they became rich when they used the offers as a wedge to remain in New York.

Some people collect stamps. Mileti was an avid collector of sports franchises. He had the Cleveland Indians of baseball, the Cleveland Cavaliers of the National Basketball Association and the Cleveland Barons of the American Hockey League. He also owned the Cleveland Arena.

Two weeks after Mileti was denied a franchise in the NHL, he was in the WHA. By then it was June, just a few months from the season's start. There was intense pressure all around. Mileti figured, quite simply, that to get the best players he had to offer the best salaries. With no general manager, he began negotiating by himself. He offered Park, Gilbert and Hadfield each about $200,000 a season for long-term deals. The three listened. They appeared to be ready to jump. At the last minute, the Rangers decided to open their pocketbooks. They kept the three players, although they didn't go quite as high as Mileti's offers. Mileti wasn't through, though.

Next, he went after the Bruins' goalie, Gerry Cheevers. Cheevers had just finished a spectacular season in which the Bruins had won the Stanley Cup. He set a record by going undefeated in the nets for 33 straight games. He inspired confidence, and with him the Bruins would feel invulnerable. Unlike most goalies, Cheevers rarely showed emotion. Once in the 1960s, after a game in which the Bruins had been shelled, he sat relaxed in the dressing room. The general manager, Hap Emms, stormed in and demanded to know what had happened.

"Simple," replied Cheevers, "Roses are red, violets are blue. They got ten, we only got two."

Mileti also got another jumper, this one on the management level. He hired Chuck Catto as his assistant general manager. Catto had been with the Golden Seals of the NHL. Soon, Catto got three Seals to jump to the Crusaders. Then to try to attract even more Seals, Mileti hired Fred Glover, who once had been the Seals' coach. But Glover didn't stay around long.

One of the Crusaders' officials describes Glover's strange tenure this way: "I was on a three-week vacation. Glover was hired while I was away. By the time I came back, he was gone." Glover went back to the Seals.

With Bill Needham behind the bench, the club began its first season lacking many big-name players. But the team was experienced, and Cheevers, as expected, starred. His club turned in the lowest goals-against average and Cheevers led all goalies with a save percentage of .912. The club finished second.

After their first season, the Crusaders found they had a reverse jumper. Catto left to become general manager of the St. Louis Blues of the NHL. Jack Vivian replaced him. With Cheevers around, Cleveland has a team that should stay in play-off contention for some time.

Gerry Cheevers backstops the Crusaders. A standout with the Boston Bruins, Cheevers found instant stardom in Cleveland, leading all WHA goalers in just about everything.

THE EDMONTON OILERS

Bill Hunter, known to colleagues as Wild Bill, would have been as comfortable in Texas as he was in Edmonton. He was the flamboyant, fast-talking, always optimistic man who got people to put up the money to bring the WHA to his beloved Alberta province. Once the team was created, Hunter became the general manager and vice president and didn't hesitate to offer coaching advice.

The club was based in Edmonton, where it played in the grandly named Edmonton Gardens—a building erected in 1906 that had been renovated just once in the intervening years. Undeterred, Hunter gathered a strange collection of players to perform in this 5,200-seat arena. In many ways he helped refurbish these players much as the arena would be refurbished with a major-league image.

"To Bill, every event was the greatest moment in sports history," says a colleague. Oh, Hunter had first-year problems. The team averaged only 3,800 fans a game, though the top admission price was only six dollars. The closest city in the WHA was Winnipeg—1,600 miles away. No team in any sport was as isolated from its opposition. The first-year Oilers found all sorts of bizarre scheduling problems. There were several bad stretches. Once the club had to play four road games in five nights. The next week the Oilers were at home five times in seven days—including back-to-back games with the same team.

Hunter looked for the sunshine. He reminded people that "my life's savings are in this team." A strong, opinionated man who had been used to having his own way, he lured nine NHL players to jump to his team. Several of them had played for his Edmonton Oil Kings, once the toast of junior hockey. To help attract the fans, he called his games "A Carnival of Fun." He even replaced the organist, a fixture at every hockey game, with a 14-piece band. Rarely did he ask for advice, operating on the premise that no one else could do things as well as he.

Who's to say he wasn't right? He successfully rescued several players from oblivion and turned them into instant heroes. His goalie, Jack Norris, was one of the players (the others were Gilles Marotte and Pit Martin) who had been traded to the Chicago Black Hawks by Boston in exchange for Phil Esposito, Ken Hodge and Fred Stanfield. Norris hadn't really been heard of since. But in the WHA he now blossomed, appearing in more games, 64, than any other goalie in the new league.

For his captain, Hunter chose Allan Hamilton, once a Hunter protégé with the Oil Kings. Hamilton had never made it with the Rangers, after a Bobby Orr buildup. But with the Oilers he became the team's second-leading scorer, even though he was a defenseman. Hamilton led the team in assists with 49.

The scoring star turned out to be Jim Harrison, also an Alberta boy. He notched 39 goals and 87 points. Harrison also had the biggest point night any professional player of modern times enjoyed. It came in a strange game against the New York Raiders. Eight New York players were to be hospitalized with injuries the day after the game. Harrison, a center, had a field day. He scored 3 goals and 7 assists for a record 10 points.

In year two, under coach Brian Shaw, the Oilers began grandly. They set a league mark of 11 straight victories. Hunter's way is a winning way.

Ron Climie (11) heads for his wing while Jim Harrison pursues the puck. Harrison became the Oilers' highest scorer and set a hockey record when he scored three goals and seven assists in a game.

OILERS
WOOD
KOHO

NEW YORK-NEW JERSEY

It originally cost about $20,000 to own the rights to a WHA franchise in the New York metropolitan area, the most expensive real estate market in the world. But in the franchise's early years, $20,000 seemed overpriced. While the area's original owner, Neil Shayne, struggled to find a place to put the team, the NHL came along and threw in another squad in Long Island, where Shayne had hoped to establish his own sextet.

The WHA finally fielded a team in New York when two lawyers, Dick Wood and Sy Siegel, bought the franchise for $50,000 from Shayne. So Shayne, who never even had a letterhead for the club, made $30,000. The new club was to be called the Raiders. Strangely, the partners in the Raiders did not hire a hockey man. Instead, they tapped a man with long administrative experience in baseball, Marvin Milkes.

Now the Raiders had to convince players to come to New York. Money was going to be tight. The Garden's costs came to about $20,000 a game–by far, the highest of any WHA team. Wood and Siegel expected to lose some money the first year, but they never were prepared for the financial woes that finally plagued them.

The management and partners wooed players constantly. If they had their eye on someone, he was invited to Fun City and wined and dined at the Playboy Club or taken to a show. It was strange seeing Camille Henry, the coach, attempting to convince marginal players to come to New York for $30,000 a year.

Unfortunately, many of those who signed changed their minds. The Raiders, in fact, set a record for reverse jumpers. Five players they signed jumped back to the Establishment, including Bill Flett of the Flyers and Mike Robitaille of the Sabres. Even a minor leaguer, who had never been given a chance to make it to the NHL, leaped back–after the Raiders had given him a $2,000 bonus and another $1,000 for expense money to come to New York. He stayed for a day and then went home, never returning the money.

Still, the Raiders had high hopes. They did get a few name players. There was Bobby Sheehan, American-born, fast and exciting, who had appeared briefly with the Canadiens. There was Norm Ferguson, another who had scored 20 goals in the NHL. There was even a former rookie of the year–Kent Douglas.

The season finally opened, and within a week the Raiders' Ron Ward, a reject from Vancouver and Toronto, scored more points than he had the previous season. He quickly became the league's leading scorer.

A dozen owners took over the club in the second year and changed the name to the Golden Blades. Jerry Delise, a long-time associate of the Canadiens, was in charge of the personnel. Andre Lacroix was traded for Ward, in an ironic twist. Lacroix had beaten out Ward for the scoring title. The veteran Harry Howell joined the team on defense after jumping from the Kings. But the same old problems cropped up. The club's skates were to be golden blades with white shoes. They didn't arrive on time, and the club started the season wearing black shoes painted white. Then the owners found that they couldn't meet the payroll. The league stepped in again and took over the squad. Howell replaced Henry as coach, and the team quit Madison Square Garden for Cherry Hill, New Jersey. The league hopes to return to New York. Baltimore also seems a possibility.

Andre Lacroix (7) looks for the puck in game against the Oilers. Lacroix was the league's highest scorer with Philadelphia, but could not fill Jersey's empty seats.

THE HOUSTON AEROS

Snow and Gordie Howe in Houston? No reasonable man would have predicted that either of these unlikely visitors would wind up in Texas. But within a year, both came. It hadn't snowed in 13 years in Houston—until the Aeros were created. As if to greet the WHA, which was bringing big league hockey to Texas for the first time, it snowed three times. Texas put out more traditional welcome mats too, making the Canadians feel right at home.

Not many fans turned out in year one at the Sam Houston Coliseum, even though the Aeros finished second in the Western Division to the powerful Winnipeg Jets. But those who showed up were noisy. They were, after all, Texans. Some people say the Houston crowds were the noisiest and most enthusiastic in the sport.

To get them interested, the chairman of the board, Paul Deneau, the president, Jim Smith, and the coach, Bill Dineen, attended dozens of civic dinners. Wherever they went they brought along hundreds of free tickets. It didn't matter to them how many people got in for free—just as long as people would see the game. Maybe the next time they'd pay.

To entice fans to listen to the games, the Aeros figured they needed a Houston personality. They found one in a fellow named Bobby Brown, a former football trainer. Brown was the color man to the experienced Jerry Trupiano who handled the play-by-play. It didn't seem to matter that Brown wasn't exactly an expert in this new game. He was a local celebrity who was in demand as an after-dinner speaker. Everyone in Houston knew him. There was a game in which the Nordiques were badly outplaying the Aeros. Trupiano mentioned on the air that Houston wasn't doing well. Brown, the expert, replied: "Well, the reason is they just can't get their wide-open conservative style untracked tonight."

As time went by, the Aeros' style did get untracked. Under Dineen, who was a regular for five years with the great Detroit Red Wing teams of the 1950s, the club spurted around mid-season. It was paced on the scoring front by Gordon Labossiere, a seasoned center who had never scored more than 13 goals in the NHL. He responded in his new surroundings with 36 scores and added 60 assists for 96 points. Only five players picked up more assists. Another veteran was Ted Taylor, who added 76 points. It was a balanced squad, helped, too, by Murray Hall, Larry Lund and Poul Popeil. John Schella was the defensive anchor, assisted by Larry Hale, Dunc McCallum and Ray Larose. Wayne Rutledge, who split the goaltending with Don McLeod, was one of the few WHA goalies to post a goals-against average under three a game.

The league and Aeros took on more of a big-league image when the Aeros lured Gordie Howe and his two boys to town. The deal for all three—Gordie, Mark and Marty—was worth about $1.5 million over four years to the Howes. Gordie was required to play for only one of those years and to spend the other three in the front office. His own contract was worth about $750,000. His boys didn't do badly either. "Each of my sons," he said proudly, "will earn more money in one year on their interest alone than I earned after ten years in the NHL." He didn't have to add that his personal four-year package came to more money than he had made in his first 20 years in the NHL.

Howe and family took the money, starting another strange saga in one of sports' greatest careers. It had a promising beginning, too. In his first exhibition game, in a roundrobin tournament in Madison Square Garden, Gordie scored within 20 seconds of touching the puck for the first time.

To solidify its franchise, Houston lured Gordie Howe, perhaps the finest player ever, out of retirement. Howe and his two sons paced the Aeros to the top.

THE QUEBEC NORDIQUES

From the time the great Jean Beliveau had been stolen from Quebec by the Montreal Canadiens, the capital city of the French province had chafed. It wanted a major league team, and it wanted an improved image. What better figure to lead the team behind the bench than Canada's greatest French-Canadian folk hero, Maurice (the Rocket) Richard? The Rocket was a magnificent presence, an intense man with fire in his eyes and the greatest goal scorer of his time. His 544 career goals stood for years as the record. Since his retirement, he had been waiting angrily for someone to tap him as a coach. No one had. Perhaps he'd been considered too temperamental, someone who would demand from lesser players the greatness he expected of himself. He had broken with his old team, the Canadiens, after hanging around the front office for several years. When the Nordiques asked him to coach, he saw a chance to vindicate himself.

After the Rocket was signed, optimistic Nordiques officials estimated he alone would sell 5,000 season tickets to the 10,000-seat Coliseum. There was, however, one seat that the Rocket lost when he signed with the new league. The Canadiens took away his season ticket to the Montreal Forum.

That must have seemed unimportant. Here, Richard was starting a new life, finally vindicated. And when the great J. C. Tremblay, the Canadiens' all-star defenseman, jumped to the Nordiques, it appeared the club was off to a fine start.

Then the troubles began. After Tremblay came along, it wasn't quite as easy to get other players. First of all, the club had no general manager. It couldn't sign one. So the vice president, Marius Fortier, attempted to deal with players.

Gradually a squad was brought together. There were hardly any recognizable names on the team except for Tremblay. But the Nordiques had the honor of opening the new league with a game at Cleveland. The Nordiques lost it, and Richard wanted to quit. Incredible as it seemed, the Rocket couldn't stand the pressure. It was his first game and it was too much. He told management that he didn't know the game after 12 years away from the ice, that the players had changed, that he was unsure of himself, that he suspected he couldn't handle the pressure.

Fortier, though, convinced the Rocket to come back for the next game, the club's home opener. A good crowd was expected. If Richard quit now, it could kill the franchise. Reluctantly, Richard agreed to return to Quebec. In his first game back in his province, the Nordiques won, shutting out Alberta.

Everything should have been perfect for the Rocket. Instead, he quit for good. He had coached for two games and his new career was over.

Maurice Filion replaced Richard as coach. Led by Tremblay, the club barely missed the play-offs. Tremblay wound up with 89 points and became the only defenseman, except for Orr, to lead a big league team in scoring.

Things changed for the better in the Nordiques second season. Another great ex-Canadien, Jacques Plante, came over. He became the general manager-coach with the possibility of playing again in 1974. He got some proven players and tapped the Canadiens to lure Rejean Houle for scoring and Dale Hoganson for defense. Serge Bernier also jumped leagues and had a fine start. Richard had quickly become a memory.

J. C. Tremblay, Nordique captain, was for a year the only big-league name on the team. In time Quebec rectified the situation, acquiring Rejean Houle and coach Jacques Plante.

THE LOS ANGELES SHARKS

There was good reason to believe that the WHA was wasting its time in attempting to move into Los Angeles. The L.A. Kings of the NHL had never quite made it as a major attraction. Yet, here were the Sharks starting their WHA careers in the L.A. Sports Arena. The president was Dennis Murphy, the league's founder, and the coach was Terry Slater, who had studied for a master's degree in child psychology.

In the land of strange religious cults and the Sunset Strip, surprises are frequent. When the Sharks opened their season, they found 11,430 fans on hand. Murphy had said he would be happy to average 3,000 fans a game. The Kings, after all, had averaged only 7,000, and they played against some of the world's best hockey teams. By the end of the Sharks' first season, the attendance had reached an average of 6,000.

But the team played poorly at home. "They're not concentrating," Slater explained. "They're either in their pools or they're entertaining friends. Heck, when your friends come in from Saskatchewan, they want to visit Disneyland."

If nothing else, dreams helped Slater. His Sharks didn't have much strength at center. One night he dreamed that one of his defensemen, Gerry Odrowski, was playing center. The next night Slater made a center of Odrowski, and Odrowski scored the winning goal.

The search for more fans propelled gimmickry to new heights with the Sharks. One day an advertisement showing three bald-headed men appeared in the paper. The three were Shark players. Under the pictures was the caption, "Can you match this?" Any bald fan was invited to the next game for free. They received wigs dyed in purple, red or orange.

No one could predict what would happen when the Sharks rescheduled a game for 11 o'clock on a Sunday morning. Had anyone ever played a big league game at that time of day? But the Sharks had to, because of television commitments. A torrential rainstorm engulfed the Los Angeles area. As one of the executives drove to the game, he wondered if anyone except the players' wives would show up. That morning, 12,804 fans were on hand. No one has ever been able to explain why. "Maybe they thought they were going to church," said an official.

The Sharks wound up with a fairly successful season. They made third place, thanks to a strong defense and goaltending. The nets were shared by Russ Gillow and George Gardner. Gillow, who had no previous professional experience, turned in the second-best goals-against average in the league, just behind Cheevers. He yielded an average of only 2.88 goals in the high-scoring circuit. The scoring was led by Gary Veneruzzo, the only Shark to get more than 20 goals. The other 20-goal man was Alton White, who became the major league's first black hockey player since 1960.

The Sharks hoped to change their image in the 1973-74 campaign by inducing Marc Tardif to leap from the Canadiens, where he had produced 78 goals in three seasons. The Sharks showed the opening week of the season that they would be battling. In a game against the Toros, both benches emptied after a fight in the penalty box. For more than 10 minutes they brawled. When the ice chips settled, eight players were kicked out of the game, and the fines totaled a whopping $3,600. It was another Hollywood spectacular.

Ron Ward on the move. With players such as Ward, later released, and Mark Tardif, the Sharks opted for an exciting style, a necessity for success in L.A.

12
VICTORIAVI

THE TORONTO TOROS

Like a band of wandering minstrels, the Toros flitted from place to place, looking for an arena they could call home. They actually began life known as the Ontario Nationals.

Naturally, the biggest place to play in Ontario is in Toronto. But the owners of Maple Leaf Gardens wanted an unheard of guarantee of $25,000 a game. That was more money than even Madison Square Garden in New York had wanted from the raiders. Next, the owners tried Hamilton, the big industrial city not far from Toronto. But the mayor of Hamilton was suspicious. He thought some big-city slickers were attempting to come in and try to get rich. He demanded more money for his arena's use than the Nationals were willing to pay.

Finally, the club found a home in Ottawa, and changed its name to the Ottawa Nationals.

For years the Ottawa 67s, the great junior team, had played in the building without having to pay a guarantee. The usual rental was about $1,000 a game, or 15 percent of the receipts. But when the Nationals moved in, they found they had to guarantee the arena $100,000 for the season. That came to an average of more than $2,500 a game. The owner looked for more financing.

In order to meet the guarantee, the Nationals had to average 5,500 a game. That would pay for expenses, salaries and rental. Instead, the season was a disaster. They averaged only 2,900 fans. And because the price scale was low the team took in only about $10,000 a game. So for the season the team took in $400,000 and had to pay $100,000, or 25 percent, in rent.

Even the varied promotions the team tried in its desperate attempt to get money backfired. For much of the season the team was far from the top, with small hopes of making the play-offs. Fans simply stayed away. There were no superstars on the club, which was spearheaded by Wayne (Swoop) Carleton, a journeyman from the NHL. "All that our promotions accomplished was to lower our prices and not bring in any more fans," moaned one official.

The general manager of the team was Buck Houle, who didn't have much money to work with. The coach was Bill Harris, who was equally starved for talented players. But Harris got his forces together by the end of the season. The team hit a stretch in which it won 11 of 12 games. Suddenly, the Toros were a play-off contender. Meanwhile, there was trouble with the arena. Ottawa wanted another $100,000 for the following season. Politicians entered the discussion and one said, "Pay, or we lock the doors."

The Maple Leafs did not make the NHL Stanley Cup play-offs, and that meant the Gardens would be empty, and the rental would be only $8,000 a game. In the meantime Ottawa changed its mind. Please come back, it asked, but the Nationals refused.

In two games in Toronto the Nationals drew 9,000 people and grossed about $50,000 —more than 10 per cent of what they had pooled in 39 games in Ottawa. That made the decision to move even easier.

The club shipped everything to Toronto. There was a new owner in a syndicate headed by Harold Bassett, Jr., whose father had once been one of the owners of Maple Leaf Gardens. The team would now be playing in the Toronto Arena, home of the University of Toronto. Eventually, said Bassett, he'd build a new arena for his team. Meanwhile, he

hoped that the newly acquired Carl Brewer—once one of the best defensemen in hockey, who then became a wanderer—and Carleton and Guy Trottier would combine to give his club more depth. In goal he had Les Binkley and Gilles Gratton. Perhaps playing in the big city would bring happy times.

Gilles Gratton sticks aside a shot from close range. The Toros, once the Ottawa Nationals, are finding Toronto more amenable. They're winning more and drawing better.

THE VANCOUVER BLAZERS

A team that started at virtually the other end of North America, in Miami Beach, eventually worked its way northwest and gave the people of Vancouver a second big league hockey team. The Miami Screaming Eagles were one of the charter members of the upstart WHA. Indeed, the first game was to be played in Florida. But the building in which the game was to be played was never finished, and the franchise was in limbo. It had one solid player, the first jumper—Bernie Parent.

A New Jersey lawyer named Jim Cooper raised the $210,000 it would take to buy the franchise for Philadelphia. The money man was a Jersey trucker, Bernie Brown.

Cooper sat down and figured what he needed. He wanted names important to Philadelphia hockey, such as Andre Lacroix. "I also wanted someone like John McKenzie and Derek Sanderson," said Cooper. "People told us that McKenzie wasn't interested, but maybe he'd think about coaching. Derek was the star we needed. He'd give us an identity instantly with a new franchise."

Before players were signed, though, Cooper needed a man to sign them, a general manager. Cooper was thrilled when the perfect man for the job called and asked to be hired. It was Murray Williamson, who had recently coached the United States Olympic squad to a surprising silver medal. Cooper believed Williamson would be perfect. He was young, intelligent, and accustomed to dealing with the new breed of hockey player. Williamson got the job.

The Blazers were a happy organization and planned a grand news conference to announce Williamson's arrival. The night before the conference Williamson went out for a few drinks with a club official. Williamson suddenly told him, "I don't think I can go through with it."

"Hey, don't be silly," Williamson was told. "The Philadelphia press is tough, but all they'll do is ask you a few questions."

"I don't mean the press conference. I mean the job," Williamson replied.

Cooper got another general manager in Dave Creighton. He got McKenzie as player-coach, then set about wooing Sanderson. Finally, after weeks of feverish negotiations, everyone came to an agreement: Derek was to get a deal worth $2.65 million to play five years with the Blazers. One of the strangest parts of the affair happened the night that Derek agreed. Cooper had been having dinner in a Chinese restaurant and asked for a fortune cookie. He opened it and the message inside read, "Tonight you will make a good business deal."

Derek joined the team but got hurt before the club played 10 games. The opener was postponed because the Zamboni went through the ice. And the prices in the Civic Center were steep. To pay Derek's salary, they had been raised a dollar.

As Derek lay in the hospital, the club floundered. Creighton had come and gone, replaced by Phil Watson. McKenzie was still the coach in name, but Watson actually guided the club. Lacroix became the league's scoring star, and Danny Lawson also produced a 100-point season. He led the league with 61 goals.

By season's end, Cooper was out and Derek was gone. Sanderson settled for $800,000 after scoring three goals and adding three assists. Soon the team was sold to Vancouver interests. Lacroix refused to move, so he was traded to New York for Ron Ward.

The new life in Vancouver started grandly. In the first four games the club averaged more than 10,000 fans a contest. McKenzie officially stepped down as coach, and Watson took over. Soon, however, the team was losing more than it was winning. Ward was traded to Los Angeles, and Andy Bathgate became coach, facing less than a promising future.

Toros' shot is stopped as Irv Spencer (23) grapples with high-scoring Wayne Carleton. Shifted from Philadelphia to Vancouver, the Blazers are building.

Coca-Cola
VICTORIAVILLE PRO.
VICTORIAVILLE

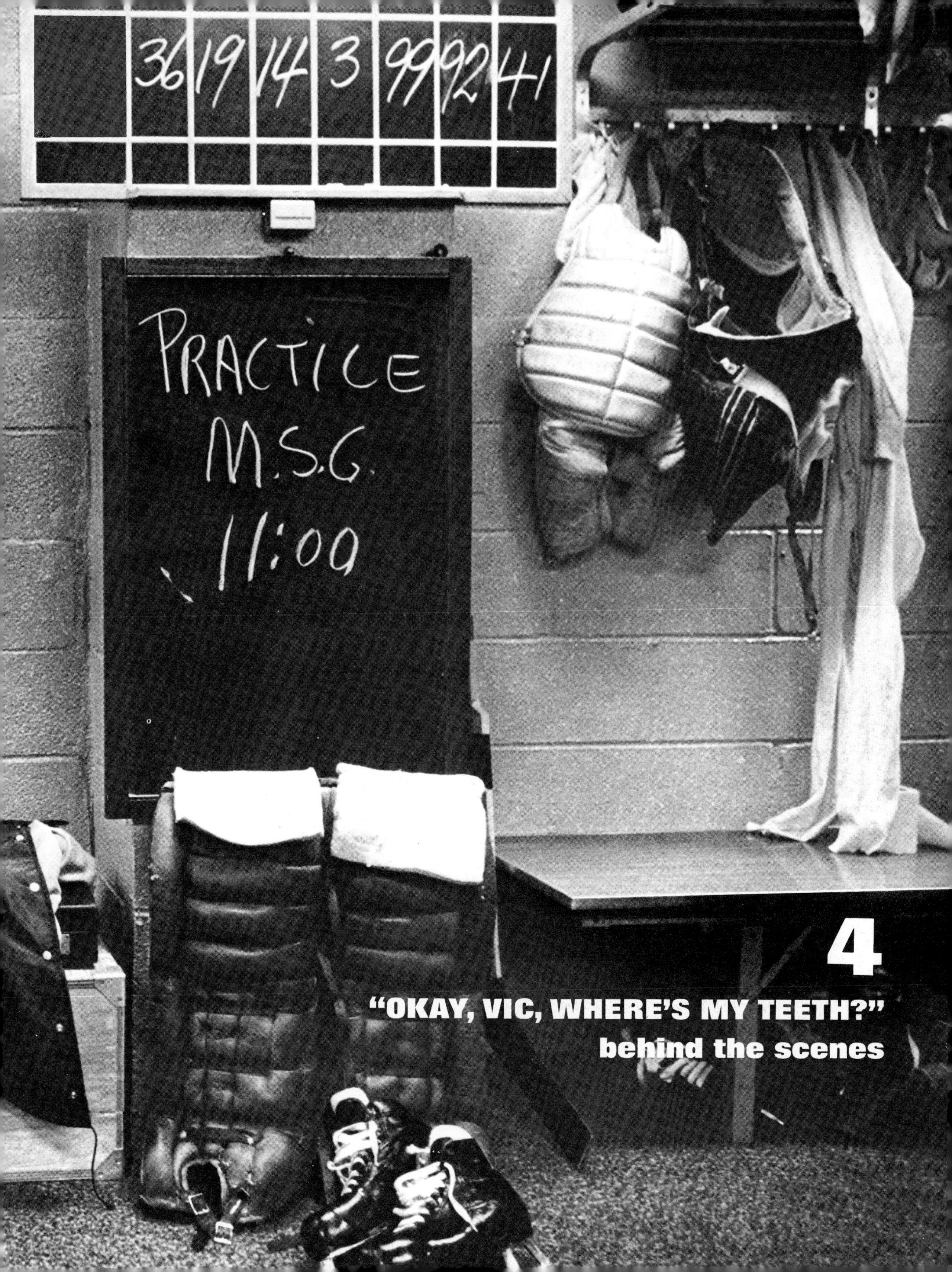

4

"OKAY, VIC, WHERE'S MY TEETH?"

behind the scenes

Coach Al Arbour (right) commands the Islanders in training camp.

TRAINING CAMP

About 60 players report to a big-league camp. Only 17, including two goalies, will be permitted to start the season. The players these days arrive in shape. At one time weight was a major problem during the early days of camp. But so many of today's athletes run summer camps and clinics, or serve as instructors, that it is convenient to work out. During the off-season, they receive a diet and exercise plan. But even if they do nothing over the summer, they are expected to be in shape.

Muscles should be firm, weight no more than three pounds above normal, wind strong. All players skate on their own for at least a week before camp. Some get together and rent a rink for their private use, others merely go down to their local rinks and skate for an hour or two a day.

The men who report include regulars, those who are virtually assured of jobs. The top minor leaguers are there, too, as well as promising amateur players. Often a club will invite a teen-ager to camp who it knows will not make the club but whom it wants to give a taste of big-league competition. Every coach and general manager will say before the start of camp that nobody is certain to start. They hope to rev up the players, trying to get maximum competition for each position.

Sometimes a player not accorded a chance will stay with the parent club just by virtue of the effort he puts out in camp. Few friendships are made in camp, at least not among players competing for one position. At a recent camp two rookies were hoping to land a job as the team's spare defenseman. "I like Allan," said one, "but I can't wait to get him in the corners."

That is the kind of talk coaches love to hear. A few years ago Ranger defenseman Rod Seiling was a mystery in camp. He was timorous, afraid to hit. Boom Boom Geoffrion, during a scrimmage, slammed into Seiling. Nothing happened. The next time Seiling had the puck Geoffrion hit him again, again with no reaction. The third time it happened, Seiling got up and rammed Geoffrion, toppling him to the ice. Geoffrion skated away smiling.

The day before camp starts is hectic and tiring, reminiscent of life in an army induction center. The players start that day at eight in the morning. First are their physicals. Each undergoes a complete medical examination and X ray. Then comes picture taking. Programs and yearbooks account for tens of thousands of dollars of revenue for each club and players' pictures must be in the pages. Also, each hometown newspaper and TV station receives a complete set of photographs as well as player biographies. The "head" shots of a player people see in their newspaper probably were taken in training camp, along with the tried-and-true pictures of players "throwing snow," those shots of skaters stopping short and sending up a burst of ice chips.

The first day of camp is not cheerful. The regulars report at 7:30 in the morning into the chilled arena, past the older men and boys playing hookey from school. Their dressing room is warm but austere and functional. They have an hour to get ready and as they slowly dress they discuss family matters, whose wives had children, what's happening in baseball or how the car is operating. Forty-five minutes later the quick dressers are on the ice, while young onlookers vie for positions behind the cages. They will not see any shooting just yet, however.

The regulars, along with a dozen good prospects, take the ice and skate in lazy laps around the rink. The coach, wearing a warm-up jacket and skates, merely watches them from the center of the rink. Many of the players are "trying on their skates," breaking in a new pair. After the workout, blades will be worked on, smoothed and sharpened. The reverie on the ice is shattered by a whistle shriek. It is time for business.

The coach gathers his men around him. There are things they should know, or have to be reminded about: curfew, meal allowance,

practice schedules, barbers, cleaners, restaurants, off limits and other details that will make the players' weeks at camp go smoother, as well as cement community relations. Except for Detroit and Toronto, which stage camp at their own rinks, most of hockey's clubs work out in cities in eastern Canada.

The short speech over, the coach lines up his men behind him and starts to skate. The players follow, exercises begin. The most common injuries early in training camp are to the groin, so this is what they must first prevent. The coach raises his right knee until his thigh is parallel to the ice. A line of players behind him do the same, some kicking higher than others. Then the left knee goes up. They continue for a minute, raising one knee, then the other. The players hold their sticks straight out, as though holding onto a bar. The coach continues to lead the parade, an uncostumed drum major, until once again he blows the whistle, signalling a new routine.

Arms flop to the side. The players stretch their backs. They have not yet seen a puck, and won't for a while. Another whistle blow, another exercise. The coach moves forward, goes into a semisplit, stops and rocks. Again, the players follow. Their legs limbered, groin muscles stretched, the players are ready for their first punishing activity of camp—wind sprints.

If they were smart, they had practiced wind sprints in the preceding weeks. The rink is 200 feet long—almost 70 yards—and they are to go full speed from one end to the other and back. All line up at one end. At the whistle's blast, they take off. The goalies strain under the weight of 40 pounds of equipment. The rookies try to burst into the lead. They know that the coach, who sees all, is watching. They also are being observed from the stands by the club's general manager, scouts and assistants. Some are looking at specific players, others the whole picture.

ABOVE: Stretching the legs for...
FACING: the skating drills to follow.

On the second day, when scrimmages start, the scouting staff will keep detailed records on each player on long sheets of ruled paper divided into columns. There they note every shot on goal, each steal of the puck, loss of the puck, "hit" (taking out the man with the puck with a body check), face-off won or lost or special maneuver or play.

Within a week, they will have an almost perfect line on the player, whether he will make it or not. The youngsters on the ice know this and hope to make a good first impression. The team leaders, the captain and his assistants, and the older players (whose jobs may be in jeopardy) try to show up the newer men. The leaders should lead. They pump furiously to lead the pack down the ice. When the pack arrives at the other end of the rink they stop short, throwing snow against the boards before they turn around and dash back.

Briefly they rest, some draped over the boards, gasping for air. Others smile and laugh. Fifteen seconds later, exercises resume. They goose-step around the rink while raising their sticks over their head. This is followed by another wind sprint, but in a special order. The goalies go first. If the coach is not pleased, if one loafs, he must go again. Then the defense shoots down ice and when they return the forwards move out. The procedure is followed for 90 minutes—skating, exercising, then skating. At the end of the session are push-ups and one last back-and-forth sprint. The players trudge off the ice, into their dressing rooms, for one final ritual —the weigh-in.

Before camp, the coach and trainer had gone over each player's acceptable reporting weight. It is most probably the weight at which a player will finish the season, for most players lose weight by the end of the year. Before the start of the workout they are weighed. Now, the first session over, they go on the scales again. The losses are remarkable.

Some drop as much as seven pounds. The weight is penciled in the "after workout" column, under the correct date. The coach compares the figure with the "before" weight and the player's projected weight. Half pounds are rounded off in the coach's favor.

The players shower and leave and the next session of the morning is given over to minor leaguers who go through the same routine. The first group's day isn't over. Far from it. Another session will follow in the afternoon. They return to their rooms and relax before a steak lunch. The lobby is filled with milling children (in places like Kitchener, London and Oshawa the arrival of a big-league team is major news) who try to get the players on the way to lunch. Some players are late for lunch, having played a round of golf after a workout that would level the average man.

The afternoon work is 60 minutes of routine identical to that of the morning session. The players still haven't touched a puck. The major social event of the day is the final meal which the players are permitted to eat out. New players stick together. Many appear lost in their first National Hockey League experience. Their dress is small-town. Brown shoes cover blue socks.

Everyone is stiff when he gets up the second day, but there is work ahead. With no consideration for unwilling ankles and aching joints, morning exercises continue. The trainer hands a pail of frozen pucks to the coach, who dumps the pail at center ice. He flips a puck to the players who skate around stickhandling the disk. The goalies he wants to watch are assigned their cages, while rough lines and new defensive combinations are formed.

First the squad practices line rushes, three men moving against two defenders. The coach has his time-honored lines, but will also mix and match and try rookies with estab-

ABOVE: Like any other athlete, a hockey player cannot escape push-ups. RIGHT: The whirlpool for a tender hand. When players are not on the ice, the whirlpool is in constant use.

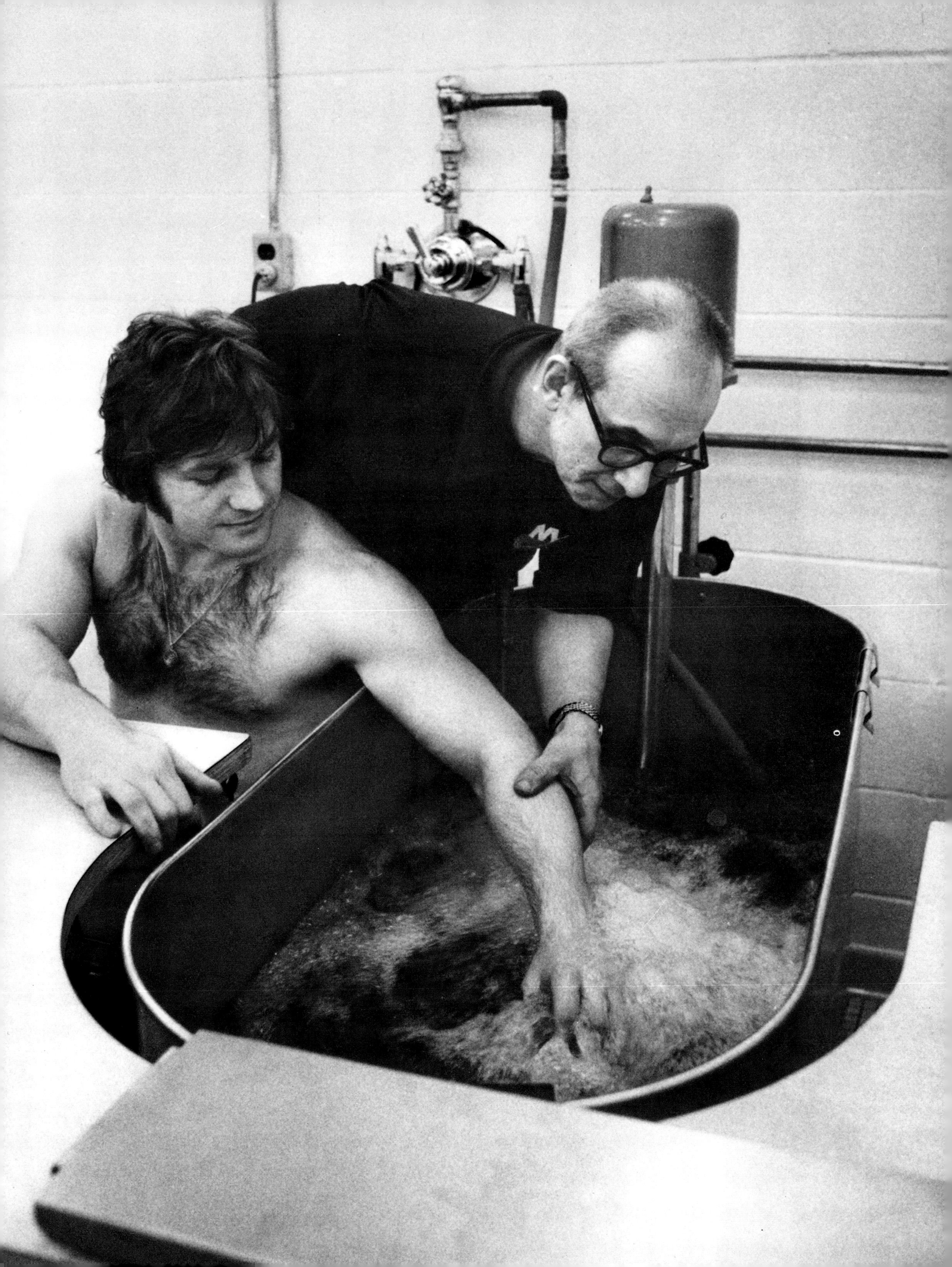

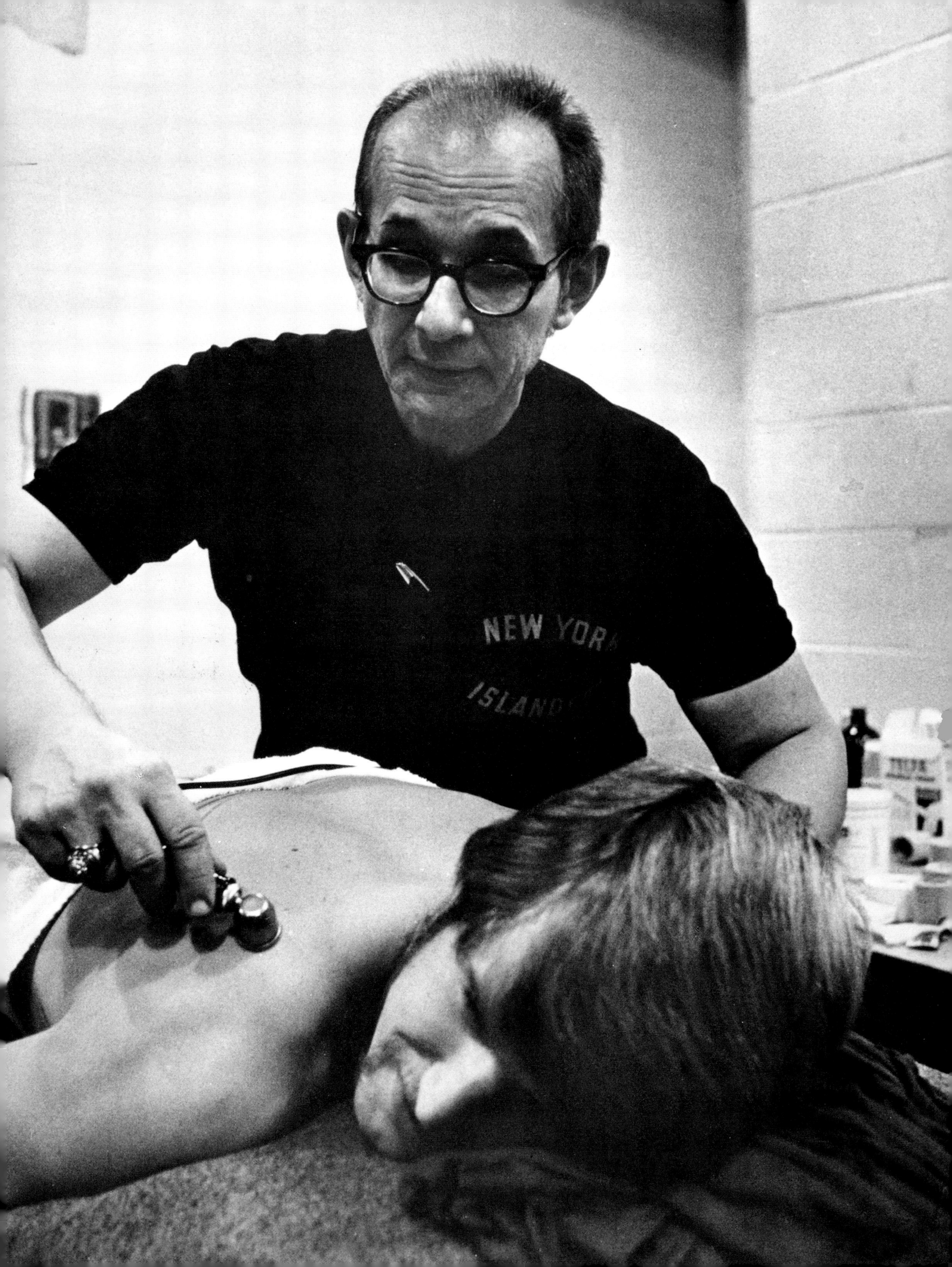
NEW YORK

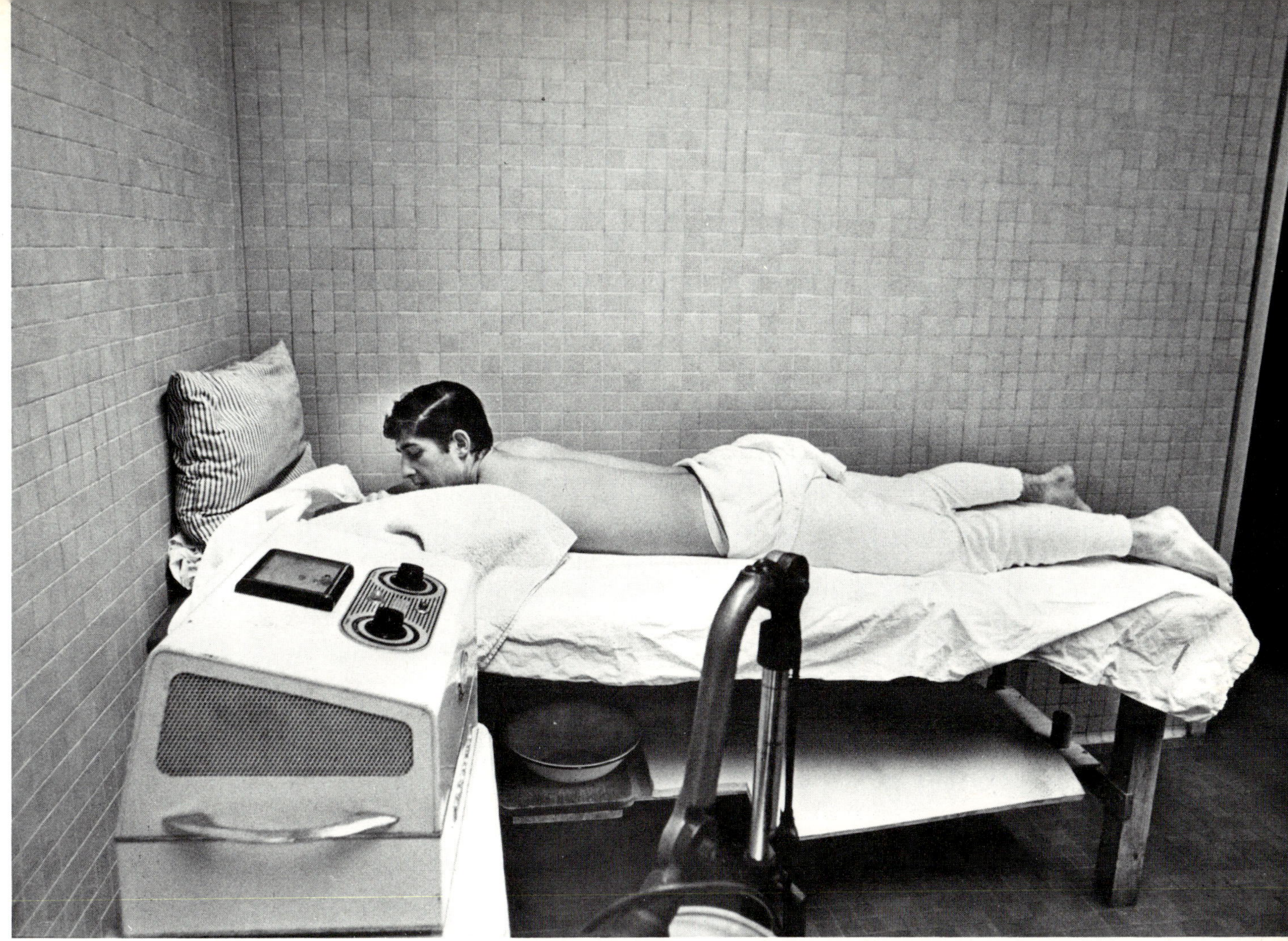

lished players. And there are rookie lines. Three-on-two rushes are watched closely by everyone in the arena—players, coach, aides in the stands and the fans. Is the center moving well with the puck? Are his wings in position? What is the defense doing to break up the rush? Are the defenders' sticks held with the blade on the ice so they can swipe at the puck easily and not have to waste the split second it takes to bring the stick down?

Club officials are busy jotting notes, talking among themselves. "Did you see the head fake?" "Did you notice how the goalie cut down the angle?" "Did you see how the defenseman took out the man with the puck?" The players also watch intently, especially the new ones. They want to pick up pointers, yes, but also learn the weak spots, for they will be rushing or defending against these same players. They will need an edge.

And so it goes, morning and afternoon, day after day for a month, the routine broken only by exhibition games. Pluses and minuses are totaled, observations made. Each night the scouting staff and executives talk over the day's happenings. The coach may have missed a minor-league workout. The staff briefs him. As they approach their first exhibition game they are reasonably certain how the team is shaping up.

But there are intangibles, the most important of which is how a player will react in a game situation. In the exhibition games, the untested player gets his chance. Often a coach can tell immediately. Sometimes, though, a player is simply nervous and a clever general manager or coach can spot that and know if the player can do better. If they think he can, he will get another chance in another game.

Coaches don't like to do much juggling in the later exhibition games. They want to put out their team and get it to work as a unit —as it will have to in the approaching season. There is little sense in working a rookie right

LEFT and ABOVE: If the whirlpool is insufficient, perhaps sound therapy will succeed in loosening tight muscles.

wing if the four established right wings are certain to be back with the team. During the weeding-out process the club must choose which amateurs, if any, it wants to turn professional, which players it wants to move up on the minor-league scale, which players it wants on the big club.

The club's needs are evaluated. Should a trade be made for a center? Can the club afford to give up a right wing in exchange? And what happens if the regular goalie gets injured? Is a promising goalie kept with the club as second string, where he might not get much experience, or is he shipped to the minors where he will see more ice time? The answers are critical in today's hockey, for there is no margin for error in picking 16 skaters to start the season (not counting the goalie and backup goalie).

There should be three lines, two sets of defensemen as well as a spare defenseman. That makes 14. A few choices are left. The remaining players will be forwards, but who and what type? The coach and general manager must decide if they have enough adequate penalty killers among the nine forwards already selected. Can they afford to choose a player whose value lies mainly in penalty-killing ability? They must also decide which of the starting forwards is most likely to come down with an injury. So the few "spare" forwards they ultimately select must be able to fill in and play any position in an emergency.

As the days grind along a player's weight stabilizes. The dramatic weight loss stops. Some of the players may have been fined for not reporting in shape, especially those with a history of delinquency. Others, also with a history of weight problem, might have received bonuses if they arrived at a predetermined weight. Ultimately it is up to each player to follow orders and do his best. The coach and his staff have followed all closely. They know that each individual has his own problems, his own ambitions. One may have been frustrated the previous season, unable to

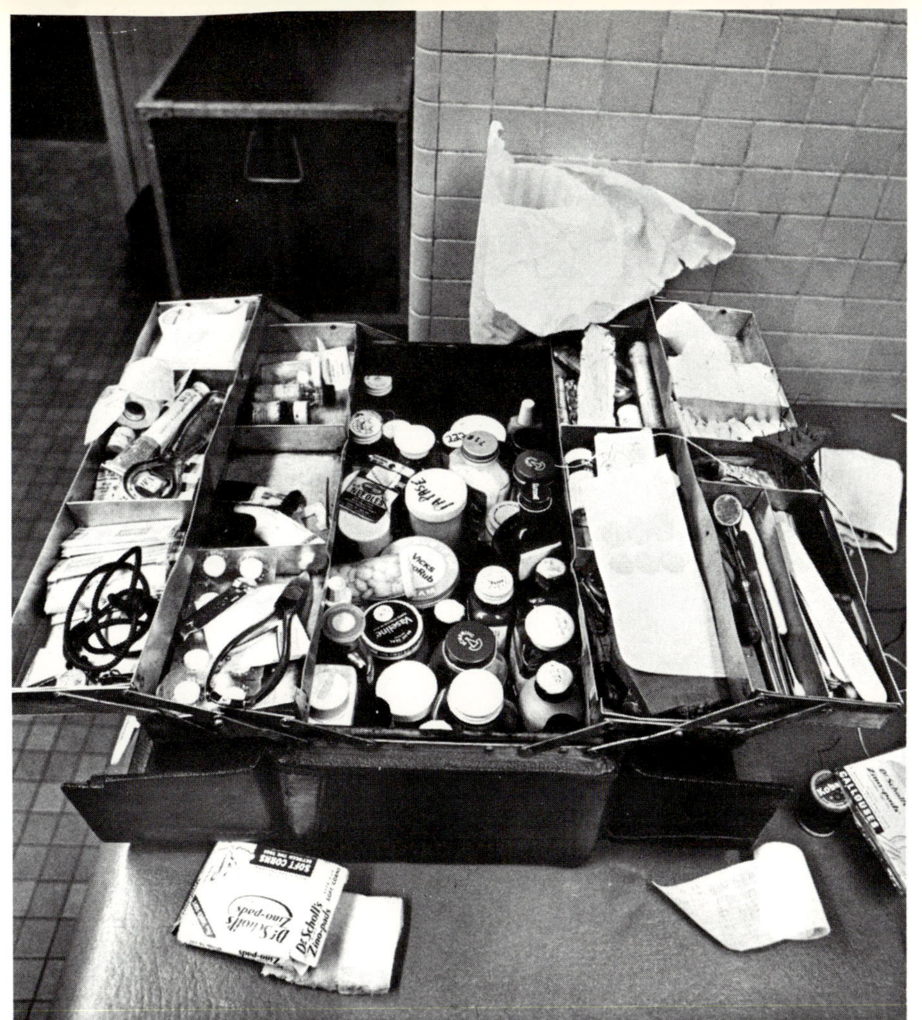

LEFT: A trainer's medicine kit weighs 30 pounds and contains everything from Gelusil and Tuf-Skin to tongue forceps. BELOW: During the game, a trainer is never without a towel. It is used primarily to absorb blood until the injured player can be taken to the dressing room where he will receive stitches, usually in time to return for the next period. FACING: Skates are sharpened after every use, for without a sharp blade, a player cannot cut quickly enough. Skates are rocked so that a minimum of blade will actually rest on a flat surface.

score consistently. Another may have had family difficulties. Still another might be concerned about prior injuries. He wonders whether he can bounce back. The job in training camp is to recognize the differences.

But one way or the other, all must be reconciled. Soon a club—a unit—must emerge from separate elements. Somehow, faster than seemed possible, a team appears. Camaraderie is essential. The team must want to protect its goaltender; they must respect their teammates. If one is going for a three-goal game, another sacrifices his own impluses for a score and feeds his teammate. If a player has a natural reluctance to hit he subverts the feeling and hits anyway. Then, and only then, does a team emerge. And a team does emerge out of training camp, which is why there is a camp in the first place.

THE DAY OF THE GAME

There probably isn't one team in the history of professional hockey that hasn't had a winning record at home, over the long haul. "It's nice to have the crowds behind you," say the players. Players become familiar with their own ice surface. At Olympia Stadium, the Detroit Red Wings were masters of the boards. They knew instinctively how the puck would react against them. A favorite Detroit play was to have the center shoot the puck off the boards behind the goalie. One of his wings would swoop down the alley and would be able to rip off a shot by being exactly in the right place for the ricochet.

But players also say that when their team is going badly they'd just as soon play on the road. Nothing is so demoralizing as having the home fans boo. Some coaches believe a player is more relaxed on the road where he is away from the pressures of home, the late-night feeding of a baby, the visits of friends and relatives.

Before a home game the player makes his own departure schedule for the rink. On

Elbows take more abuse in hockey than in any other sport. Huge elbow pads, made of leather and plastic, slip over the arms.

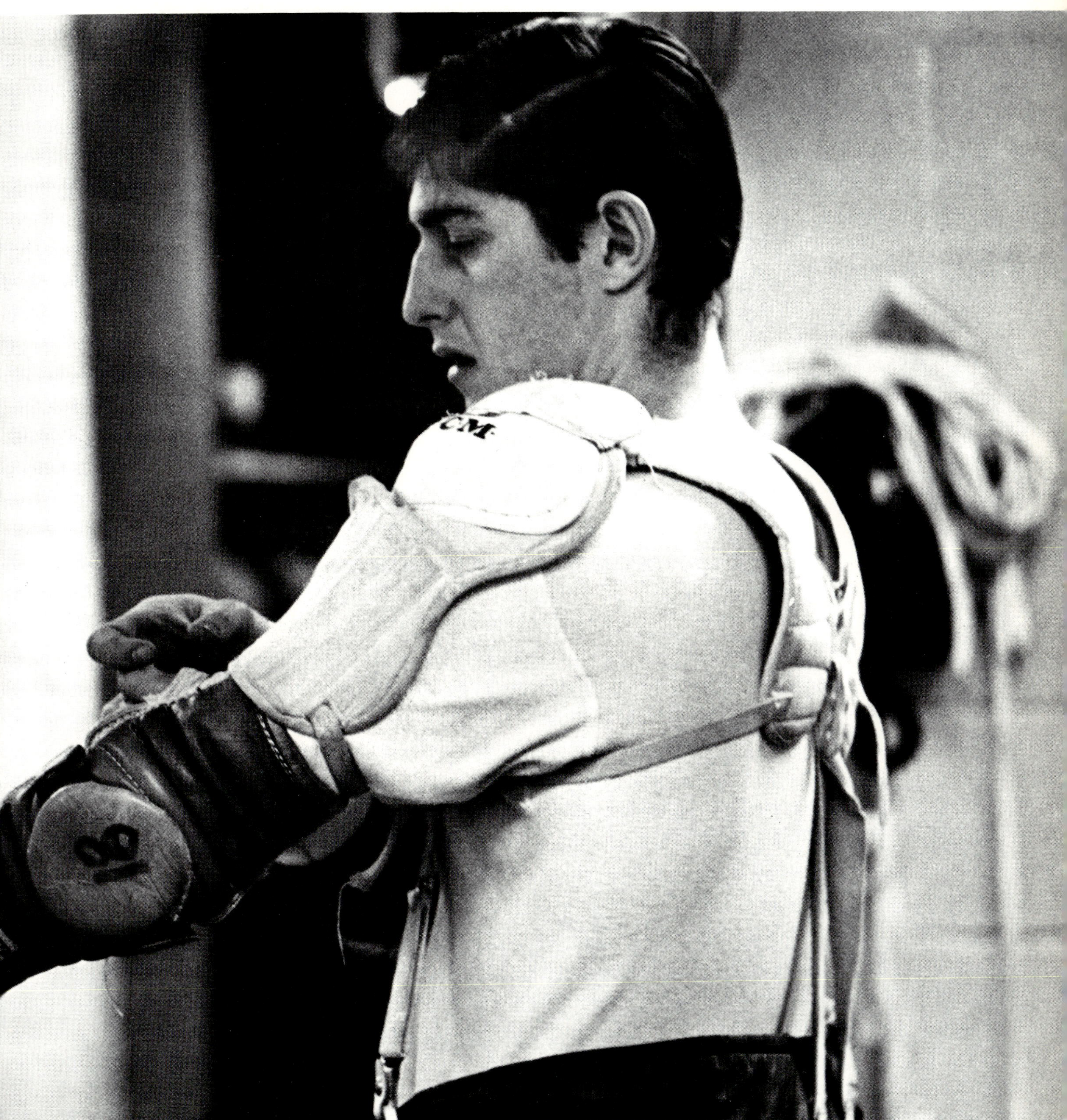

the road the team usually meets in a hotel lobby and leaves together. Life away from home revolves around a hotel, a steak meal and afternoon nap. A team meets in the coach's suite either before or after lunch. The conversation is not startling, rarely is a hitherto unknown quantity revealed. Perhaps the coach will discuss what happened the last time these two clubs met, what one team did better than the other. He'll talk about the importance of the game. And he'll stress each player's plus and minus figures, numbers which indicate if a player has been on the ice for more of his team's goals or for more of the other team's scores at equal strength.

If, say, he has been in action while his club has scored 100 goals and the other team scored 96, he is plus four. It is one of the better yardsticks with which to judge a regular. The figures, though, may be deceptive for a player with a bad team or for a player who sees action mostly as a spare, since he is likely to be on the ice when players for both sides let down and get sloppy.

The steak meal, eaten home and away, is lunch. It includes baked potato, coffee or tea and ice cream. Then comes the nap. It is a wonder that grown men can sleep for three hours before a game. "It's a question of conditioning your body to it," one player once said. "We're pros and we know our livelihood depends on our staying in condition. So we do it."

For a seven o'clock game, the players must report to the dressing room by 5:45. They may be fined if they are late. Most players are there by 5:30. The first thing they do is remove their teeth. Most started losing their teeth in grade school. When they were youngsters a gap between teeth was a badge of courage. Badges have become bridges. They slip them out matter-of-factly and drop them in paper cups provided for the purpose. The cups go on a shelf above the clothes

ABOVE: Shin guards are bulky but light. Stockings are pulled tight and held in place by a garter.
FACING: Goalie is heavily protected on legs and chest.

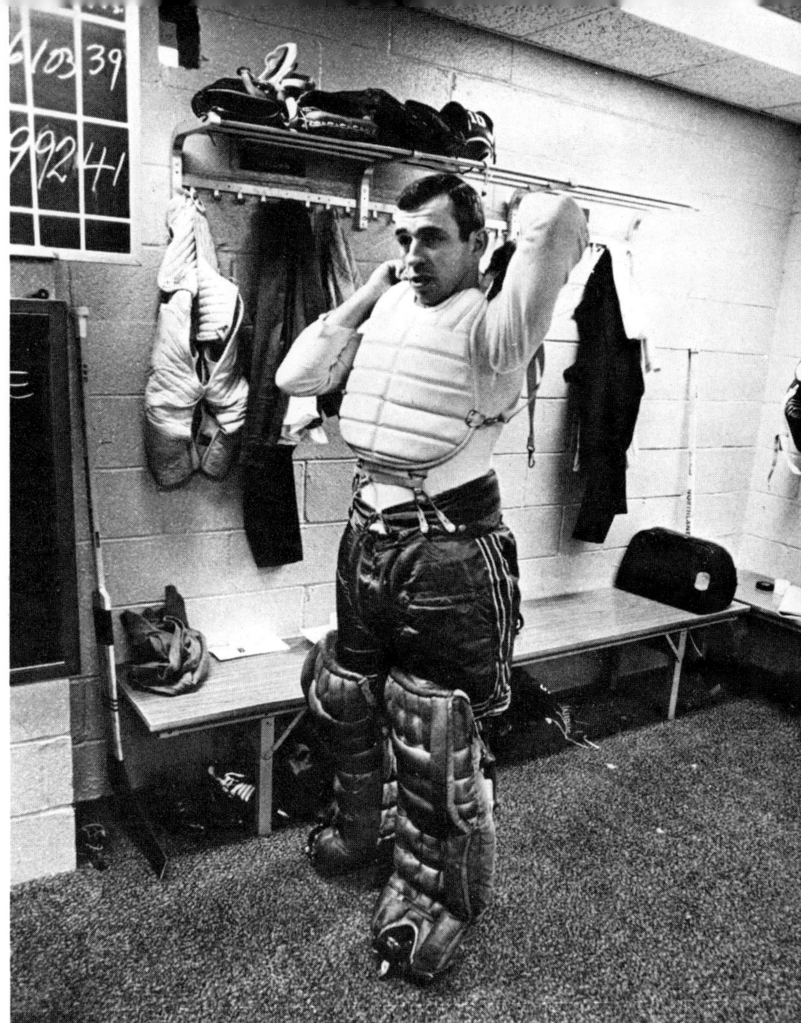

hooks, forming a row of almost 18 cups on the shelves, mutely symbolizing hockey's rigors. The Rangers' Vic Hadfield likes to switch around cups. Whenever a Ranger unsuccessfully tries to slip a teammate's bridge back in his own mouth after a game he immediately howls, "Okay, Vic, where's my teeth?"

The trainer and assistant trainer are too busy to share in pre-game talk. It has been said that a trainer is a man who practices medicine without a license. Several trainers in the past have stitched injured players. Even an experienced surgeon will say that a sports trainer probably can sew up a player quicker than he can.

Most trainers are former bush-league players who loved hockey enough to try to remain in the game in some capacity. In their makeup is something of the mother hen. They scurry to and fro before a game, making sure there are enough towels, enough soap, enough clean gear. They are psychologists practicing group therapy. They can sense the mood of a team before a game. If it is loose and jovial, they are part of it, cracking a joke, constantly smiling. If the atmosphere is tense, they know enough to keep quiet.

If it is a home game, the host trainer is in charge of freezing the pucks. He puts three dozen of them into a freezer five hours before game time to insure the hard rubber remains hard. During a game 18 to 24 pucks may be used (the number is increasing because of the curved stick).

A trainer's medicine kit, weighing 30 pounds, is open during pre-game dressing. It contains almost every kind of remedy a well-stocked drug cabinet should have, as well as many more that the average person never heard of or considered. There is nasal mist for head colds, Kaopectate, antacids, spirits of ammonia, gauze bandages, foot powder, petroleum jelly, corn pads, cold pills, eye wash, razors, adhesive tape, cough medicine, baby

oil, items named Tuf-Skin and Atomic Balm, corn plaster. In his pocket the trainer keeps an oral screw to pry open the mouth of a player who has swallowed his tongue, as well as a pair of tongue forceps to reach the tongue.

Tuf-Skin is applied to any bandaged area. It toughens and coats the skin so that when bandaging is removed the area will not be as sensitive. Atomic Balm is rubbed into a sore area or the back. When the player's pores open, the balm will penetrate, warming the area. Petroleum jelly is applied to the player's face and neck. When he perspires the salt water will not chafe his neck but run right off.

If the club is on the road, the trainer will take along a tool kit filled with saws and rasps for fixing skates and sticks. Once upon a time rival trainers were known to "fix" a player's skates when asked to sharpen them. Now each team's trainers take care of their players' equipment on the road. At home are all the tools they need: grinding machines for smoothing skate edges, vises for shaping the correct individual curve to a stick.

Players dress slowly. Proper fit of all equipment is essential. If a skate is tied loosely, disaster may result. They strip completely from street clothing before starting the laborious job of getting dressed in hockey gear. They first step into long underwear, under which is placed a protective cup for the groin. Shoulder pads, similar in design to football shoulder pads, slip over their heads. The pads are softer and lighter than football players' gear and are connected to shoulder and chest padding. Elbow pads are put in place as are shin pads. Some players also use kidney pads. Defensemen place shin guards under their skates since they block so many shots with their feet.

Thigh pads also are part of the equipment. Heavy knee socks cover feet and pants extend from the bottom of the rib cage to the knees. Suspenders hold up pants, jerseys are slipped on after suspenders are in place. The $70 skates go on last, lace-tying is critical. Finally, the players pick up their thick gloves which are connected to a gauntlet that covers the wrist and forearm. They are now ready to play, 25 pounds heavier. The stick they choose from their number in a rack may be no longer than 55 inches from the heel (where the stick meets the blade) to the end of the shaft. If the stick is curved, it may not have a curve of more than a half inch from the blade out.

It takes the goaltenders quite a bit longer to dress. Whatever a forward or defenseman wears, a goalie wears at least twice that. The upper half of his body is completely encased in padding, including a chest protector similar to that of a catcher's in baseball, shoulder pads and quilting that extends from the wrists, under the shoulder pads, up to the neck. Outside protection is considerable. Overstuffed pads, tied around his calf, protect him from the tips of his skates to above the knees. These leg pads may be as much as 10 inches wide and in addition to protecting him are vital in kicking away shots.

He wears two different kinds of gloves. On his free hand he wears a glove that is almost a duplicate of a first baseman's mitt but has a long cuff that reaches halfway up his arm. The hand that holds the stick fits into a five-finger glove but is backed by an elbow-length, wide pad that is used for stopping shots. The blade on his skates is flat, not the rocker type used by forwards and defensemen, who have to do the turning and fast skating. A goalie's skate blades must be flat and thick for balance. The front and rear of the shoe are covered with rubber cups, which give him added protection for shot blocking.

His stick, too, is different. It also is 55 inches long at most, but midway down the shaft it becomes wider, up to 3½ inches wide. The blade is also 3½ inches across and gives the goaltender the use of the stick as a further defensive weapon. Virtually all of today's goalies wear a mask, molded of Fiberglas, with cutouts for eyes, nose and mouth, as well as air holes along the sides.

The only really vulnerable spot in a hockey player is his face. Shoulder pads are smaller and lighter than most because contact on shoulder tops is minimal and players carry too much weight.

As the players trudge through the walkway and the crowd gets its first glimpse, it appears that the athletes are lumbering. Skaters off the ice look rather clumsy. As seen from bench level, they look like oversized strong men. In actuality, the average player is smaller than one expects from most professional athletes. Feared shooters Yvan Cournoyer, Marcel Dionne and Rod Gilbert are only 5-7, 5-9 and 5-9, respectively. Two of the NHL's "giants," Phil Esposito and "the Big M," Frank Mahovlich, stand 6-1 and 6-0, respectively. Padding, huge pants and the extra inches skates add give the illusion of size.

Following warm-ups, the players who will not start go to the bench, sitting down in front of the coach after the national anthem. Players do not get overly excited on the bench during normal play. The coach masks his feelings by pacing, sometimes letting out an expletive on a missed shot or a call that went the wrong way. The trainer stays near, a towel draped around his neck in case an injury causes bleeding. An equipment boy hovers near, passing out a plastic bottle filled with water which the players sip through a straw. When a coach wants to throw out a new line or defensive combination, he taps the players if he's close to them, or hollers at them.

Players with the same first names are given nicknames. When a new line is ready to go over the boards, the players pounce to attention. Some drape a foot over the side. As soon as the situation permits a line change—either when play has been stopped or the action is centered near the opposition goal—they take the ice.

Between periods they relax, some munching on oranges or sipping one of the high-energy liquids that have become popular in recent years. A player might mumble something about rotten luck or blame himself for a goal. They are silent when the coach speaks. It is difficult to make corrections in the heat of the game, but now they are somewhat relaxed and can listen to reason or take orders.

Hockey dressing room often appears as if a tornado had just hit. Each player has dozens of sticks for his use.

NORTHLAND
VICTORIAVILLE

After the 15-minute break (longer in some arenas so more food can be sold) the entire team again goes on the ice for a brief warm-up. Before each of the nonstarters leaves, he goes over to his goalie and gives him a tap on the pads, telling him to hang in there and be tough. "We're with you," the gesture says.

At game's end, the trainer is the busiest member of the club. If the team is leaving to catch a plane, equipment must be packed, the medicine kit stocked. Skates and padding go into a giant-sized overnight bag. The players will not need their home jerseys on the road (clubs have different-colored uniforms for home and away). If the club will be home for its next game, the trainer puts the jerseys and underwear into washing machines near the locker room.

According to National Hockey League rules, a team must be en route to its next game by the night before the scheduled game. If Chicago, for example, has a game at Detroit on Wednesday night and another in New York on Thursday, it must leave immediately after the Detroit contest. Airlines will hold up a regularly scheduled flight for a team, but the players still must rush. Their road uniforms have been packed since afternoon and have been loaded on the chartered bus that will take the team to the airport. When a club is leaving for another city immediately after a game, it misses a meal. If it is traveling from west to east, past a time zone, it loses sleeping time. Clubs that play in Minnesota one night and in an eastern city the next arrive at three in the morning local time and some clubs are not able to get into bed until after 4 A.M. They arise sometime in mid-morning.

Yet they are due on the ice that night and the fans who paid money to see them expect a top performance. "You just can't go out there and say, 'I'm sorry, folks, I'm tired tonight.' Even though you might be," said one player. "You know you've got to try your best. After all, you're among the best and if you're not going to give 100 percent, the other team will."

HOCKEY, INC.

Old values die hard. In hockey, the *laissez-faire* attitude of owners is slowly changing. Some believe not quickly enough. Old guard thinking was typified by Conn Smythe's belief that his Toronto players owed him complete allegiance. That meant signing the contract he put before them without consulting a lawyer or business manager.

Hockey today is a multimillion-dollar business. Salaries soared dramatically after the WHA came along. In the NHL the average salary rose from about $25,000 a year in 1971 to $44,000 a year by 1974. The WHA averaged about $25,000 a man. Most of the NHL clubs play in arenas built in the 1960s. Others were refurbished during those years.

It costs $1.5 million a year to run an NHL franchise. The structure of the game has changed almost completely in recent seasons, the cost going up sharply. Before the universal draft, players were signed in their early teens. The boys signed an amateur card, which made them club property and started them on the road to hockey. A scout saw a bright prospect playing on a local, unsponsored team. With his parents' consent, he was signed by an NHL team and assigned to a certain club, depending on his ability. It might be a midget team, or junior B or, if he were good, Junior A.

The best teams were usually in the east, so it was not unlikely that if the boy did not live near a midget or junior B team he could be shipped hundreds of miles from home to play with his new team. This was the way Bobby Hull started, and even today he tells stories of how homesick he was, of the nights he cried himself to sleep.

The boy's moving expenses were paid for.

His room, board and tuition in school were provided and he received $10 a week for spending money. On Christmas and Easter, he was given a vacation home. If he elected not to go to school, his $10 a week spending money was increased to $60, since the club didn't have to pay tuition. It was an incentive for a 16-year-old to quit school, for that amount of money in many cases was as much as the boy's father earned. The clubs, though, usually took good care of the youngsters. But principally the boys were there to play hockey, and that's what they did.

By the time a boy was ready to turn professional, he had played hundreds of games in league competition, received expert coaching, learned the tricks of hockey. Despite the money he may have received, he was still considered an amateur, because the Canadian Amateur Hockey Association made the rules and permitted the practice. As long as a boy played for an amateur team (one that fitted their definition of amateur) he was an amateur.

Territorial rights preserved and protected dynasties in Montreal and Toronto. No club could come within a 50-mile radius of an NHL team and sponsor a junior program without the permission of the club in that territory. A sponsored club allowed 54 players to be tied up. If a team had a junior A squad as its sponsored club, it also could have two farm teams—a junior B and a midget club. Naturally, a large percentage of players and would-be players came from a 50-mile radius of Montreal and Toronto (What good did it do the Rangers to have exclusivity in Hoboken?) and that made it difficult for other teams to compete.

The face of hockey changed in more than one way with expansion. The practice of sponsored clubs ended. If it hadn't, the new teams would never have achieved equality, for the established clubs would have had an overwhelming backlog of players, a ready reserve for many years. As of January 1, 1966, player lists were frozen—every player on that list remained the property of the parent club. After that, players were put in a pool.

In 1967 all the franchises which had been sponsored were turned over to local control. Since then they have been jointly underwritten by the Canadian Amateur Hockey Association and the National Hockey League. Junior A and junior B teams each get $5,000 in subsidies. The universal draft was instituted (only those players on the January 1, 1966, list are exempt) and is run similarly to drafts in other sports. And only boys 20 years old or older may be drafted. No players under 20 are likely to see NHL action anymore.

The first three years of the draft favored the West Division clubs. Each of the 12 clubs may draft as many as six players. The West Division clubs were allowed to go first, teams with the worst records getting first choice. Starting in 1969, the 12 clubs, then 14, chose in order, starting with the teams with the poorest records. For every player drafted, the team picking the player reimburses the CAHA for $3,000. The NHL spends more than $1 million a year (almost $80,000 a club) helping the CAHA administer the far-reaching amateur program.

Drafting a player doesn't guarantee an NHL team a certain player. It must now negotiate with him on his professional contract. The average bonus to get a boy to sign is $15,000 and his playing contract varies. The minimum salary in the NHL is $10,000 a year, but no players in years received the minimum. The pay scale is lower in the minors, of course, and a first-year pro usually will not receive $10,000 a season.

Each club today has about 60 players under professional contract, including those on the parent club, but costs do not stop there. Some minor-league franchises run the parent team $100,000 a year, a necessity for the club's development. An NHL team also must contribute $250,000 a year as its share of running the National Hockey League. The cost covers the salaries of league officials and workers, administrative costs, trophies, monetary awards given for all-star games, trophy recipients and Stanley Cup play-off money. Travel expense has been increased to a scale never imagined in the 1950s.

Before expansion and the necessity of air travel, teams often took overnight trains. The farthest trip was between Montreal and Chicago. A club could use its sleepers for the players' rooms and save on hotel bills. The cost of getting to the station from the stadium was much less than going from the stadium to an airport located outside of town.

The general manager calls in local airline executives in the summer when he gets his schedule for the coming season. Since each of the NHL clubs is in a major city, there are several major airlines serving his city and the general manager usually is able to take care of most of his reservations. But there are exceptions. There are no late (postgame) flights out of Montreal and Toronto to Philadelphia, for example, and the Flyers have to charter flights from there when they have a game the following night.

All is not outgo, of course. Attendance at hockey generally has been remarkable, the price scale usually quite high. Average attendance for the 1966-1967 season, the last one before expansion, was 14,689. For the two seasons after expansion the 12 clubs averaged about 12,000, including relatively poor attendance in Pittsburgh and Oakland and the fact that only one of the expansion arenas was as large as an East Division arena. If an average club played before an average crowd of 12,000 it will have played before almost half a million home fans. At an average price of $5, that is a gross of $2.4 million.

Revenues from local radio and television can mean $60,000 to $400,000 a year to a club. Network television adds $70,000 a year to each of the 11 United States teams. Toronto, Montreal and Vancouver split a private Canadian TV deal, with $750,000 each for the first two and $400,000 for Vancouver. Home clubs keep all gate receipts—there is no split with the visitors.

There are also concessions—hot dogs, soft drinks, programs. Some clubs sell 7,000, 75-cent programs *a game*. Some clubs may own the concessions outright; others may receive a flat rate. Almost all clubs play pre-season exhibitions in their own rink. Season's subscribers must buy the exhibition games as well as regular-season contests.

Some clubs' gross, then, is as high as $5 million. Allowing for splits on gross attendance income with arenas, there still is a comfortable margin over the $1.5 million it costs to operate a club. But there is still more potential revenue—the play-offs. Salaries have been paid. Virtually everything won in the play-offs is gravy. And now it takes four extended series before the Stanley Cup can be won. Take Madison Square Garden in New York as an example. It seats 17,500 for hockey. During the play-offs, its prices are raised by 40 percent—as are ticket prices for play-offs in every other city. If the Rangers last only one round and their series goes only the minimum of four games, they still will have two games at home.

During the play-offs, the Garden is scaled for $150,000 for a full house—a minimum of $300,000 more that the Rangers take in than if they hadn't made the play-offs. Carried to extremes, if they get to the finals after an opening-round best-of-three affair and then three best-of-seven series, they might play fourteen games in New York—worth more than $2.1 million. It is easy to see why hockey people hunger for the Stanley Cup.

In recent years, especially under the direction of vice president Don Ruck, the NHL has become highly promotion-conscious and has been cashing in to a greater degree on the value its imprimatur has on a product. Games and equipment that bear the NHL seal deliver hundreds of thousands of dollars to the league annually and the market is getting broader.

If a player in an advertisement or commercial wears his team uniform, the club gets a cut. If a player is even identified in an ad as being with a specific team, the team comes in for a piece of the action. The situation was different in Toronto, where the Leafs gave a flat $1,500 to each player in exchange for using his name for commercial endorsements. The Leafs in turn received a handsome fee from their advertising agency. The practice has been abandoned there.

To make sure the public likes the NHL product and thinks favorably about the league, Ruck is closely involved with the network telecasts which reach millions of people that have never seen hockey. Ruck or an aide is at every "Game of the Week" in the control tower. His function is to make sure that commercials do not interrupt the flow of play. It was not an easy task, since it was necessary to get major advertisers to cut down their commercials' time. As most advertisers believe, a longer commercial is more effective than a shorter one.

A linesman at a Game of the Week is equipped with a beeper, hidden in his shirt. When there is a natural stoppage of play–a face-off, say – Ruck will signal the linesman that a commercial is coming on. If the commercial goes over the normal time it would take for a face-off to start, the referee holds up play. At first, fans booed the procedure. They have gotten used to it.

For Ruck it has meant a new way of thinking. He freely admits he came to the sport minus a deep hockey background. He did know something about the medical aspects of the sport–his previous job was with Blue Cross in Connecticut. Ruck has had to learn tempo and pace. It would be unfair to run a commercial after an offside when a team has been attacking strongly. The club's momentum might be hurt, the flavor of the whole game changed, if play was halted until the commercial were finished.

All broadcasters have to be approved by the clubs whose games they air and in the case of network television, the league approves. When any television broadcasters–even the color men–are nominated by the networks, the league must okay them. Owners are finnicky. One complained about a broadcaster who touched Derek Sanderson in an interview.

The players are fully aware of how much money their team makes. And that helps them (they hope) when it comes to contract time. The general manager sends out contracts in July. In two weeks, the counter-offers come in. The mail not being the easiest way of settling differences, a general manager usually will take a few days off and set up shop in Montreal, then Toronto, for person-to-person talks with his players. Most general managers use three criteria for arriving at a salary: length of service, ability and value to team, box-office appeal.

Contracts are sweetened in many ways, primarily through bonuses. There seem to be bonuses for everything in the sport. Credit for starting a bonus system is claimed by Frank Selke at Montreal. Selke complained that Boom Boom Geoffrion did not shoot enough. "With a shot like yours, you should be blasting the puck when you're 15 feet out instead of passing to some guy who couldn't put the puck in the ocean." To give the Boomer incentive, he offered him $100 for every goal scored. "He was sorry he did," said Geoffrion 371 goals later.

Every player today is eligible for some type of bonus. Goal scorers generally get one for every goal they score over a set figure. Most get $100 for every one over 20. Defensemen get extra money if the opposition scores less than a predetermined figure over the season. Goalies get money for shutouts. Many general managers also give additional money to each player if the club finishes better than fourth, or is first after half a season, or finishes higher than the previous season.

A player who hasn't scored a lot, hasn't had a long career, isn't a smash at the box office, will often point to the team's finish, if it was a good one, and show what part he played. Emile Francis once had an argument with his general manager when the former was playing with the Black Hawks. "You're weak on your right side," claimed the general manager. "That's a lie," said Francis, and promptly produced a record card that proved him right.

Contract negotiations these days are more complex. The personal touch may not always be there as it was in the old days. But the old days weren't ideal by far. Those who believed in organizing for players' rights were quickly branded as troublemakers and either traded to another club or eased out of hockey. Under Clarence Campbell's presidency there has been more open talk about contracts, while at the same time players organized even more strongly than before. In the 1960s pressure for a Players Association reached its peak and finally was formed with Alan Eagleson as its head. The Players Association claimed contracts were archaic, looked to other sports and consulted with other leaders to see how their own association might be strengthened.

In 1967 a summit conference was held at which player representatives from football, basketball, hockey and baseball got together to examine ways of increasing bargaining power and of determining what was the best type of contract for each sport. The NHL thought itself already fair and above board. Every team put in $1,500 a year for each player into the pension fund, a figure matched by the player. In the event of disputes over salary, Campbell served as a mediator if either party requested arbitration and the owners felt he generally gave the player the benefit of the doubt.

But the players wanted self-determination and contracts similar to other sports. In particular, they wanted a clause that would allow a player to play out his option for a year at his previous salary and then become a free agent. In 1967 they wanted to test the legality of contracts and to fight the ambiguous wording that the owners interpreted this way: a player must report to camp and play even if he hasn't signed a contract.

One month before the 1967-1968 season, the first under expansion, was the great confrontation. The gap between management and labor grew wider than ever. The split was symbolized by—and indeed was focused on—the Ranger training camp in Kitchener, Ontario. Rod Gilbert, the Rangers' top name, Arnie Brown, a defenseman, and Orland Kurtenbach, a center, failed to skate with the club and were fined $500 each.

The date was September 13, the birthday of the Rangers' coach-general manager, Emile Francis. They were the first such fines levied in Ranger history. Francis called them "contract breakers," and said that according to their contracts they were signed from October 1, 1966, to October 1, 1967. He also fined Don Simmons, a goalie, and Wayne Hall, a left wing, $300 apiece. Brown was the only one of the five to report to camp. He sat alone in the balcony of the Kitchener Memorial Auditorium and watched his teammates skate. Brown's room later became the command post for Alan Eagleson, a Toronto member of Parliament who had been hired as the Players Association executive director.

Eagleson sat near a telephone while Brown, unsure of the consequences, watched moodily from his bed. Eagleson was on the phone for hours, making and taking calls as he contacted players on each of the 12 clubs. That day, Tim Horton of Toronto was fined $500 for reporting late; Ed Van Impe of the new Philadelphia club reportedly was also fined, but Clarence Campbell supposedly intervened with the Flyers' brass; Earl Ingarfield and Al MacNeil, the Pittsburgh Penguins' first two draft choices, had not reported; Norm Ullman was not skating with Detroit; Pat Stapleton, Ken Wharram and Pit Martin had not reported to Chicago's camp.

Eagleson assured each of the players that the Association would stand behind them. But he had inadvertently created confusion that permeated all the training camps. The players misunderstood him. They thought that they should not play unless they had signed contracts for the coming season. He had meant to convey the thought that they could work out with the club, even without a contract. Some players were bitter about the affair afterward since nothing of significance was resolved. The players paid their fines and reported. Eagleson said he did "not want to hold a knife to the owners' throats. The players don't want a nickel more or a nickel less than they're entitled to—especially a nickel less."

It appeared to many people that the confrontations were going to be just a start, that eventually the players would threaten to strike as did those in the other major sports. They wanted to bargain for more TV revenue, the pension fund, the right to free themselves from binding contracts. If nothing else, that day made it clear to both sides that they would have to keep a way open for talk.

The Rangers found themselves embroiled in a situation before the 1970-71 season started when four key players—Brad Park, Jean Ratelle, Vic Hadfield and Walt Tkaczuk —were suspended after they had hired lawyers to negotiate for them and talks bogged down. Hockey first saw the lawyer in 1950, when the great Jean Beliveau was coaxed into turning pro and signed with the Montreal Canadiens. Then Orr refused to sign unless his own lawyer approved before Orr's rookie season.

Beliveau had been earning $20,000 a year with the Quebec Senior Aces and was considered an amateur since the Aces' league was amateur. A god in Quebec, his name and face were on most of the milk containers sold in the city. To induce him to turn professional, the Canadiens, through some maneuvering, turned the whole league pro. Then they got Beliveau, who showed up for the talks with a business manager, to sign a long-term contract calling for $20,000 a season.

Orr signed another contract in 1968, and the rumors about the deal, believed to be for three years, varied from $200,000 to $400,000. Bobby Hull, meanwhile, had been viewing the Orr speculation with interest. He knew that the top stars in every other sport were earning $100,000 (or more) a year, that rookies were signed to bonuses that made them wealthier than established stars. Before the 1968-1969 season, following a 44-goal year, Hull decided to make his move. He would ask the Chicago Black Hawks for $100,000. The Hawks and Hull talked over the summer. They talked again in the fall. Lester Stanford, Hull's business manager, sat in on the talks. They could not believe that the Hawks were refusing to meet Hull's terms, which included deferred payments for tax reasons.

Hull suddenly called a press conference the week the season was to begin. He announced he was quitting hockey. He was shocked and saddened, his friends said, that the Hawks would treat him as if he were just another player. What bothered him most was the Hawks' requesting mediation with Campbell, breaking a private agreement with Chicago that their talks would never go beyond the conference room.

Hull also was upset over the ramification of mediation. The Players Association had won a point in their contracts that stipulated if a player and his club went to mediation, the player would be represented by Eagleson. That would be fine for the average player, thought Hull. But not for him. Eagleson was Orr's attorney, and in order to represent Hull effectively, he would have to know the Golden Jet's business structure inside and out.

Hull and his advisers rebelled. Orr and Hull were the two players most in demand for commercial endorsements in Canada and Hull and his associates felt they would be represented by an attorney for a rival. The Hull case never went to Campbell. He missed only the Hawks' first game, before the front office relented on the $100,000. Ninety minutes before their second game, he signed. All the players took the ice, except Hull. Then he came out, whereupon the crowd gave him a five-minute standing ovation. He scored the game's final goal as the Hawks won.

Even if there hadn't been a Players Association, today's National Hockey League skater has more ways to make money than ever before. The leisure-time explosion has made millions of people sports fans. There is an inclination for the average fan to buy something that a star athlete uses or wears. Thus, Hull is closely associated with Lincoln-

Mercury in Canada, which ties in new-car promotions closely with the handsome skater. Gordie Howe owns a skating rink in Detroit, Orr sells his own equipment, Stan Mikita has patented a helmet, Rod Gilbert wears a certain brand of support hose.

Speaking fees for dinners range from $100 to $1,500. There are almost more dinners than players. Many name players run their own summer camps or teach at them. But hockey players haven't even scratched the surface of the rich United States advertising market. Since their names are household words only in Canada you won't see a hockey player (except, perhaps, for a few) model clothing, trying a new hair tonic or using a certain razor. Hockey players are always amazed when they hear of the contracts athletes in other sports sign for the use of their name. With continued national exposure, as more fans become acquainted with the sport, hockey players will soon be taking their share of the market.

Even if a player fails to sign a single outside contract, there is enough reward inside the sport to more than compensate for it. The league distributed $1.3 million after its 1973-74 season:

Stanley Cup Play-offs—Every player on a club losing the quarterfinals earned $2,500. Every player on a club losing the semifinals earned $5,000. The losers of the finals were richer by $10,000 a man. And the Cup champions earned $15,000 apiece—double the amount that the winners earned two years before. Since so many clubs are involved in the play-offs, more than half the players in the league earn extra thousands.

Final Standings—Every player on the club finishing first in its division picked up $4,000. Second place was worth $2,000, third $1,250 and fourth $750.

All-Star Game—Every member of the winning squad earns $500, each member of the losing team earns $250; ties are split.

All-Star Teams—The squad, in the past composed of players selected by compiling votes the first half and second half of the season, is now elected at the end of the season. Selection to the first team is worth $2,000; to the second team, $1,000.

Trophies—The Art Ross Trophy, for the league's scoring leader, is worth $500 to the leading scorer the first half of the season, $500 to the leading scorer the second half of the season, $1,000 to the final leader. If one player leads all the way, he earns $2,000. The runner-up to the scoring leader is worth $250 for each half, $500 for final standing.

The Vezina Trophy goes to the goaltender, or goaltenders, playing at least 25 games for the team having the fewest goals scored against it. The leader for each half earns $250, the overall winner takes home $1,500. The runner-up gets $750.

The Hart Memorial Trophy, for the league's most valuable player, carries an award of $1,500. The runner-up earns $750.

The Lady Byng Memorial Trophy, for clean and effective play, is worth $1,500, $750 for the runner-up.

The James Norris Memorial Trophy, for best defenseman, is worth $1,500, $750 for the runner-up.

The Calder Memorial Trophy, for best rookie, is worth $1,500, $750 for the runner-up.

The Conn Smythe Trophy, for the outstanding player in the play-offs, is worth $1,500.

Take Yvan Cournoyer, the Canadiens' superstar, as an example. His team finished first in the 1972-73 season. That was worth $4,000 to him. Montreal won the Stanley Cup. That was worth an additional $15,000. He won the Smythe Trophy for $1,500. He was a second-team all-star—$1,000. He played in the all-star game, worth $500. So in 1973, Cournoyer earned an additional $22,000. He also got a car for his play-off performance.

The coach (who shares in all prize money won by the club) and the general manager are at the helm of the squad, but there are dozens

Arnie Brown of the Rangers sits alone and watches his teammates start summer practice at their rink in Ontario. Brown had gone on strike against inflexible contracts.

more behind the scenes. There are few people today who hold the once-common title of coach and general manager. Expansion, the universal draft, travel have made it extremely difficult to keep up with the paperwork, scouting reports and finances—and coach a team. The general manager is in charge of the operation of the club and its minor-league affiliates. His job even includes passing on the types of stories that will be in the programs and yearbooks. To keep abreast of the far-flung operations, he needs many aides.

There is a public relations staff which may also handle promotion and publicity. Hockey teams generally combine the three titles, conferring them on one man. Publicity is just that. Press releases on upcoming games have to be sent out, stories geared for a specific newspaper or writer or television or radio personality have to be thought up. Questions on an upcoming game have to be answered. In the press box the publicist keeps a set of notes that may have interest for the specific game—a player's 300th goal is near, a player's 500th consecutive game.

To help newsmen in their jobs, he has compiled a press guide which gives a rundown on every player. It contains such items as height and weight, date of birth, position played, marriage status and playing record. In addition, the guide will have the club's records through the years—how it finished, Cups won, individual team marks. If a player scores four goals in a game, the reporter or announcer merely has to look into the guide to see how many other players in the team's history scored as many in a game. The guides, which generally cost $1, are also available to the public.

The promotional aspects of the publicist's job include getting players to speak at banquets or before youth and church groups. A sports organization has an obligation to the public of which the P.R. head should be cognizant. The public relations part of his job includes answering letters to the team. They may be complaints about ticket prices, or a happy letter complimenting the club. He must always present a smiling face to the public.

The bulk of the 40 or so people employed by a club (in addition to the players) is made up of the scouting staff. A club may have as many as 30 full-time and part-time scouts. There is a chief scout and two major assistants —one for eastern Canada, the other for western Canada. They in turn have bird dogs of their own. When a player worth watching—someone they might want to draft—is brought to their attention, a regional scout will take a look. If he likes him, he will bring in another opinion—a scout for the other region will watch the player, and perhaps the chief scout as well. If the player is prized, the general manager will also look him over. The scouts crisscross Canada constantly and if they spot an exceptional player, they will follow him for weeks. It is not enough to see a player at home. He must be judged on the road as well.

Some players with superstar potential fizzle on the road. Even if the team doesn't select the player, it has learned something about him. The information may be useful if another club drafts him. The regional scouts and the chief scout travel as much as 100,000 miles a year. Worse, they travel in winter, when the game is played, to places like Kirkland Lake, Ontario, where temperatures consistently hover at 40 below. Most of the traveling is done by car since most of the cities are hundreds of miles from an airport.

The scouting staff doesn't only look for unknowns. It must constantly reevaluate the minor leaguers in their system to determine who are ready to move, who should be sent even lower, who should be discarded. Because no club goes through a season without some major injuries to key players, the scouting staff must know which players in the minors are ready to come up to the big club. The other teams in the NHL must also be scouted. With today's scheduling, it is possible that a club might not play all its opponents at least once until two months after the season starts. It has to know what to look for.

A club also has a road secretary who may or may not travel with the team. He prepares an itinerary for the general manager's office before every trip—where the bus leaves from, departure time, arrival time, how the team gets from airport to hotel, what time the game starts, checkout time at the hotel.

There are several other "executives" on a team—captains and alternate captains. Often the captain is a natural leader. He receives a bonus for serving in this capacity, which gives him a major privilege over the other players. Only he or his alternates, of all the players, may question a referee on a decision. In some cases the captain is not by inclination a leader, but is appointed to the post by his coach to give him leadership qualities as well as a sense of responsibility.

As with any million-dollar operation there are secretaries, office boys, attorneys and accountants. But NHL clubs usually are not independent entities. They are generally part of the corporation that owns the arena so that bookkeeping and legal work are done by the parent corporation.

THE MINOR OFFICIALS

Although their names are announced before each game, minor officials are unknown to the public and their method of operation is generally unknown to the average fan. They are called minor officials only because the referee and two linesmen are known as major officials. There is nothing minor about their duties. The five include two goal judges, the penalty timekeeper, the game timekeeper and the scorer.

No minor officials in the National Hockey League are salaried. They are appointed by the league as men of high standing in their community. Actually, each official gets two tickets for every game and usually receives $5 to cover the cost of parking and supper. Minor officials are homegrown. They generally have spent their lives in the city they are working. The league does not rotate them, except for the Stanley Cup play-offs. Before each season, the local supervisor of officials goes over the list with the team's general manager. The names are then submitted to the league office in Montreal, which grants or withholds approval. Approval is almost automatic.

The goal judges are the most intriguing of the group. They are closest to the game, physically and spiritually. They are men with long experience, usually having worked their way up from amateur and minor-league hockey. The judge sits in a booth built flush against the protective glass ten feet behind the cage. There is a footstool in the three-foot-square box and a switch in front of him that looks like a simple wall switch found in any house. The goal judge has one duty—to signal a goal. He does this by flipping the switch which puts on the red goal light atop his cage.

Judges have different styles, just as goalies do. There are puck watchers and cage watchers. The judge who follows the puck needs the quicker reflexes. He must not be bothered by flashing skates, sticks or uniforms, any one of which can conceal the disk. The goal watcher, on the other hand, has his eyes riveted to the area behind the goalie. Many judges prefer this method, especially with the coming of the slap shot in recent years. "The puck travels too fast for you to try and follow it," they say. Of course, the cage watcher is also alert for the puck when it's not near the cage. His peripheral vision can follow a wing with the puck and he can see the shot ripped off.

Whichever style is followed, the judge must make the same decision: a goal is scored if the *whole* puck is over the goal line. Halfway in doesn't count. Even when a save is made the goal judge's job isn't over. When Chuck Rayner played for the Rangers he once pulled his hand back—over the line—to toss the puck out to a teammate. The red light flashed—the puck had crossed the line. To avoid getting trigger-happy, the judge keeps his hands away from the switch. Once he is confident a goal has been scored, he signals. In the closing seconds of a period, though, he will keep his hand near the switch in order to beat the automatic clock which signals the end of a period.

Once the period ends a green light flashes automatically, locking the goal light. This doesn't mean that if a player scores with one second to go and the goal judge doesn't signal quickly enough, the goal doesn't count. It does. But to avoid confusion and arguments, a judge must be especially quick at the end of a period.

Arthur Reichert of New York City may be typical of the goal judges. He is a certified public accountant, with offices in midtown Manhattan. He has been a goal judge at Ranger games since World War II. Reichert's station is the same for all games, for every period. A cage watcher, the slender, narrow-faced Reichert has incredibly sharp, beady, piercing eyes. When the play hovers near, he strains forward, his mouth moves furiously around a wad of gum, his eyes stare at the area behind the goalie, peripherally watching play. All goal judges manifest this tenseness when the play is at their end. During the 60 minutes of play, they will see from 20 to 40 shots taken at the goalie. And even when shots aren't taken, they still must be alert to the possibility that a pass will ricochet off a skate toward the cage.

The official scorer in hockey carries more responsibility than does his counterpart in any other sport. For one thing, he decides who scored the goal and who got the assist or assists. But not all goals are clear-cut scores. Many are put in during a scramble from in front of the net. Others bounce in off someone's skate or shoulders or are deflected in by a stick. Many times fans are surprised when they hear the goal scorer's name announced, convinced someone else had put in the goal.

After a goal the referee usually will tell one of the scorer's aides who scored and players will tell the referee, if he didn't see the play, who did it (a large percentage of goals are deflections). But the referee's opinion on the goal merely reinforces the official scorer's, whose ability to credit the correct player is uncanny. The official scorer must also credit a goal to an attacking team player when a defender or a goalie inadvertently puts the puck in his own net. Say the goaltender tries to clear the puck, but instead hits it off the back of one of his own defensemen, and the puck bounces back and into the cage. The scorer credits the goal to the player on the other team who was closest to the cage.

It is especially difficult to remember the sequence of a play, but it is necessary because assists are credited to the two previous attacking players who have touched the puck before the goal was scored. A favored method is quite simple, but extremely tedious. The official scorer keeps a sheet of paper in front of him and merely writes down the number of the player touching the puck. It must be done quickly, of course. A play may go this way: 10-6-11-5-3-4-goal. Player No. 4 gets the goal, Nos. 3 and 5 receive assists. If the sequence doesn't result in a score and the other team gets possession, the scorer then draws a line under the numbers and starts again.

Numbers don't help when there is a clutch of players in front of the net and the scorer's view is blocked. He must then consult with the bench and the referee to determine who claimed the goal and who assisted. A scorer may change assists and even goals during a game, but once the contest has ended he must leave his last selections as official.

In the final game of the 1966-1967 season, Stan Mikita, who had tied the single-season scoring record of 97 points, argued that he should have received credit for an assist on a goal against the Rangers. The official scorer disagreed. "At least look at the films," said Mikita. The films could not have changed the official decision, but the scorer agreed. As they usually do, the films corroborated the judgment of the official scorer—Mikita had not figured in the goal.

After each game the scoring (including

assists and the time of the goals), the number of goaltenders' saves as well as the penalties are sent to the league office in Montreal, where Campbell's staff keeps a complete table. Records are compared, for example, on the assists a player receives at home and on the road. Teams almost always do better on their own ice and so more players should be credited with assists. But if a player gets a strongly disproportionate number of assists at home, the league might begin to wonder if the scorers favor a hometown player. It was said that in Montreal Rocket Richard regularly received an assist while he was sitting on the bench. The same rumors were spread about Mikita in Chicago.

In some old arenas players in the penalty box were separated only by a three-foot-wide aisle. Tempers were not easily controlled in the close atmosphere and the penalty timekeeper—also known as the penalty box attendant—often acted as peacemaker. The job now is quite simple. He opens the gate for the penalized player or players, and lets him out when the penalty is up. To make sure the player serves his allotted time, the penalty timekeeper keeps a stopwatch in case something goes wrong with the penalty clock. With ten seconds to go in the penalty box, he will open the latch to the door. When the penalty is over, and not a second before, the player may leave. Some jump over the boards, but most skate out through the open gate.

Players rarely fuss or fume in the penalty box. They sit quietly, an aisle in front of the fans, and take abuse from the opposition's followers. In smaller rinks penalized players are practically joined by the fans. In Commack, Long Island, where a minor league team plays, the owner's wife always takes a seat behind the penalty bench. When a member of the opposition is penalized and takes his place on the bench, she needles him constantly with such questions as, "Why were you charging? You couldn't pay cash?" Or if a player has fought with another, she might ask, "What would your mother say?" A player who keeps his cool in this situation while his team struggles one man short must truly be considered a man of tolerance.

The game timekeeper, the fifth member of the minor officials' staff, operates the clock and scoreboard. He puts the score on the board, the number of the player penalized (and for which team) and the duration of the penalty. All clubs use a statistician, but he is not an official. He keeps track of home-team shots on net (which usually vary widely with the official shots), face-offs won and lost, who was on ice for the goals, who lost the puck.

The officials for all-star games are the officials always used by the host team. Only during the play-offs are neutral officials employed. If Detroit plays at Toronto in the play-offs, for example, none of the minor officials may be from either city. In the play-offs the league authorizes first-class travel accommodations for its officials and pays each man $50 a day.

It is to the minor officials' credit that their natural hometown interest doesn't interfere with objectivity. Most will admit to being fans for their home team, but their skill is high and they are proud of their selection by the league. As one official remarked, "Sure I root for my team. I'm a fan. But when I'm working, all I look at is the puck."

THE ICE

Much of the glamor of hockey has to do with ice colors—the white of the ice itself, red and blue lines, symmetrical red circles, colorful home insignias. The surface is a product of eight hours of work by four men.

Rinks in Montreal and Toronto are covered by ice most of the season. But New York's Madison Square Garden is an example of the activity that goes on when the ice is to be prepared. Like many of the other arenas in the United States, the Garden is used for basketball, boxing, entertainment shows, benefits, rallies. There is usually a basketball game one night, a hockey game the next. On a typical

Tuesday night, the Knickerbockers are playing basketball. While the game is in progress, brine is circulated through 13 miles of pipe embedded in the concrete floor.

After the game the floor boards are removed and the dasher boards for hockey are installed which give the rink its dimensions—200 feet by 85 feet. A compressor, with freon used as a refrigerant, cools the brine which has a freezing point of 20 degrees below zero. It is cooled to 10 degrees above zero. When the desired temperature is reached, about two o'clock in the morning, the workmen roll out a hose.

One worker directs the six-inch nozzle, the other three hold the hose. He puts on what is known as the first spray—400 gallons of water, which leave a thin layer of film on the concrete. When this freezes the process is repeated two more times. After the third spray, the entire surface is painted white. Three hundred gallons of a water solution containing calcimine powder (a whitening agent) are applied. Three more water sprays cover the paint. Then the markings are put on, some by hand.

There are five major face-off circles, one at center ice, the others divided in the two ends. The paint is applied with a brush. One worker holds a string at the center of the circle (he looks at a reference point through the ice) and the painters merely follow the edge of the string, completing the circle. The four smaller face-off spots also are done by hand.

The rink-wide blue lines and center red line are applied with the aid of a frame. The goal line, the referee's crease (the semicircle near the announcer's table which a player may not enter when the referee is consulting with other officials) and the goalie's crease (that area directly in front of the cage, eight feet wide and extending four feet out from the goal line) also are painted in. A form is used to paint the team's symbol on either side of the center face-off circle. Another 14 water sprayings are applied after the painting.

Eight hours and 6,000 gallons of water later the surface is ready. It is five-eighths of an inch thick.

Between periods the Zamboni—the surface-clearing machine used in all rinks—takes the ice. Named for its inventor and maker, the Zamboni scrapes the surface and gathers the loose snow into the van via a chain belt. It resurfaces the ice at the same time by spraying a thin layer of hot water over the area it has cleared.

When the game is over the ice has to be removed for another event and the scraping starts. It takes an hour and three quarters to undo. The men chip the ice away while a truck equipped with a snow plow breaks it up. The workers push the broken layers to a huge pit outside the rink area. The ice melts and eventually the water finds its way to the city sewers.

LEFT: Every club has a Zamboni to scrape, clean and resurface the ice. ABOVE: When a period starts, ice is glassy clear.

14

5

HOCKEY AND WHEAT

great moments

Rarely has a country's spirit been captured by one sports event as Canada's was by the Team Canada-Soviet Union games in September, 1972. Before the series had ended, it had become one of the game's great spectacles, with far-reaching effects that changed the course of hockey both in North America and in the Soviet Union.

For years most entrenched members of hockey's Establishment hadn't thought it fit to mention the Russians and the National Hockey League in the same breath. Sure, the Russians were fast and in good condition, but whom did they beat? It didn't seem to matter that the Russians were the perennial world amateur champions. Their success in international competition left Westerners unimpressed because the Russians had had obviously unfair advantages over their opponents. There is no distinction between amateur and professional in Russia, and consequently, the Russians were by Western standards amateurs in name only. North America had sent only patchwork, young, second-line teams against the Russians, who were experienced and had played together for years.

In the early 1970s, as more and more hockey executives finally got to see the Russians, they were intrigued. How good were the Russians really? Canadian and American collegians who played them said they were very good. At least one NHL general manager didn't think so. After a game in the United States against the American national team, the G.M. became angry when a writer suggested the Russians might give some of the NHL teams a battle. "I'm sick and tired of hearing that baloney about the Russians," he shouted. "None of them are in our class."

The games were to work like this: only Canadian nationals would compete for Team Canada. Four games would be staged in Canada and then four in Moscow. Though it seemed a simple enough format, problems soon arose. The NHL had been asked to direct the selection, conditioning and coaching of the Team Canada squad. Suddenly, the WHA was on the scene, and the WHA had lured Bobby Hull. The great goal scorer was not going to be on the squad. There was a public outcry, but the NHL was unmoved. Hull can be on the team, it said, but then we'll pull out. So Hull and several other jumpers that probably would have made the team were excluded.

The coach and general manager of Team Canada was Harry Sinden, who had been out of hockey since quitting the Bruins after winning the Stanley Cup. His assistant was John Ferguson, once the brawny belter of the Canadiens.

After the grumbling about the snubbing of WHA players, there were more complaints: training camp for the series was starting in the middle of August. Some stars felt it was too early.

The grumbling soon stopped, though, once camp began in Toronto. Players such as Frank Mahovlich, Phil Esposito, Brad Park, Yvan Cournoyer and Bobby Clarke became teammates. As the days passed, a sense of excitement and nervousness infused the squad. This was becoming a bigger deal than anyone had believed possible. "Canada is first in the world in two things: hockey and wheat, in that order," said Sinden. It was obvious he and his players wanted to keep it that way.

Finally, the day before the first game, which was to be played in Montreal, the Canadians got their first look at the Russians. There were two noteworthy things about the

PRECEDING PAGES: J. P. Parise cocks for slap shot in Team Canada series against Russia. RIGHT: Russian goalie Vladislav Tretiak is congratulated by team after 7-3 victory.

25
26

visitors: their conditioning and their strange practices. They were, first of all, in extraordinary shape. "No one even takes a drink of water during the workouts," said Esposito. Then there was their practice style. They didn't bother shooting much, and when they did, their goalies simply waved at the puck. And their equipment made some of the NHL stars laugh. The goalies' masks were the old-fashioned cage masks that only the junior players wore. The skates weren't even the pro models. They were second best. The sticks were things called "Scandinavian Surprise."

The psychological warfare started. Perhaps it was only in the minds of Team Canada players, but they believed the Russians were attempting to psych them out. Little things bothered them. On the afternoon of game one, the Russians stayed on the ice long past their allotted time before allowing the NHL to have its time. "You see," said Mahovlich, "they'll do anything to psych us."

Just before game time, Sinden asked the official scorer for the Soviet lineup. In the NHL, the visiting team discloses its lineup before receiving the home team's. The Russians refused to part with theirs and instead asked for Team Canada's lineup. This upset Sinden, who finally prevailed after a heated debate.

These pregame unpleasantries seemed to matter little once the game started. After 30 seconds, Team Canada had a 1-0 lead on Esposito's deflection. Soon it became 2-0. But Sinden and the other Canadians were worried. The Russians didn't give up. They didn't permit their game to become unglued after they trailed so quickly. "I wanted to believe that they weren't doing these things, that it was a mistake," said Sinden. "But I realized they were everything I didn't want them to be." Soon it was tied, and then Kharlamov, Russia's best, put in two second-period goals. The Canadians never recovered. Frustrated at the end, they got chippy, running at every Russian. It was a 7-3 rout.

Afterward, the Russians remained on the ice for the traditional ceremony that marks international competition—the post-game handshakes. But most of the Team Canada players trudged to their dressing room. The stunned capacity crowd at the Forum watched silently. Only a few players, including Ken Dryden and Red Berenson, remained on the ice. "Hey, get on the ice," shouted Alan Eagleson, the head of the Players Association and the man who had set up the series. He ran into the Canadians' dressing room and tried to collect all the players, but by the time they reached the ice the Russians had left. Team Canada was booed. Many fans thought their heroes had acted like anything but sportsmen.

Later, one of the Russian coaches effectively put down the Canadian team. He said, in a pseudo-sympathetic tone, "I understand many of your best players weren't here tonight." He spoke again of his hoping "to learn" from the Canadians. Instead, his Russians had taught "the world's best hockey players" a lesson.

The loss shocked Canada. Front page headlines across the country screamed the news of Canada's defeat. Sinden was under fire. The team was under fire. The players quickly started to wonder just what had happened. Had they been suckered into this affair? So much about the Russians was unknown. Their goalie, Vladislav Tretiak, was supposed to be weak on long shots. But then it was discovered that he had been practicing against shots fired from a cannonlike device that blew the puck at him at 130 miles an hour, considerably faster than the NHL's best shots.

The Russians seemed strange as they drank glass after glass of Coca-Cola and mineral water in their rooms. And their coaches always sat in the stands watching the Canadian workouts, never saying anything. "Hey, what's the Canadian equivalent for Siberia?" the Rangers' Rod Gilbert wondered after the defeat.

The Canadians weren't going to take the Russians lightly again. As Sinden prepared for the second game in Toronto, he felt good after the workout. He had decided to use such "diggers" as Wayne Cashman and Bill Goldsworthy, instead of his flashy, faster forwards. The fast players weren't fast enough to keep up with the Russians. When the workout ended, Sinden saw the Russian coaches in the stands, presumably stealing secrets. That got him so angry, he said, "that I wanted to take a bite out of the boards."

The Canadians' new tactics worked, and they skated away with a 4-1 victory. But they were less than jubilant afterward. "I don't know whether I could do that for seventy-eight games," said a tired Pete Mahovlich. Many of the players thought the Russians could.

Instead of an exhibition series, this suddenly became the Stanley Cup, the World Series and the Super Bowl rolled into one. Now everyone was keeping score. It was a best-of-eight series and it was tied at one game each. That wasn't good enough for many Canadians. Sinden was barraged with telegrams, including one that read, "We're waiting for you to bring your clowns to town." It was signed "Barnum and Bailey."

The result of the third game at Winnipeg didn't help: a 4-4 tie, after Canada had led 4-2. The Russians were gloating. "Tretiak isn't even our best goalie," said one of the Russian reporters. The Canadians were practically in awe of these opponents who never tired, never got rattled no matter how many times they were hit, and who didn't like to fight. Instead, when they were angry they'd spit. "If someone gave the Russians a football," said Frank Mahovlich, "they'd win the Super Bowl in two years."

In this atmosphere the teams prepared for game four in Vancouver, and it was the low point in Canadian fortunes. The team was booed unmercifully and lost 5-3. Esposito, angry and saddened, went on television after the game to berate his countrymen who didn't stand by their team. "We're all in this together," he said.

The first phase of the "exhibition" was over, and the Canadians had won only once in four games. Now the next four would be in Moscow. "We were troops going off to fight for Canadian glory," Esposito recalled.

The Canadian players were given the VIP treatment when they arrived in Moscow, but their wives were treated as ordinary tourists. In contrast to the player's fare, the wives' food was rather meager. So many of the players smuggled extra bits of steak up to their rooms after supper to keep their spouses happy. When the Russian games opened the next night, the Russians stormed back twice from three-goal deficits and won, 5-4. Now they led this series, 3-1-1. To win the Canadians would have to capture the remaining three games, a seemingly impossible task.

After this loss the Canadiens had a party in Esposito's room, and Eagleson managed to get hold of some roast turkey. Esposito doesn't remember how it happened, but when he woke up the next morning, he found turkey under his bed, on the walls, in the bed.

The task in front of Team Canada was formidable, at the least. The Rangers' Vic Hadfield, angered at not being used as a regular, had left the team. Sinden got him a ticket back to Canada before the first Russian game was played. Richard Martin of the Sabres and Jocelyn Guevremont of the Canucks also deserted the squad. Then, after the opening defeat in Moscow, the Sabres' Gil Perreault also left, and Sinden was moved to say, "I'll never pick twenty-year-olds again for a series like this."

Withal, Team Canada won the next game, and Esposito knew that the following game, number seven, "would be the most important one I ever played. I figured if we could take this, the final game would take care of itself."

Esposito hadn't scored in the first two games in Moscow, and he decided it was about time. He felt that without Bobby Orr, who had missed the series following knee surgery, it was up to him.

In some ways the sixth game was one of the most dramatic. The officials were West

Germans whom Sinden didn't want around. He claimed that they were the worst officials he had ever seen. Penalty after penalty was called against Team Canada, and soon Ferguson and Sinden were screaming nonstop from the bench. The players on the ice kept looking quizzically at the bench, from which towels and curses were flying. After the second period, with Team Canada leading 3-2, Orr shoved one of the referees. Soon, Team Canada was surrounded by Soviet police and ushered into the dressing room.

Sinden kept his team together a long time before the final period started. He knew that after the first period the Soviets had thrown a heavy layer of water on the ice. Sinden believed it had been done deliberately to slow down the Canadians. He told Stan Mikita to walk to the ring and see whether the water had frozen yet. It hadn't. So Sinden kept his team an extra 10 minutes. Finally, he led them out. Team Canada won, and Esposito didn't disappoint himself or his countrymen. He scored the first two goals. The club didn't play too well but still came away with a victory. It set up the final game. The clubs now were tied at 3-3-1. "I think," said Sinden, "that the next game may be the greatest ever played."

It may have been. But first there was more trouble even before the first puck was dropped. The Canadians had been so angered at the West German officials that they got the Russians to agree that only Czech or Swedish referees would be used. At the last minute, though, the Russians insisted on using two Germans. Finally, there was a compromise—one German and one Czech would be used. The Soviet star, Kharlamov, meanwhile, was spotted limping into the arena. He took a couple of shots of novocaine and was ready to play. "I don't want any of you guys to go out of your way," Sinden told his players, "but if Kharlamov happens to skate by and gets in your way—well, give him a tickle."

Early in the game, the Canadians' worst fears about the officiating were realized. J. P. Parise was called for interference. When Parise slammed his stick on the ice in disgust, the German referee gave him a misconduct. Incensed, Parise raced over to the official and threatened him. Parise was thrown out of the game. The 500 fans from Canada in the stands began screaming, "Let's go home!" Sinden picked up a stool and tossed it onto the ice. Then he grabbed another chair and threw it out, shattering the ice. When play was resumed, the Canadians lost their poise. After two periods they were trailing by 5-3, the Russians dominating them.

Early in the final period, Esposito cut the lead to 5-4. Then midway through the session, Cournoyer scored, but the red light didn't go on. Eagleson immediately ran to the timer's bench to protest. He started punching, and soon he was surrounded by Soviet plainclothesmen who punched him. Pete Mahovlich immediately jumped over the side of the boards and ran to the melee, brandishing his stick. Other players followed, with Sinden close behind. They grabbed Eagleson and led him back across the ice to their bench. Finally, the goal light was put on.

The Russians had changed their style in the final period. They didn't seem as goal-oriented, and there was a good reason for it. Under their system of play, if a series ends in an equal number of victories, the team with more goals overall is declared the winner. They went into the final period with a 3-goal overall edge. So even if the game ended in a tie, they would still win the series. It appeared it would end this way as the seconds ticked away with the score tied at 5-all.

In the final minute Sinden wanted Bobby Clarke's line on the ice and Esposito off. "But there was no way I was going to get off the ice with the game ending like that," Esposito was to say later. Luckily for the Canadians, he didn't. Paul Henderson, who was supposed to skate with Clarke, came on the ice. Esposito passed the puck to Henderson, it was knocked back to Esposito, who shot from a difficult angle. The puck rebounded in front of the goal to Henderson, who swiped at it. Tretiak made the save. But the rebound again came out, and Henderson scored. Only 34 seconds remained. Team Canada had won, and in a sense the Canadians had vindicated themselves and their country.

When the buzzer sounded, Sinden turned to his players and said, "Never in doubt, was it, fellas?"

THE KLONDIKE CHALLENGE

In the early days of the twentieth century, the Ottawa Silver Seven squad was conceded to be the best team across Canada. Some people believed that when Lord Stanley donated his cup, he had it earmarked for this club, which played in the nation's capital. But the Silver Seven didn't take the trophy until 1903, when it defeated a club with the astounding name of the Rat Portage Thistles.

Meanwhile, in the Yukon, a group of proud men was annoyed with the idea that these weaklings from the East were calling themselves world champions. The Yukon had attracted a burly collection of gold prospectors who had made the long trip to nowhere and had endured hardships. Certainly, they believed, they would be just as tough on ice. So they decided to challenge hockey's mightiest team for the Stanley Cup.

No one had ever heard of the players. The goalie was a 17-year-old named Albert Forest, the youngest player ever to play for the Stanley Cup. He would be playing in front of a collection of people that no one had heard of, and facing a team with almost legendary players: Frank McGee, Alf Smith and Harvey Pulford.

They didn't frighten the men from the heart of the Yukon, who formed a team called the Dawson City Klondikers. They nicknamed themselves the Golden Seven. In the winter of 1904, they issued the challenge, and the Silver Seven accepted. The problem was that the Klondikers were 4,000 miles away. They had to raise money and find a way to get to Ottawa. Along came a prospector named Colonel Joe Boyle, a theatrical man who had struck it rich. He said he would put up the $3,000 it would cost to send the team to Ottawa. It was to be quite a journey.

Dawson City was festive as their heroes started out in 20-degrees-below-zero weather. Their destination for the first part of the trip was Skagway, 350 miles away. Their transportation: dog sled. The bands played and thousands of people in the thriving city lined the streets. Children waved banners, young girls threw kisses. The players waved. Someone shouted "Mush!" and the caravan was off.

Fortified with whiskey and the plaudits of the crowd, the Klondikers made good time the first day, traveling 46 miles. They moved well the second day, crossing 41 miles of tundra. But by the third day they were slowing down. Frostbite had begun to set in. Their feet were blistered. They wrapped newspapers, socks and cloth around their feet and removed their boots.

Eventually, they reached Skagway, a port city that offered their only way out of the Yukon by boat. The delays had cost them valuable time. A boat left for Seattle only once every five days, and they had just missed the boat by two hours. They had to spend five days in this strange city, preparing for a Stanley Cup challenge against a rested team that was lying in wait. There was only one rink in Skagway on which to practice, and it was the size of a small pool. It measured only 40 by 50 feet. Worse, it had sand on it, so they couldn't use it. They did no skating.

The boat that finally arrived provided another strange means of transportation. It was a coal scow. But it was their only way to make the trip to Seattle, another key point on the journey. From Seattle they would have to backtrack to Vancouver, where they'd board the train to take them to Ottawa. The cold, long days passed, and finally they were on board their train. Yet, they found another problem. They were getting stiff from lack of exercise. Luckily, they were able to work out in the smoking car, though it was big enough for only a few players at a time. But at least they were able to do some rope-skipping.

Their incredible trip finally ended on January 12, 1905—24 days after it started. They had just one day before the opening game. The Klondikers made a futile attempt to get Ottawa to postpone the game for a few days so that the visitors could get some rest. Their hosts refused.

The first game was staged in Dey's Gladstone Avenue Rink. The new Governor-General, Earl Grey (for whom Canadian football's Grey Cup is named) was among the 2,200 fans who packed the matchbook-sized arena. The team from the Yukon took the ice grandly attired in black and gold.

The game was a rout, a 9-2 trouncing by Ottawa. But one of the Klondikers was boasting after the game. "Who's this guy McGee?" he asked. McGee hadn't done much in the opener. But a few days later the visitors found out who he was. He scored the absurd total of 14 goals, and the Silver Seven demolished the Golden Seven by 23-2. Afterward, the losers returned to the Yukon, to remain alive in legend.

THE GREATEST COMEBACK

One thing has always been said about the Toronto Maple Leafs: they have a tradition as a great clutch team. In fact, in some ways they may overall be the best clutch team that hockey has produced. True, Montreal has won more Stanley Cups and finished first more times. But the Leafs are the only team to have won the Stanley Cup more times than they have finished first. Through its first 56 seasons, the club won the cup 13 times but finished first only 7 times. If the club wasn't good enough to make it to the top during the regular season, it was at its best during Stanley Cup play, when emotions are at their highest and many players choke.

The 1942 play-offs perhaps provide the clue to their success. They didn't finish first in the regular season. That honor went to the Rangers. But the Leafs knocked off the Rangers in the first round.

They faced the Detroit Red Wings for the championship. The Leafs had manhandled the Wings during the regular season and finished 15 points ahead of them. But the Wings somehow captured the first three games. It was over after that third game. How could the team possibly have any spirit left?

After Toronto absorbed a 5-2 drubbing in game three, coach Hap Day of the Leafs thought he had discovered the problem. But was it too late? The Wings, a younger club, had been dumping the puck in the Leafs' end and beating the slow Toronto defensemen to it. For the fourth game, then, Day benched two of his stars, Gordie Drillon and Bucko McDonald. He inserted a utility player, Don Metz, and another unknown, Ernie Dickens. Day also resorted to the oldest of coaching tactics: a bit of psychology. Before the fourth game he received a letter from a 14-year-old girl, who told Day that she was praying for the team to win. Day read the letter to the team. When he finished, Sweeney Schriner shouted, "Don't worry, coach. We'll win it for that little girl." Such are the legends of hockey.

At first, there were some problems. The Wings took a 2-0 lead. Back came the Leafs to tie the score. Then the Wings went ahead again, with only about 10 minutes remaining. But the Leafs tied it again. And then Metz, of all people, put in the winning goal. The buzzer sounded and the Leafs had won. Two of the Detroit players, angry at the calls of referee Mel Harwood, began arguing with him. Jack Adams, the Wings' coach, jumped off the bench to his players' defense. He dashed across the ice and began slugging Harwood. After the game, NHL President Frank Calder, suspended Adams for the remainder of the series. Detroit was now without its coach-general manager, the man who had nursed many of the Red Wings players from hockey infancy and who could inspire and lead them.

Ebbie Goodfellow, an excellent player but not a coach, succeeded Adams behind the bench for the fifth game. The despondent Detroiters were trounced, 9-3. The pressure, suddenly, was on the Wings. In the next game the Leafs' surge continued. With Turk Broda in the nets, they triumphed 3-0. The series was tied at three games apiece.

Broda was back in the nets as the series went to its seventh and deciding game at Maple Leaf Gardens. Broda was superb and the Leafs won, 3-1, to win the Cup. It marked the first time any club had been down by three games to none and won. Indeed, through the first 80 years of Cup play, no other club has come close to equaling that feat.

THE YEAR THE CANADIENS MISSED THE PLAY-OFFS

It was the final day of the 1969-70 season, a topsy-turvy year in which the Hawks would bow out of the East Division finishing first. On this last Sunday, the Canadiens began the day with a two-point edge over the fifth-place Rangers. The Canadiens had been locked in a tight race for the play-offs all year, perhaps the tightest race in the league's history. Still, the Frenchmen had made the play-offs for a record 21 straight seasons, and there was no reason, it appeared, why they wouldn't now make it 22. Even if the Rangers won and the Canadiens lost, in which event the two teams would be tied in points, the club with more goals would make the play-offs, and the Canadiens had a five-goal edge, 242 to 237. It was unlikely that the Canadiens would be shut out, even though they were playing the stingy Chicago Black Hawks. But even if they were, the Rangers needed five goals to tie. And the Rangers, who were closing the season in an awful slump, hadn't scored five goals in a game in months.

On this final day the Rangers would play the Red Wings at Madison Square Garden in an afternoon game televised across North America. The Canadiens would play at night in Chicago. Brad Park, the Rangers' leader, had a premonition. He told his mother, "Well, Ma, it looks like we'll have to get nine goals."

Before the game, coach Emile Francis of the Rangers gathered his forces around him in the dressing room. He stood in front of a sign that read, "We Supply Everything But Guts." Then Francis spoke. "I've been in sports a number of years," he said. "And I've seen athletes with their backs against the wall, and I've seen funny things happen. If we can score six, seven, eight goals, this is one of those times."

In the next few minutes, the 17,250 fans at Madison Square Garden saw the Rangers turn into tigers. After 36 seconds, Gilbert tipped in a shot—his first goal in a month. The Wings scored, but still the Rangers attacked, sending shots at Roger Crozier, the Detroit goalie, from every angle. Jack Egers gave the Rangers a 2-1 edge, and Dave Balon made it 3-1. The organist played "More." Egers scored again, and at the end of the period the Rangers had a 4-1 lead.

The Rangers kept it up and, incredibly, finished with a 9-5 victory after pulling their goalie with a 9-3 lead in an attempt to score even more. When it ended, the Rangers had set a club record by taking 65 shots, including 26 in the final period.

"If I were the coach of the Canadiens," said Francis after the game, "I would have locked all my players up in a room without a television."

In Chicago, Sam Pollock, the Canadiens' general manager, and coach Claude Ruel turned off the television set in disgust. They knew then that they would play under pressure. They were angry because the Wings hadn't played better, and later they would charge that Detroit had celebrated the night before, after it had clinched a play-off berth.

Ruel and Pollock then discussed a possible strategy, one of the oddest ever devised: starting the game without a goalie. After all, they would be the underdogs anyway at Chicago. But if they played without a goalie, they'd have a sixth attacker on the ice. It wouldn't matter how many goals Chicago scored as long as Montreal got five. Ruel and Pollock discussed the possibility, then dismissed it. Meanwhile, the players were angry too. They felt that the Wings had fallen down for the Rangers. As the bus took them to Chicago Stadium the Canadiens cursed Detroit.

The game at the Stadium was as bizarre as the game earlier in the day in New York. Midway through the game Montreal trailed 3-2. They had half a game to score three more goals, and everyone knew they could no longer worry about defense. In New York, fans tried to pick up the broadcast of the game in Chicago. Bill Jennings, the Rangers' president, called the president of the Black Hawks, William Wirtz, and asked him to put his radio next to a telephone. Jennings listened to the game by long distance.

The Canadiens didn't score for the remainder of the second period and early in the final session. The Hawks played better and took a 5-2 lead. Then Ruel made his decision. He pulled his goalie, Rogatien Vachon with 9 minutes, 16 seconds remaining. The Canadiens were to go the rest of the way without a goalie—longer than any other team has ever played without one. Ruel didn't care how many goals the Hawks scored as long as his boys got three more, but the Hawks remained poised in the face of the swarming Canadiens. They started pumping home goals at the empty net—five in a row. The Canadiens' strategy had backfired. The Hawks won, 10-2. The Canadiens missed the play-offs for the first time in 22 years. On the radio the Montreal announcer told his listeners, "This is a black day for Canada."

ABOVE: Phil Esposito scores first goal against Tretiak in Canada's first victory of series. RIGHT: Winning goal is scored against Canada in the fourth game of series.

ONE MAN: THREE GOALS IN 21 SECONDS

There wasn't too much excitement on the night of March 23, 1952, the last day of the season. The Chicago Black Hawks, who were about to finish last, were facing the Rangers, who were finishing fifth. But that night an absurd series of circumstances led to a record: Bill Mosienko scoring three goals in 21 seconds—the fastest hat trick in history.

The Rangers' regular goalie, the great Chuck Rayner, had been sidelined for some time with an injury. His replacement was Emile Francis, later to be the team's coach and general manager. But the Rangers needed Francis less this particular evening than did a Ranger farm club, which was starting playoffs in the minor leagues. Francis went down to help out, leaving the Rangers without an experienced netminder. That afternoon another Ranger farm team, the Rovers, had played at Madison Square Garden. The goalie was Lorne Anderson. Even though he had played in the afternoon, the Rangers picked him to play that night. Anderson had played in only two NHL games.

A Ranger defenseman, Hy Buller, also wanted to see action. Buller had been sidelined for several weeks with a broken ankle, but he was only one point away from a Ranger record for points by a defenseman. This was his last chance and he asked the coach, Bill Cook, for an opportunity to play. It was granted.

So on that final evening the Black Hawks would be skating against a goalie who had played just a few hours before and who was being protected by a defenseman with a broken ankle.

Yet, by early in the final period the Rangers had surprised the Garden crowd by taking a 6-2 edge. Fewer than 14 minutes remained in the game, when Mosienko suddenly found himself free at center ice. His center, Gus Bodmar, spotted him and delivered a lead pass. Mosienko went around the disabled Buller and pushed home a low shot. The time was 6:09. There was the usual center-ice face-off. The Hawks controlled the puck. Bodnar again slipped Mosienko the disk, again Mosienko found Buller in front of him, and again he rapped the puck low and to Anderson's right. Another goal. The time was 6:20. There was a third face-off, and once again Bodner spotted Mosienko. Who did he have to beat? Buller. That was no problem. Once more he confronted Anderson, who now was expecting the low shot. Instead Mosienko ripped off a high one—another goal. The time was 6:30. Mosienko had scored his third goal in 21 seconds.

Lost in the legend was the fact that Bodnar also set a record—for the fastest three assists. Ironically, less than a minute after the third goal Mosienko again found himself in front of Anderson but shot wide with Anderson out of position. The Hawks, eventually won, 7-6. One final footnote: Buller failed to pick up one point.

At a Glance: Statistics

NATIONAL HOCKEY LEAGUE

THE STANLEY CUP

In the most trophy-filled sport of all, the Stanley Cup, a magnificent three-foot-high trophy, is the most glamorous. Teams have been after it since 1894. "Amateur" teams paid players to try and capture it, a ring in Montreal once tried to steal it. A squad from the Yukon once traveled thousands of miles, much of the way by dogsled, to battle for it. It costs more to engrave the names of the winning players on it for one season ($150) than the Cup cost (less than $50). It was donated by Frederick Arthur, Lord Stanley of Preston, who never saw a Stanley Cup game. It is presented annually, immediately following the final game, to the team winning the National Hockey League play-offs.

SEASON	CLUB	GEN. MANAGER	COACH
1972-73	Montreal Canadiens	Sam Pollock	Scotty Bowman
1971-72	Boston Bruins	Milt Schmidt	Tom Johnson
1970-71	Montreal Canadiens	Sam Pollock	Al MacNeil
1969-70	Boston Bruins	Milt Schmidt	Harry Sinden
1968-69	Montreal Canadiens	Sam Pollock	Claude Ruel
1967-68	Montreal Canadiens	Sam Pollock	Toe Blake
1966-67	Toronto Maple Leafs	Punch Imlach	Punch Imlach
1965-66	Montreal Canadiens	Sam Pollock	Toe Blake
1964-65	Montreal Canadiens	Sam Pollock	Toe Blake
1963-64	Toronto Maple Leafs	Punch Imlach	Punch Imlach
1962-63	Toronto Maple Leafs	Punch Imlach	Punch Imlach
1961-62	Toronto Maple Leafs	Punch Imlach	Punch Imlach
1960-61	Chicago Black Hawks	Tommy Ivan	Rudy Pilous
1959-60	Montreal Canadiens	Frank Selke	Toe Blake
1958-59	Montreal Canadiens	Frank Selke	Toe Blake
1957-58	Montreal Canadiens	Frank Selke	Toe Blake
1956-57	Montreal Canadiens	Frank Selke	Toe Blake
1955-56	Montreal Canadiens	Frank Selke	Toe Blake
1954-55	Detroit Red Wings	Jack Adams	Jimmy Skinner
1953-54	Detroit Red Wings	Jack Adams	Tommy Ivan
1952-53	Montreal Canadiens	Frank Selke	Dick Irvin
1951-52	Detroit Red Wings	Jack Adams	Tommy Ivan
1950-51	Toronto Maple Leafs	Conn Smythe	Joe Primeau
1949-50	Detroit Red Wings	Jack Adams	Tommy Ivan

SEASON	CLUB	GEN. MANAGER	COACH
1948-49	Toronto Maple Leafs	Conn Smythe	Hap Day
1947-48	Toronto Maple Leafs	Conn Smythe	Hap Day
1946-47	Toronto Maple Leafs	Conn Smythe	Hap Day
1945-46	Montreal Canadiens	Tommy Gorman	Dick Irvin
1944-45	Toronto Maple Leafs	Conn Smythe	Hap Day
1943-44	Montreal Canadiens	Tommy Gorman	Dick Irvin
1942-43	Detroit Red Wings	Jack Adams	Jack Adams
1941-42	Toronto Maple Leafs	Conn Smythe	Hap Day
1940-41	Boston Bruins	Art Ross	Cooney Weiland
1939-40	New York Rangers	Lester Patrick	Frank Boucher
1938-39	Boston Bruins	Art Ross	Art Ross
1937-38	Chicago Black Hawks	Bill Stewart	Bill Stewart
1936-37	Detroit Red Wings	Jack Adams	Jack Adams
1935-36	Detroit Red Wings	Jack Adams	Jack Adams
1934-35	Montreal Maroons	Tommy Gorman	Tommy Gorman
1933-34	Chicago Black Hawks	Tommy Gorman	Tommy Gorman
1932-33	New York Rangers	Lester Patrick	Lester Patrick
1931-32	Toronto Maple Leafs	Conn Smythe	Dick Irvin
1930-31	Montreal Canadiens	Cecil Hart	Cecil Hart
1929-30	Montreal Canadiens	Cecil Hart	Cecil Hart
1928-29	Boston Bruins	Art Ross	Cy Denneny
1927-28	New York Rangers	Lester Patrick	Lester Patrick
1926-27	Ottawa Senators	Dave Gill	Dave Gill
1925-26	Montreal Maroons	Eddie Gerard	Eddie Gerard
1924-25	Victoria Cougars	Lester Patrick	Lester Patrick

1925
B. CAMERON
BOBBY BOUCHER
CANADIANS
SEATTLE
1915-16
Detroit Red Wings 1935.6
Boston Bruins 1940-1

1923-24	Montreal Canadiens	Leo Dandurand	Leo Dandurand
1922-23	Ottawa Senators	Tommy Gorman	Pete Green
1921-22	Toronto St. Pats	Charlie Querrie	Eddie Powers
1920-21	Ottawa Senators	Tommy Gorman	Pete Green
1919-20	Ottawa Senators	Tommy Gorman	Pete Green
1918-19	*No decision.	—	—
1917-18	Toronto Arenas	Charlie Querrie	Dick Carroll
1916-17	Seattle Metropolitans	Pete Muldoon	Pete Muldoon
1915-16	Montreal Candiens	George Kennedy	George Kennedy
1914-15	Vancouver Millionaires	Frank Patrick	Frank Patrick
1913-14	Toronto Ontarios	Jack Marshall	Scotty Davidson
1912-13	**Quebec Bulldogs	M. J. Quinn	Joe Malone
1911-12	Quebec Bulldogs	M. J. Quinn	C. Nolan
1910-11	Ottawa Senators	—	Bruce Stuart
1909-10	Montreal Wanderers	Dick Boon	Pud Glass
1908-09	Ottawa Senators	—	Bruce Stuart

*Final series between Canadiens and Seattle called off because of Canada-wide flu epidemic after each club had two victories and a tie.

**Not officially recognized. Victoria defeated Quebec in a challenge series.

1907-08	Montreal Wanderers	Dick Boon	Cecil Blachford
1906-07	Montreal Wanderers (March)	Dick Boon	Cecil Blachford
1906-07	Kenora Thistles (January)	F. A. Hudson	Tommy Phillips
1905-06	Montreal Wanderers	—	—
1904-05	Ottawa Silver Seven	—	Alf Smith
1903-04	Ottawa Silver Seven	—	Alf Smith
1902-03	Ottawa Silver Seven	—	Alf Smith
1901-02	Montreal AAA	—	Dick Boon
1900-01	Winnipeg Victorias	—	—
1899-1900	Montreal Shamrocks	—	Harry Trihey
1898-99	Montreal Shamrocks	—	Harry Trihey
1897-98	Montreal Victorias	—	F. Richardson
1896-97	Montreal Victorias	—	Mike Grant
1895-96	Winnipeg Victorias	—	—
1894-95	Montreal Victorias	—	Mike Grant
1893-94	Montreal AAA	—	—

THE CALDER MEMORIAL TROPHY

This award—for the rookie of the year—was donated by the league president, Frank Calder, in 1936. To be eligible, a player may not have competed in more than 25 games in any single preceding season, or in six or more games in any two preceding seasons.

SEASON	PLAYER
1972-73	Steve Vickers, New York Rangers
1971-72	Ken Dryden, Montreal
1970-71	Gil Perreault, Buffalo
1969-70	Tony Esposito, Chicago
1968-69	Danny Grant, Minnesota
1967-68	Derek Sanderson, Boston
1966-67	Bobby Orr, Boston
1965-66	Brit Selby, Toronto
1964-65	Roger Crozier, Detroit
1963-64	Jacques Laperrière, Montreal
1962-63	Kent Douglas, Toronto

SEASON	PLAYER
1961-62	Bobby Rousseau, Montreal
1960-61	Dave Keon, Toronto
1959-60	Bill Hay, Chicago
1958-59	Ralph Backstrom, Montreal
1957-58	Frank Mahovlich, Toronto
1956-57	Larry Regan, Boston
1955-56	Glenn Hall, Detroit
1954-55	Ed Litzenberger, Chicago
1953-54	Camille Henry, New York
1952-53	Lorne Worsley, New York
1951-52	Bernie Geoffrion, Montreal

1950-51	Terry Sawchuk, Detroit
1949-50	Jack Gelineau, Boston
1948-49	Pentti Lund, New York
1947-48	Jim McFadden, Detroit
1946-47	Howie Meeker, Toronto
1945-46	Edgar Laprade, New York
1944-45	Frank McCool, Toronto
1943-44	Gus Bodnar, Toronto
1942-43	Gaye Stewart, Toronto
1941-42	Grant Warwick, New York
1940-41	Johnny Quilty, Montreal
1939-40	Kilby MacDonald, New York
1938-39	Frank Brimsek, Boston
1937-38	Cully Dahlstrom, Chicago
1936-37	Syl Apps, Toronto
*1935-36	Mike Karakas, Chicago
1934-35	Dave Schriner, N. Y. Americans
1933-34	Russ Blinco, Montreal Maroons
1932-33	Carl Voss, Detroit

*Karakas and previous winners selected as top rookies before Calder Trophy was presented.

THE HART MEMORIAL TROPHY

This award, to the most valuable player, started in 1923 when Dr. David A. Hart donated a trophy. His original trophy was retired to the Hockey Hall of Fame in Toronto in 1960, when the league struck a new trophy.

SEASON	PLAYER	CLUB
1972-73	Bobby Clarke	Philadelphia
1971-72	Bobby Orr	Boston
1970-71	Bobby Orr	Boston
1969-70	Bobby Orr	Boston
1968-69	Phil Esposito	Boston
1967-68	Stan Mikita	Chicago
1966-67	Stan Mikita	Chicago
1965-66	Bobby Hull	Chicago
1964-65	Bobby Hull	Chicago
1963-64	Jean Beliveau	Montreal
1962-63	Gordie Howe	Detroit
1961-62	Jacques Plante	Montreal
1960-61	Bernie Geoffrion	Montreal
1959-60	Gordie Howe	Detroit
1958-59	Andy Bathgate	New York
1957-58	Gordie Howe	Detroit
1956-57	Gordie Howe	Detroit
1955-56	Jean Beliveau	Montreal
1954-55	Ted Kennedy	Toronto
1953-54	Al Rollins	Chicago
1952-53	Gordie Howe	Detroit
1951-52	Gordie Howe	Detroit
1950-51	Milt Schmidt	Boston
1949-50	Chuck Rayner	New York
1948-49	Sid Abel	Detroit
1947-48	Buddy O'Connor	New York
1946-47	Maurice Richard	Montreal
1945-46	Max Bentley	Chicago
1944-45	Elmer Lach	Montreal
1943-44	Babe Pratt	Toronto
1942-43	Bill Cowley	Boston
1941-42	Tom Anderson	New York Americans
1940-41	Bill Cowley	Boston
1939-40	Ebbie Goodfellow	Detroit
1938-39	Toe Blake	Montreal
1937-38	Eddie Shore	Boston
1936-37	Babe Siebert	Montreal
1935-36	Eddie Shore	Boston
1934-35	Eddie Shore	Boston
1933-34	Aurel Joliat	Montreal
1932-33	Eddie Shore	Boston
1931-32	Howie Morenz	Montreal
1930-31	Howie Morenz	Montreal
1929-30	Nels Stewart	Montreal Maroons
1928-29	Roy Worters	New York Americans
1927-28	Howie Morenz	Montreal
1926-27	Herb Gardiner	Montreal
1925-26	Nels Stewart	Montreal Maroons
1924-25	Billy Burch	Hamilton Tigers
1923-24	Frank Nighbor	Ottawa Senators

THE VEZINA TROPHY

The award, presented by the Montreal Canadiens to the league in 1927 in memory of their outstanding goalie, Georges Vezina, goes to the goaltender, or goaltenders, who has played a minimum of 25 games for the team with the fewest goals scored against it.

SEASON	PLAYER	AVERAGE
1973-74	Bernie Parent and Bob Taylor, Philadelphia Tony Esposito and Mike Veisor, Chicago	2.10 2.10
1972-73	Ken Dryden, Montreal	2.26
1971-72	Tony Esposito and Gary Smith, Chicago	2.12
1970-71	Ed Giacomin and Gilles Villemure, New York	2.26
1969-70	Tony Esposito, Chicago	2.17
1968-69	Glenn Hall and Jacques Plante, St. Louis	2.07
1967-68	Lorne Worsley and Rogatien Vachon, Montreal	2.26
1966-67	Glenn Hall and Denis DeJordy, Chicago	2.43
1965-66	Lorne Worsley and Charlie Hodge, Montreal	2.47
1964-65	Terry Sawchuk and Johnny Bower, Toronto	2.47
1963-64	Charlie Hodge, Montreal	2.26
1962-63	Glenn Hall, Chicago	2.54
1961-62	Jacques Plante, Montreal	2.37
1960-61	Johnny Bower, Toronto	2.50
1959-60	Jacques Plante, Montreal	2.54
1958-59	Jacques Plante, Montreal	2.18
1957-58	Jacques Plante, Montreal	2.11
1956-57	Jacques Plante, Montreal	2.02
1955-56	Jacques Plante, Montreal	1.86
1954-55	Terry Sawchuk, Detroit	1.94
1953-54	Harry Lumley, Toronto	1.85
1952-53	Terry Sawchuk, Detroit	1.90
1951-52	Terry Sawchuk, Detroit	1.94
1950-51	Al Rollins, Toronto	1.75
1949-50	Bill Durnan, Montreal	2.20
1948-49	Bill Durnan, Montreal	2.10
1947-48	Turk Broda, Toronto	2.38
1946-47	Bill Durnan, Montreal	2.30
1945-46	Bill Durnan, Montreal	2.60
1944-45	Bill Durnan, Montreal	2.42
1943-44	Bill Durnan, Montreal	2.18
1942-43	Johnny Mowers, Detroit	2.48
1941-42	Frank Brimsek, Boston	2.47
1940-41	Turk Broda, Toronto	2.06
1939-40	Dave Kerr, New York	1.64
1938-39	Frank Brimsek, Boston	1.58
1937-38	Tiny Thompson, Boston	1.85
1936-37	Normie Smith, Detroit	2.12
1935-36	Tiny Thompson, Boston	1.72
1934-35	Lorne Chabot, Chicago	1.81
1933-34	Charlie Gardiner, Chicago	1.72
1932-33	Tiny Thompson, Boston	1.81
1931-32	Charlie Gardiner, Chicago	2.11
1930-31	Roy Worters, N.Y. Americans	1.67
1929-30	Tiny Thompson, Boston	2.22
1928-29	George Hainsworth, Montreal	0.97
1927-28	George Hainsworth, Montreal	1.09
1926-27	George Hainsworth, Montreal	1.52
*1925-26	Alex Connell, Ottawa	1.2
1924-25	Georges Vezina, Montreal	1.9
1923-24	Georges Vezina, Montreal	2.0
1922-23	Clint Benedict, Ottawa	2.3
1921-22	Clint Benedict, Ottawa	3.5
1920-21	Clint Benedict, Ottawa	3.1
1919-20	Clint Benedict, Ottawa	2.7
1918-19	Clint Benedict, Ottawa	3.0
1917-18	Georges Vezina, Montreal	4.0

*Trophy not awarded until 1926-27.

THE ART ROSS TROPHY

Arthur Howie Ross, the Boston Bruins' first general manager, donated the trophy in 1947, to be awarded to the player who leads the league in total points. If there is a tie at the end of the season, then the trophy is awarded to the player with more goals. If there still is a tie, then the player with the fewer number of games played, or the player scoring the earlier goal, wins the trophy.

SEASON	PLAYER	GAMES PLAYED	GOALS	ASSISTS	TOTAL POINTS
1973-74	Phil Esposito, Boston	78	68	77	145
1972-73	Phil Esposito, Boston	78	55	75	130
1971-72	Phil Esposito, Boston	76	66	67	133
1970-71	Phil Esposito, Boston	78	76	76	152
1969-70	Bobby Orr, Boston	76	33	87	120
1968-69	Phil Esposito, Boston	74	49	77	126
1967-68	Stan Mikita, Chicago	72	40	47	87
1966-67	Stan Mikita, Chicago	70	35	62	97
1965-66	Bobby Hull, Chicago	65	54	43	97
1964-65	Stan Mikita, Chicago	70	28	59	87
1963-64	Stan Mikita, Chicago	70	39	50	89
1962-63	Gordie Howe, Detroit	70	38	48	86
1961-62	Bobby Hull, Chicago	70	50	34	84
1960-61	Bernie Geoffrion, Montreal	64	50	45	95
1959-60	Bobby Hull, Chicago	70	39	42	81
1958-59	Dickie Moore, Montreal	70	41	55	96
1957-58	Dickie Moore, Montreal	70	36	48	84
1956-57	Gordie Howe, Detroit	70	44	45	89
1955-56	Jean Beliveau, Montreal	70	47	41	88
1954-55	Bernie Geoffrion, Montreal	70	38	37	75
1953-54	Gordie Howe, Detroit	70	33	48	81
1952-53	Gordie Howe, Detroit	70	49	46	95
1951-52	Gordie Howe, Detroit	70	47	39	86
1950-51	Gordie Howe, Detroit	70	43	43	86
1949-50	Ted Lindsay, Detroit	69	23	55	78
1948-49	Roy Conacher, Chicago	60	26	42	68
1947-48	Elmer Lach, Montreal	60	30	31	61
1946-47**	Max Bentley, Chicago	60	29	43	72
1945-46	Max Bentley, Chicago	47	31	30	61
1944-45	Elmer Lach, Montreal	50	26	54	80
1943-44	Herbie Cain, Boston	48	36	46	82
1942-43	Doug Bentley, Chicago	50	33	40	73
1941-42	Bryan Hextall, New York	48	24	32	56
1940-41	Bill Cowley, Boston	46	17	45	62
1939-40	Milt Schmidt, Boston	48	22	30	52
1938-39	Toe Blake, Montreal	48	24	23	47
1937-38	Gordie Drillon, Toronto	48	26	26	52
1936-37	Dave Schriner, N.Y. Americans	48	21	25	46
1935-36	Dave Schriner, N.Y. Americans	48	19	26	45
1934-35	Charlie Conacher, Toronto	48	36	21	57
1933-34	Charlie (Chuck) Conacher, Toronto	42	32	20	52
1932-33	Bill Cook, New York	48	28	22	50
1931-32	Harvey Jackson, Toronto	48	28	25	53
1930-31	Howie Morenz, Montreal	39	28	23	51
1929-30	Cooney Weiland, Boston	44	43	30	73
1928-29	Ace Bailey, Toronto	44	22	10	32
1927-28	Howie Morenz, Montreal	43	33	18	51
1926-27	Bill Cook, New York	44	33	4	37
1925-26	Nels Stewart, Montreal Maroons	36	34	8	42
1924-25	Babe Dye, Toronto	29	38	6	44
1923-24	Cy Denneny, Ottawa	21	22	1	23
1922-23	Babe Dye, Toronto	22	26	11	37
1921-22	Punch Broadbent, Ottawa	24	30	14	44
1920-21	Newsy Lalonde, Montreal	24	33	8	41
1919-20	Joe Malone, Quebec	24	39	6	45
1918-19	Newsy Lalonde, Montreal	17	23	9	32
1917-18	Joe Malone, Montreal	20	44	*	44

*Assists not recorded.

**Trophy not awarded prior to 1947-48 season.

Note: In 1917-18, the teams played a 22-game schedule; in 1918-19, schedule was lowered to 18 games; in 1919-20, schedule increased to 24 games. Schedule increased to 30 games in 1924-25; to 36 games in 1925-26; to 44 games in 1926-27; to 48 games in 1931-32; to 50 games in 1942-43; to 60 games in 1946-47; to 70 games in 1949-50; to 74 games in 1967-68; to 76 games in 1968-69; to 78 games in 1970-71.

THE JAMES NORRIS MEMORIAL TROPHY

The newest of the NHL's achievement awards for regular-season play (it was presented in 1953), this trophy goes to the best defenseman in the league. It was donated by the four children of the late James Norris, the Red Wings' former owner.

SEASON	PLAYER
1972-73	Bobby Orr, Boston
1971-72	Bobby Orr, Boston
1970-71	Bobby Orr, Boston
1969-70	Bobby Orr, Boston
1968-69	Bobby Orr, Boston
1967-68	Bobby Orr, Boston
1966-67	Harry Howell, New York
1965-66	Jacques Laperrière, Montreal
1964-65	Pierre Pilote, Chicago
1963-64	Pierre Pilote, Chicago
1962-63	Pierre Pilote, Chicago
1961-62	Doug Harvey, New York
1960-61	Doug Harvey, Montreal
1959-60	Doug Harvey, Montreal
1958-59	Tom Johnson, Montreal
1957-58	Doug Harvey, Montreal
1956-57	Doug Harvey, Montreal
1955-56	Doug Harvey, Montreal
1954-55	Doug Harvey, Montreal
1953-54	Red Kelly, Detroit

THE LESTER PATRICK TROPHY

To commemorate the Rangers' first coach-general manager, one of the sport's dominant figures, the Rangers donated the trophy in 1966 to honor either a player, official, coach, executive or referee for outstanding service to United States hockey. The award is presented annually at a dinner in New York.

YEAR	RECIPIENT
1974	Alex Delvecchio Murray Murdoch Weston W. Adams, Sr. (posthumously) Charles L. Crovat (posthumously)
1973	Walter L. Bush, Jr.
1972	Clarence S. Campbell John Kelley Ralph (Cooney) Weiland James D. Norris (posthumously)
1971	William Jennings Terry Sawchuk (posthumously) John B. Sollenberger (posthumously)
1970	Eddie Shore Jim Hendy (posthumously)
1969	Bobby Hull Edward Jeremiah (posthumously)
1968	Tom Lockhart Walter A. Brown (posthumously) General John Reed Kilpatrick (posthumously)
1967	Gordie Howe Charles F. Adams (posthumously) James Norris, Sr. (posthumously)
1966	Jack Adams

THE BILL MASTERTON MEMORIAL TROPHY

This is the first award donated by the National Hockey League Writers Association, in memory of the Minnesota North Stars player who was the first NHL skater to die as a result of a game injury. It is presented annually to the player "who best exemplifies the qualities of perseverance, sportsmanship and dedication to hockey." All players who participate in a minimum of 50 games are eligible.

The trophy carries a cash award of $1,000.

SEASON	PLAYER
1972-73	Lowell MacDonald, Pittsburgh
1971-72	Bobby Clarke, Philadelphia
1970-71	Jean Ratelle, New York
1969-70	Pit Martin, Chicago
1968-69	Ted Hampson, Oakland
1967-68	Claude Provost, Montreal

CONN SMYTHE TROPHY

This is the first individual award given for Stanley Cup play. It goes to the most valuable player in the tournament, not necessarily to a player who is a member of the finalists. It was presented by Maple Leaf Gardens in 1965 in honor of the man who built the Maple Leafs.

YEAR	PLAYER
1973	Yvan Cournoyer, Montreal
1972	Bobby Orr, Boston
1971	Ken Dryden, Montreal
1970	Bobby Orr, Boston
1969	Serge Savard, Montreal
1968	Glenn Hall, St. Louis
1967	Dave Keon, Toronto
1966	Roger Crozier, Detroit
1965	Jean Beliveau, Montreal

THE LADY BYNG TROPHY

The wife of Canada's governor-general presented the trophy in 1925, to be awarded annually to the player who combines sportsmanship and gentlemanly conduct with a high degree of skill. Frank Boucher of the Rangers, after winning the trophy seven times in eight years, was given the trophy to keep, and Lady Byng donated a new one in 1936.

SEASON	PLAYER	TOTAL POINTS	PENALTY MINUTES
1972-73	Gil Perreault, Buffalo	88	10
1971-72	Jean Ratelle, New York Rangers	109	4
1970-71	John Bucyk, Boston	116	8
1969-70	Phil Goyette, St. Louis	78	16
1968-69	Alex Delvecchio, Detroit	83	8
1967-68	Stan Mikita, Chicago	87	14
1966-67	Stan Mikita, Chicago	97	12
1965-66	Alex Delvecchio, Detroit	69	16
1964-65	Bobby Hull, Chicago	71	32
1963-64	Ken Wharram, Chicago	71	18
1962-63	Dave Keon, Toronto	56	2
1961-62	Dave Keon, Toronto	61	2
1960-61	Red Kelly, Toronto	70	12
1959-60	Don McKenney, Boston	69	28
1958-59	Alex Delvecchio, Detroit	54	6
1957-58	Camille Henry, New York	56	2
1956-57	Andy Hebenton, New York	44	10
1955-56	Earl Reibel, Detroit	56	10
1954-55	Sid Smith, Toronto	54	14
1953-54	Red Kelly, Detroit	49	18
1952-53	Red Kelly, Detroit	46	8
1951-52	Sid Smith, Toronto	57	6
1950-51	Red Kelly, Detroit	54	24
1949-50	Edgar Laprade, New York	44	2
1948-49	Bill Quackenbush, Detroit	23	0
1947-48	Buddy O'Connor, New York	60	8
1946-47	Bobby Bauer, Boston	54	4
1945-46	Toe Blake, Montreal	50	2
1944-45	Bill Mosienko, Chicago	54	10
1943-44	Clint Smith, Chicago	72	4
1942-43	Max Bentley, Chicago	70	2
1941-42	Syl Apps, Toronto	41	0
1940-41	Bobby Bauer, Toronto	39	2
1939-40	Bobby Bauer, Toronto	43	2
1938-39	Clint Smith, New York	41	2
1937-38	Gordie Drillon, Toronto	52	4
1936-37	Marty Barry, Detroit	44	6
1935-36	Doc Romnes, Chicago	38	6
1934-35	Frank Boucher, New York	45	2
1933-34	Frank Boucher, New York	44	4
1932-33	Frank Boucher, New York	35	4
1931-32	Joe Primeau, Toronto	50	25
1930-31	Frank Boucher, New York	39	20
1929-30	Frank Boucher, New York	62	16
1928-29	Frank Boucher, New York	26	8
1927-28	Frank Boucher, New York	35	15
1926-27	Billy Burch, N. Y. Americans	27	40
1925-26	Frank Nighbor, Ottawa	25	40
1924-25	Frank Nighbor, Ottawa	7	18

PRINCE OF WALES TROPHY

Presented annually to the team finishing first in the East Division. The trophy was donated by the Prince of Wales to the NHL in 1924. From 1927 to 1938 it was presented to the team finishing first in the league's American Division. From 1938 until the expansion of 1967, the award was given to the team winning the NHL regular-season title. Following expansion, it again became a divisional trophy.

SEASON	CLUB	COACH
1973-74	Boston Bruins	Bep Guidolin
1972-73	Montreal Canadiens	Scotty Bowman
1971-72	Boston Bruins	Tom Johnson
1970-71	Boston Bruins	Tom Johnson
1969-70	Chicago Black Hawks	Billy Reay
1968-69	Montreal Canadiens	Claude Ruel
1967-68	Montreal Canadiens	Toe Blake
1966-67	Chicago Black Hawks	Billy Reay
1965-66	Montreal Canadiens	Toe Blake
1964-65	Detroit Red Wings	Sid Abel
1963-64	Montreal Canadiens	Toe Blake
1962-63	Toronto Maple Leafs	Punch Imlach
1961-62	Montreal Canadiens	Toe Blake
1960-61	Montreal Canadiens	Toe Blake
1959-60	Montreal Canadiens	Toe Blake
1958-59	Montreal Canadiens	Toe Blake
1957-58	Montreal Canadiens	Toe Blake
1956-57	Detroit Red Wings	Jimmy Skinner
1955-56	Montreal Canadiens	Toe Blake
1954-55	Detroit Red Wings	Jimmy Skinner
1953-54	Detroit Red Wings	Tommy Ivan
1952-53	Detroit Red Wings	Tommy Ivan
1951-52	Detroit Red Wings	Tommy Ivan
1950-51	Detroit Red Wings	Tommy Ivan
1949-50	Detroit Red Wings	Tommy Ivan
1948-49	Detroit Red Wings	Tommy Ivan
1947-48	Toronto Maple Leafs	Hap Day
1946-47	Montreal Canadiens	Dick Irvin

SEASON	CLUB	COACH
1945-46	Montreal Canadiens	Dick Irvin
1944-45	Montreal Canadiens	Dick Irvin
1943-44	Montreal Canadiens	Dick Irvin
1942-43	Detroit Red Wings	Jack Adams
1941-42	New York Rangers	Frank Boucher
1940-41	Boston Bruins	Cooney Weiland
1939-40	Boston Bruins	Cooney Weiland
1938-39	Boston Bruins	Art Ross
1937-38	Toronto Maple Leafs	Dick Irvin
1936-37	Detroit Red Wings	Jack Adams
1935-36	Detroit Red Wings	Jack Adams
1934-35	Toronto Maple Leafs	Dick Irvin
1933-34	Detroit Red Wings	Jack Adams
1932-33	Toronto Maple Leafs	Dick Irvin
1931-32	New York Rangers	Lester Patrick
1930-31	Montreal Canadiens	Cecil Hart
1929-30	Boston Bruins	Art Ross
1928-29	Boston Bruins	Art Ross
1927-28	*New York Rangers	Lester Patrick
1926-27	*Ottawa Senators	Dave Gill
1925-26	Montreal Maroons	Eddie Gerard
1924-25	Montreal Canadiens	Leo Dandurand
1923-24**	Montreal Canadiens	Leo Dandurand
1922-23	Ottawa Senators	Pete Green
1921-22	Toronto St. Pats	Eddie Powers
1920-21	Ottawa Senators	Pete Green
1919-20	Ottawa Senators	Pete Green
1918-19	Montreal Canadiens	George Kennedy
1917-18	Toronto Arenas	Dick Carroll

CLARENCE S. CAMPBELL BOWL

Originally presented each year to the club finishing first during the regular season in the West Division. It is named for the league president who was a guiding figure in expansion, and it was presented for the first time in 1968.

SEASON	CLUB	COACH
1973-74	Philadelphia Flyers	Fred Shero
1972-73	Chicago Black Hawks	Billy Reay
1971-72	Chicago Black Hawks	Billy Reay
1970-71	Chicago Black Hawks	Billy Reay

SEASON	CLUB	COACH
1969-70	St. Louis Blues	Scotty Bowman
1968-69	St. Louis Blues	Scotty Bowman
1967-68	Philadelphia Flyers	Keith Allen

*No playoffs these years. Rangers finished second American Division, 1927-28, and Ottawa finished first, Canadian Division, 1926-27.

**No trophy awarded prior to the 1924-25 season.

STANLEY CUP RECORDS

Records inclusive through the 1970 season

TEAM

Most cups won: 14, Montreal Canadiens; 11, Toronto Maple Leafs; 7, Detroit.

Most final series appearances: 20, Montreal.

Most years in play-offs: 40, Montreal.

Most consecutive Cup championships: 5, Montreal (1956 to 1960).

Most consecutive play-off appearances: 21, Montreal (1949-1969).

Longest overtime: 116 minutes 30 seconds, Detroit-Montreal Maroons at Montreal, March 24, 1936. Mud Bruneteau scored at 16:30 of sixth overtime, or 176 minutes 30 seconds after start of game, to give Detroit 1-0 victory.

Most consecutive play-off game victories: 11, Montreal. Streak started April 16, 1959 at Toronto. Montreal won all eight play-off games in 1960, and streak ended March 23, 1961, against Chicago, in second game of series.

Most consecutive victories one play-off year: 10, Boston, 1970.

INDIVIDUAL

Most years in play-offs: 19, Red Kelly, Detroit-Toronto; Gordie Howe, Detroit.

Most consecutive years in play-offs: 16, Jean Beliveau, Montreal.

Most goals in play-offs: 82, Maurice Richard, Montreal; 73, Jean Beliveau, Montreal; 67, Gordie Howe, Detroit.

Most play-off games: 164, Red Kelly, Detroit-Toronto; 154, Gordie Howe, Detroit.

Most points in play-offs: 158, Gordie Howe, Detroit (67 goals, 91 assists); 154, Jean Beliveau, Montreal (73 goals, 81 assists).

Most assists in play-offs: 91, Gordie Howe, Detroit.

Most penalty minutes in play-offs: 224, John Ferguson, Montreal.

Most shutouts in play-offs: 14, Jacques Plante, Montreal-St. Louis, 14 years, 105 games.

Most play-off games by goaltender: 112, Glenn Hall, Detroit-Chicago-St. Louis.

Most points one play-off year: 27, Phil Esposito, Boston, 1970 (13 goals, 14 assists in 14 games).

Most goals one play-off year: 13, Phil Esposito, Boston, 1970, 14 games.

Most assists one play-off year: 15, Stan Mikita, Chicago, 12 games, 1962.

Most goals by a defenseman one play-off year: 9, Bobby Orr, Boston, 1970, 14 games.

Most penalty minutes one play-off year: 80, John Ferguson, Montreal, 1969, 14 games.

Most goals final series: 7, Jean Beliveau, Montreal, 5 games, 1956, vs. Detroit.

Most points in final series: 12, Gordie Howe, Detroit, 7 games vs. Montreal (5 goals, 7 assists).

Most shutouts one play-off year: 4, Clint Benedict, Montreal Maroons, 9 games, 1928; Dave Kerr, N. Y. Rangers, 9 games, 1937; Frank McCool, Toronto, 13 games, 1945; Terry Sawchuk, Detroit, 8 games, 1952.

Most consecutive shutouts: 3, Frank McCool, Toronto, 1945.

Longest shutout sequence: 248 minutes 32 seconds, Norm Smith, Detroit, 1936.

Most points one game: 6, Dickie Moore, Montreal, March 25, 1954 (2 goals, 4 assists); Phil Esposito, Boston, April 2, 1969 (4 goals, 2 assists).

Most goals one game: 5, Maurice Richard, Montreal, March 23, 1944, at Montreal. Montreal defeated Toronto, 5-1.

Most assists one game: 5. Record held by many.

Most points by a defenseman one game: 5, Eddie Bush, Detroit, April 9, 1942, at Toronto (1 goal, 4 assists). Detroit won, 5-2.

Most penalties one game: 8, Forbes Kennedy, Toronto, April 2, 1969, at Boston. Four minors, two majors, one 10-minute misconduct, one game misconduct.

Most penalty minutes one game: 38, Forbes Kennedy, Toronto, April 2, 1969, at Boston. Four minors, two majors, one 10-minute misconduct, one game misconduct.

Most goals one period: 3, Busher Jackson, Toronto, 1932; Maurice Richard, Montreal, 1944; Ted Lindsay, Detroit, 1955.

Fastest 2 goals: 5 seconds, Norm Ullman, Detroit, April 11, 1965, against Chicago. Ullman scored at 17:35 and 17:40 of second period at Detroit. Detroit won, 4-2.

Fastest goal from start of game (and period): 9 seconds, Gordie Howe, Detroit, 1954; Ken Wharram, Chicago, 1967; Bill Collins, Minnesota, 1968; Dave Balon, Minnesota, 1968.

Most game-winning goals: 18, Maurice Richard, Montreal, in 15 play-off years.

Most overtime goals: 6, Maurice Richard, Montreal (1 in 1946, 3 in 1951, 1 in 1957, 1 in 1958).

Most 3-goal games: 7, Maurice Richard, Montreal (includes one 5-goal game, 2 4-goal games, 4 3-goal games).

Most Cup victories by coach: 8, Toe Blake, Montreal, 13 seconds.

THE ALL-STAR GAME

Until the great expansion of 1967-68, the National Hockey League's all-star game was hardly that. Most of the contests involved the Stanley Cup defender against a team of all-stars—none of whom, of course, could be players from the defender's team. The reason for this structure was that there weren't two divisions. All-star games in other sports are held between leagues or rival divisions. Hockey's all-star game first was staged in 1947, when there was only one division. Except for 1951 and 1952, when the first and second teams played one another, all the games through 1968 were between the defender and the previous season's all-stars. There was a radical change in 1969. The game was between the East and the West Divisions, and players were chosen in midseason for the contest. Starting in 1970, the game site was rotated among teams in the two divisions.

YEAR	SCORE
1974	West 6, East 4
1973	East 5, West 4
1972	East 3, West 2
1971	West 2, East 1
1970	East 4, West 1
1969	East 3, West 3
1968	Toronto 4, All-Stars 3
*1967	Montreal 3, All-Stars 0
1965	All-Stars 5, Montreal 2
1964	All-Stars 3, Toronto 2
1963	All-Stars 3, Toronto 3
1962	Toronto 4, All-Stars 1
1961	All-Stars 3, Chicago 1
1960	All-Stars 2, Montreal 1
1959	Montreal 6, All-Stars 1
1958	Montreal 6, All-Stars 3
1957	All-Stars 5, Montreal 3
1956	All-Stars 1, Montreal 1
1955	Detroit 3, All-Stars 1
1954	All-Stars 2, Detroit 2
1953	All-Stars 3, Montreal 1
1952	First Team 1, Second Team 1
1951	First Team 2, Second Team 2
1950	Detroit 7, All-Stars 1
1949	All-Stars 3, Toronto 1
1948	All-Stars 3, Toronto 1
1947	All-Stars 4, Toronto 3

SUMMARIES —	WON	LOST	TIED
All-Stars	9	7	3
Montreal	3	4	1
Toronto	2	4	1
Detroit	2	0	1
Chicago	0	1	0
First Team	0	0	2
Second Team	0	0	2
East Division	1	1	1
West Division	1	1	1
East Division	3	2	1
West Division	2	3	1

*Game changed to midseason instead of being held at start of season.

ALL-TIME STANDINGS OF CURRENT NHL TEAMS

TEAM	GAMES	WON	LOST	TIED	GOALS FOR	GOALS AGST.	PCTGE.*
Montreal	3,074	1,555	1,021	498	9,495	7,706	.587
Detroit	2,848	1,277	1,093	478	8,119	7,540	.532
Toronto	3,074	1,395	1,209	470	8,945	8,280	.530
Boston	2,914	1,293	1,165	456	8,662	8,335	.522
St. Louis	460	195	181	84	1,269	1,233	.515
New York Rangers	2,848	1,149	1,209	490	7,987	8,290	.489
Chicago	2,848	1,122	1,283	443	7,813	8,161	.472
Minnesota	460	166	203	91	1,261	1,397	.460
Philadelphia	460	159	203	98	1,247	1,346	.452
Buffalo	234	77	109	48	677	799	.432
Atlanta	78	25	38	15	191	239	.417
Pittsburgh	460	152	229	79	1,264	1,469	.416
Los Angeles	460	145	252	63	1,230	1,627	.384
California	460	123	256	81	1,169	1,644	.355
Vancouver	234	66	143	25	665	932	.335
New York Islanders	78	12	60	6	170	347	.192

*Computed by dividing possible points into actual points.

CLUB SHOOTING PERCENTAGE LEADERS

SEASON	CLUB	SHOTS TAKEN	GOALS SCORED	PERCENTAGE
1972-73	Montreal	2,496	329	13.1
1971-72	Boston	2,620	330	12.6
1970-71	Boston	3,167	399	12.6
1969-70	Chicago	2,450	250	10.2
1968-69	Boston	2,590	303	11.7
1967-68	Boston	2,466	259	10.5

SEASON	CLUB	SHOTS TAKEN	GOALS SCORED	PERCENTAGE
1966-67	Chicago	2,207	264	12.0
1965-66	Chicago	2,087	240	11.5
1964-65	Chicago	2,102	224	10.7
1963-64	Chicago	2,347	218	9.3

POWER-PLAY PERCENTAGE LEADERS

SEASON	TEAM	ADVANTAGES	POWER-PLAY GOALS	PERCENTAGE
1973-74	N.Y. Rangers	222	66	29.7
1972-73	Philadelphia	257	74	28.8
1971-72	Boston	256	74	28.9

SEASON	TEAM	ADVANTAGES	POWER-PLAY GOALS	PERCENTAGE
1970-71	Boston	289	80	27.68
1969-70	Boston	279	81	29.00
1968-69	Boston	266	60	22.60
1967-68	New York	217	46	21.20

PENALTY-KILLING LEADERS

SEASON	TEAM	MAN SHORT	POWER-PLAY GOALS AGAINST	PERCENTAGE PENALTIES KILLED
1973-74	Philadelphia	422	49	88.4
1972-73	Los Angeles	229	31	86.5
1971-72	Chicago	240	35	85.4
1970-71	Montreal	319	49	84.70

SEASON	TEAM	MAN SHORT	POWER-PLAY GOALS AGAINST	PERCENTAGE PENALTIES KILLED
1969-70	Chicago	247	32	87.10
1968-69	Boston	351	54	84.60
	Philadelphia	286	44	84.60
1967-68	Toronto	230	28	87.83

MOST GAMES PLAYED WITH ONE TEAM

PLAYER	TEAM	SEASONS	GAMES
Gordie Howe	Detroit	25	1,687
Alex Delvecchio	Detroit	22	1,538
George Armstrong	Toronto	20	1,187
Tim Horton	Toronto	17½	1,185
Henri Richard	Montreal	18	1,165
Harry Howell	New York Rangers	17	1,160

PLAYERS WITH MORE THAN ONE TEAM

PLAYER	TEAM	SEASONS	GAMES
Harry Howell	New York Rangers-California-Los Angeles	21	1,411
Tim Horton	Toronto-New York Rangers-Pittsburgh-Buffalo	21	1,391
Dean Prentice	New York Rangers-Boston-Detroit-Pittsburgh-Minnesota	21	1,354
Ron Stewart	Toronto-Boston-St. Louis-New York Rangers-Vancouver-New York Islanders	21	1,353
Red Kelly	Detroit-Toronto	20	1,316
Doug Mohns	Boston-Chicago-Minnesota	20	1,287
Norm Ullman	Detroit-Toronto	18	1,252
Bill Gadsby	Chicago-New York Rangers-Detroit	20	1,248
Allan Stanley	New York Rangers-Chicago-Boston-Toronto-Philadelphia	21	1,244
Eric Nesterenko	Toronto-Chicago	20	1,219

THE 50-GOAL CLUB

PLAYER	SEASON	GAMES PLAYED	GOALS
Phil Esposito, Boston	1972-73	78	55
Mickey Redmond, Detroit	1972-73	76	52
Rick MacLeish, Philadelphia	1972-73	78	50
Phil Esposito, Boston	1971-72	76	66
Vic Hadfield, New York Rangers	1971-72	78	50
Bobby Hull, Chicago	1971-72	78	50
Phil Esposito, Boston	1970-71	78	76
John Bucyk, Boston	1970-71	78	51
Bobby Hull, Chicago	1968-69	74	58
Bobby Hull, Chicago	1966-67	66	52
Bobby Hull, Chicago	1965-66	65	54
Bobby Hull, Chicago	1961-62	70	50
Bernie Geoffrion, Montreal	1960-61	64	50
Maurice Richard, Montreal	1944-45	50	50

LEADING GOALTENDERS IN SHUTOUTS

SEASON	PLAYER	GAMES PLAYED	SHUTOUTS
1973-74	Bernie Parent, Philadelphia	73	12
1972-73	Roy Edwards, Detroit	52	6
	Ken Dryden, Montreal	54	6
1971-72	Tony Esposito, Chicago	48	9
1970-71	Ed Giacomin, New York	45	8
1969-70	Tony Esposito, Chicago	63	15
1968-69	Glen Hall, St. Louis	41	8
1967-68	Ed Giacomin, New York	65⅔	8
1966-67	Ed Giacomin, New York	66⅓	9
1965-66	Roger Crozier, Detroit	62⅓	7
1964-65	Roger Crozier, Detroit	69½	6
1963-64	Charlie Hodge, Montreal	62	8
1962-63	Glenn Hall, Chicago	65⅓	5
1961-62	Glenn Hall, Chicago	70	9
1960-61	Glenn Hall, Chicago	70	6
1959-60	Glenn Hall, Chicago	70	6
1958-59	Jacques Plante, Montreal	66	9
1957-58	Jacques Plante, Montreal	56⅓	9
1956-57	Jacques Plante, Montreal	61	9
1955-56	Glenn Hall, Detroit	70	12
1954-55	Terry Sawchuk, Detroit	68	12
1953-54	Harry Lumley, Toronto	70	13
1952-53	Harry Lumley, Toronto	70	10
1951-52	Terry Sawchuk, Detroit	70	12
1950-51	Terry Sawchuk, Detroit	70	11
1949-50	Turk Broda, Toronto	68	9
1948-49	Bill Durnan, Montreal	60	10
1947-48	Harry Lumley, Detroit	60	7
1946-47	Chuck Rayner, New York	58	5
1945-46	Bill Durnan, Montreal	40	4
1944-45	Mike Karakas, Chicago	48	4
1944-45	Frank McCool, Toronto	50	4
1943-44	Paul Bibeault, Toronto	29	5
1942-43	John Mowers, Detroit	50	6
1941-42	Turk Broda, Toronto	48	6
1940-41	Frank Brimsek, Boston	48	6
1939-40	Dave Kerr, New York	48	8
1938-39	Frank Brimsek, Boston	43	10
1937-38	Dave Kerr, New York	48	8
1936-37	Norman Smith, Detroit	48	6
	Cecil Thompson, Boston	48	6
1935-36	Cecil Thompson, Boston	48	10
1934-35	Alex Connell, Montreal	48	9
1933-34	Charles Gardiner, Chicago	48	10
1932-33	Cecil Thompson, Boston	48	11
1931-32	Cecil Thompson, Boston	43	9
1930-31	Charles Gardiner, Chicago	44	12
1929-30	Lorne Chabot, Toronto	43	6
1928-29	George Hainsworth, Montreal	44	22
1927-28	Alex Connell, Ottawa	44	15
	Hal Winkler, Boston	44	15
1926-27	George Hainsworth, Montreal	44	14
1925-26	Alex Connell, Ottawa	36	15
1924-25	Vernon Forbes, Hamilton	30	6
1923-24	Clint Benedict, Ottawa	22	3
	Georges Vezina, Montreal	24	3
1922-23	Clint Benedict, Ottawa	24	4
1921-22	Clint Benedict, Ottawa	24	2
1920-21	Clint Benedict, Ottawa	24	2
1919-20	Clint Benedict, Ottawa	24	5
1918-19	Clint Benedict, Ottawa	18	2
1917-18	Georges Vezina, Montreal	21	1
	Clint Benedict, Ottawa	22	1

INDIVIDUAL PENALTY LEADERS

SEASON	PLAYER	GAMES PLAYED	PENALTIES IN MINUTES
1973-74	Dave Schultz, Philadelphia	73	348
1972-73	Dave Schultz, Philadelphia	76	259
1971-72	Bryan Watson, Pittsburgh	75	212
1970-71	Keith Magnuson, Chicago	76	291
1969-70	Keith Magnuson, Chicago	76	213
1968-69	Forbes Kennedy, Phil.-Toronto	77	219
1967-68	Barclay Plager, St. Louis	49	153
1966-67	John Ferguson, Montreal	67	177
1965-66	Reg Fleming, Boston-New York	69	166
1964-65	Carl Brewer, Toronto	70	177
1963-64	Vic Hadfield, New York	69	151
1962-63	Howie Young, Detroit	64	273
1961-62	Lou Fontinato, Montreal	54	167
1960-61	Pierre Pilote, Chicago	70	165
1959-60	Carl Brewer, Toronto	67	150
1958-59	Ted Lindsay, Chicago	70	184
1957-58	Lou Fontinato, New York	70	152
1956-57	Gus Mortson, Chicago	70	147
1955-56	Lou Fontinato, New York	70	202
1954-55	Fern Flaman, Boston	70	150
1953-54	Gus Mortson, Chicago	68	132
1952-53	Maurice Richard, Montreal	70	112
1951-52	Gus Kyle, Boston	69	127
1950-51	Gus Mortson, Toronto	60	142

SEASON	PLAYER	GAMES PLAYED	PENALTIES IN MINUTES
1949-50	Bill Ezinicki, Toronto	67	144
1948-49	Bill Ezinicki, Toronto	52	145
1947-48	Bill Barilko, Toronto	57	147
1946-47	Gus Mortson, Toronto	60	133
1945-46	Jack Stewart, Detroit	47	73
1944-45	Pat Egan, Boston	48	86
1943-44	Mike McMahon, Montreal	42	98
1942-43	Jimmy Orlando, Detroit	40	89
1941-42	Jimmy Orlando, Detroit	48	81
1940-41	Jimmy Orlando, Detroit	48	99
1939-40	Red Horner, Toronto	30	87
1938-39	Red Horner, Toronto	48	85
1937-38	Red Horner, Toronto	47	82
1936-37	Red Horner, Toronto	48	124
1935-36	Red Horner, Toronto	43	167
1934-35	Red Horner, Toronto	46	125
1933-34	Red Horner, Toronto	42	126
1932-33	Red Horner, Toronto	48	144
1931-32	Red Dutton, N. Y. Americans	47	107
1930-31	Harvey Rockburn, Detroit	42	118
1929-30	Joe Lamb, Ottawa	44	119
1928-29	Red Dutton, Montreal Maroons	44	139
1927-28	Eddie Shore, Boston	44	166
1926-27	Nels Stewart, Montreal Maroons	44	133

CAREER PENALTY-MINUTE LEADERS

PLAYER	TEAM	SEASONS	GAMES	PENALTY MINUTES
Ted Lindsay	Detroit-Chicago	17	1,068	1,808
Gordie Howe	Detroit	25	1,687	1,643
Tim Horton	Toronto-New York Rangers-Pittsburgh-Buffalo	21	1,391	1,558
Bill Gadsby	Chicago-New York Rangers-Detroit	20	1,248	1,539
Bob Baun	Toronto-California-Detroit	17	964	1,493
Reg Fleming	Montreal-Chicago-Boston-New York Rangers-Philadelphia-Buffalo	11	749	1,468
Gus Mortson	Toronto-Chicago-Detroit	13	797	1,370

PLAYER	TEAM	SEASONS	GAMES	PENALTY MINUTES
Fern Flaman	Boston-Toronto	15	910	1,370
Eddie Shack	New York Rangers-Toronto-Boston-Los Angeles-Buffalo-Pittsburgh	15	962	1,352
Harry Howell	New York Rangers-California-Los Angeles	21	1,411	1,298
Maurice Richard	Montreal	18	978	1,285
Eric Nesterenko	Toronto-Chicago	20	1,219	1,273
Red Horner	Toronto	12	490	1,254
Pierre Pilote	Chicago-Toronto	14	890	1,251
Lou Fontinato	New York Rangers-Montreal	9	535	1,247

SHOOTING PERCENTAGE LEADERS

SEASON	PLAYER	SHOTS TAKEN	GOALS	PER-CENTAGE
1973-74	John Bucyk, Boston	139	31	22.3
1972-73	John Bucyk, Boston	168	40	23.8
1971-72	Jean Ratelle, New York Rangers	183	46	25.1
1970-71	John Bucyk, Boston	225	51	22.6
1969-70	Phil Goyette, St. Louis	152	29	19.1
1968-69	John McKenzie, Boston	123	29	23.6
1967-68	Dick Duff, Montreal	111	25	22.6
1966-67	Paul Henderson, Detroit	101	21	20.8
1965-66	Yvan Cournoyer, Montreal	89	18	20.2
1964-65	Camille Henry, New York-Chicago	108	26	24.7
1963-64	Ken Wharram, Chicago	191	39	20.4

TOP 20 CAREER LEADERS IN GOALS-PER-GAME AVERAGE

PLAYER	GAMES PLAYED	GOALS SCORED	PER-CENT-AGE
Cy Denneny, Ottawa-Boston	326	250	.767
Babe Dye, Toronto-Chicago-New York Americans	271	200	.738
Bobby Hull, Chicago	1,036	604	.583
Phil Esposito, Chicago-Boston	691	398	.576
Maurice Richard, Montreal	978	544	.556
Nels Stewart, Montreal Maroons-Boston-New York Americans	650	324	.498
Howie Morenz, Montreal-Chicago-New York Rangers	550	273	.496
Charlie Conacher, Toronto-Detroit-New York Americans	459	225	.490
Bill Cook, New Rangers	474	229	.483
Syl Apps, Toronto	423	201	.475
Gordie Howe, Detroit	1,687	786	.466
Roy Conacher, Boston-Detroit-Chicago	490	226	.461
Frank Mahovlich, Toronto-Detroit-Montreal	1,110	502	.452
Yvan Cournoyer, Montreal	611	276	.452
Jean Beliveau, Montreal	1,125	507	.451
Bernie Geoffrion, Montreal-New York Rangers	883	393	.445
Sweeney Schriner, New York Americans-Toronto	484	201	.415
Stan Mikita, Chicago	976	401	.411
Aurel Joliat, Montreal	654	269	.411
Toe Blake, Montreal Maroons-Montreal Canadiens	577	235	.407

CAREER TOTAL-POINT LEADERS

PLAYER	GAMES	GOALS	ASSISTS	TOTAL POINTS
Gordie Howe, Detroit	1,687	786	1,023	1,809
Alex Delvecchio, Detroit	1,538	455	821	1,276
Jean Beliveau, Montreal	1,125	507	712	1,219
Bobby Hull, Chicago	1,036	604	549	1,153
Norm Ullman, Detroit-Toronto	1,252	459	666	1,125
Stan Mikita, Chicago	976	401	673	1,074
John Bucyk, Detroit-Boston	1,207	435	634	1,069
Frank Mahovlich, Toronto-Detroit-Montreal	1,110	502	521	1,023
Henri Richard, Montreal	1,165	336	642	978
Andy Bathgate, New York Rangers-Toronto-Detroit-Pittsburgh	1,069	349	624	973
Maurice Richard, Montreal	978	544	421	965
Phil Esposito, Chicago-Boston	691	398	500	898
Dean Prentice, New York Rangers-Boston-Detroit-Pittsburgh-Minnesota	1,354	389	466	855
Ted Lindsay, Detroit-Chicago	1,068	379	472	851
Red Kelly, Detroit-Toronto	1,316	281	542	823
Bernie Geoffrion, Montreal-New York Rangers	883	393	429	822
Dave Keon, Toronto	910	324	422	746
George Armstrong, Toronto	1,187	296	417	713
Doug Mohns, Boston-Chicago-Minnesota	1,287	246	440	686
Rod Gilbert, New York Rangers	748	269	408	677

GOAL-SCORING LEADERS EACH SEASON

SEASON	PLAYER	GAMES PLAYED	GOALS
1973-74	Phil Esposito, Boston	78	68
1972-73	Phil Esposito, Boston	78	55
1971-72	Phil Esposito, Boston	76	66
1970-71	Phil Esposito, Boston	78	76
1969-70	Phil Esposito, Boston	76	43
1968-69	Bobby Hull, Chicago	74	58
1967-68	Bobby Hull, Chicago	71	44
1966-67	Bobby Hull, Chicago	66	52
1965-66	Bobby Hull, Chicago	65	54
1964-65	Norm Ullman, Detroit	70	42
1963-64	Bobby Hull, Chicago	70	43
1962-63	Gordie Howe, Detroit	70	38
1961-62	Bobby Hull, Chicago	70	50
1960-61	Bernie Geoffrion, Montreal	64	50
1959-60	Bronco Horvath, Boston	68	39
	Bobby Hull, Chicago	70	39
1958-59	Jean Beliveau, Montreal	64	45
1957-58	Dickie Moore, Montreal	70	36
1956-57	Gordie Howe, Detroit	70	44
1955-56	Jean Beliveau, Montreal	70	47
1954-55	Bernie Geoffrion, Montreal	70	38
	Maurice Richard, Montreal	67	38
1953-54	Maurice Richard, Montreal	70	37
1952-53	Gordie Howe, Detroit	70	49
1951-52	Gordie Howe, Detroit	70	47
1950-51	Gordie Howe, Detroit	70	43
1949-50	Maurice Richard, Montreal	70	43
1948-49	Sid Abel, Detroit	69	28
1947-48	Ted Lindsay, Detroit	60	33
1946-47	Maurice Richard, Montreal	60	45
1945-46	Gaye Stewart, Toronto	50	37

SEASON	PLAYER	GAMES PLAYED	GOALS
1944-45	Maurice Richard, Montreal	50	50
1943-44	Doug Bentley, Chicago	50	38
1942-43	Doug Bentley, Chicago	50	33
1941-42	Lynn Patrick, New York	47	32
1940-41	Bryan Hextall, New York	48	26
1939-40	Bryan Hextall, New York	48	24
1938-39	Roy Conacher, Boston	47	26
1937-38	Gordie Drillon, Toronto	48	26
1936-37	Larry Aurie, Detroit	45	23
	Nels Stewart, Boston-N. Y. Americans	43	23
1935-36	Bill Thoms, Toronto	48	23
	Charlie Conacher, Toronto	44	23
1934-35	Charlie Conacher, Toronto	48	36
1933-34	Charlie Conacher, Toronto	42	32
1932-33	Bill Cook, New York	48	28
1931-32	Charlie Conacher, Toronto	45	34
1930-31	Charlie Conacher, Toronto	40	31
1929-30	Cooney Weiland, Boston	44	43
1928-29	Ace Bailey, Toronto	44	22
1927-28	Howie Morenz, Montreal	43	33
1926-27	Bill Cook, New York	44	33
1925-26	Nels Stewart, Montreal Maroons	36	34
1924-25	Babe Dye, Toronto	29	38
1923-24	Cy Denneny, Ottawa	21	22
1922-23	Babe Dye, Toronto	22	26
1921-22	Punch Broadbent, Ottawa	24	30
	Babe Dye, Toronto	24	30
1920-21	Babe Dye, Toronto-Hamilton	24	35
1919-20	Joe Malone, Quebec	24	39
1918-19	Odie Cleghorn, Montreal	17	24
1917-18	Joe Malone, Montreal	20	44

CAREER ASSIST LEADERS

PLAYER	GAMES	ASSISTS
Gordie Howe, Detroit	1,687	1,023
Alex Delvecchio, Detroit	1,538	821
Jean Beliveau, Montreal	1,125	712
Stan Mikita, Chicago	976	673
Norm Ullman, Detroit-Toronto	1,252	666
Henri Richard, Montreal	1,165	642
John Bucyk, Detroit-Boston	1,207	634
Andy Bathgate, New York Rangers-Toronto-Detroit-Pittsburgh	1,069	624
Bobby Hull, Chicago	1,036	549
Red Kelly, Detroit-Toronto	1,316	542

PLAYER	GAMES	ASSISTS
Frank Mahovlich, Toronto-Detroit-Montreal	1,110	521
Phil Esposito, Chicago-Boston	691	500
Ted Lindsay, Detroit-Chicago	1,068	472
Phil Goyette, Montreal-New York Rangers-St. Louis-Buffalo	941	467
Dean Prentice, New York Rangers-Boston-Detroit-Pittsburgh-Minnesota	1,354	466
Doug Harvey, Montreal-NewYork Rangers-Detroit-St. Louis	1,113	452
Doug Mohns, Boston-Chicago-Minnesota	1,287	440
Bill Gadsby, Chicago-New York Rangers-Detroit	1,248	437
Bobby Orr, Boston	467	432
Bernie Geoffrion, Montreal-New York Rangers	883	429

CAREER GOAL-SCORING LEADERS

PLAYER	SEASONS	GAMES	GOALS
Gordie Howe, Detroit	25	1,687	786
Bobby Hull, Chicago	15	1,036	604
Maurice Richard, Montreal	18	978	544
Jean Beliveau, Montreal	18	1,125	507
Frank Mahovlich, Toronto-Detroit-Montreal	16	1,110	502
Norm Ullman, Detroit-Toronto	18	1,252	459
Alex Delvecchio, Detroit	22	1,538	455
John Bucyk, Detroit-Boston	18	1,207	435
Stan Mikita, Chicago	14	976	401
Phil Esposito, Chicago-Boston	10	691	398
Bernie Geoffrion, Montreal-New York Rangers	16	883	393
Dean Prentice, New York Rangers-Boston-Detroit-Pittsburgh-Minnesota	21	1,354	389
Ted Lindsay, Detroit-Chicago	17	1,068	379
Andy Bathgate, New York Rangers-Toronto-Detroit-Pittsburgh	16	1,069	349
Henri Richard, Montreal	18	1,165	336
Nels Stewart, Montreal Maroons-Boston-New York Americans	15	650	324
Dave Keon, Toronto	13	910	324
George Armstrong, Toronto	20	1,187	296
Dick Duff, Toronto-New York Rangers-Montreal-Los Angeles-Buffalo	17	1,030	283
Bob Pulford, Toronto-Los Angeles	16	1,079	281
Red Kelly, Detroit-Toronto	20	1,316	281
Camille Henry, New York Rangers-Chicago-St. Louis	14	727	279
Ralph Backstrom, Montreal-Los Angeles-Chicago	15	1,032	278
Yvan Cournoyer, Montreal	9	611	276
Ron Stewart, Toronto-Boston-St. Louis-New York Rangers-Vancouver-New York Islanders	21	1,353	276
Howie Morenz, Montreal-Chicago-New York Rangers	14	550	273
Aurel Joliat, Montreal	16	654	269
Rod Gilbert, New York Rangers	11	748	269
Jean Ratelle, New York Rangers	11	702	267
Don Marshall, Montreal-New York Rangers-Buffalo-Toronto	18	1,176	265
Dickie Moore, Montreal-Toronto-St. Louis	14	719	261
Bill Mosienko, Chicago	13	711	258
Claude Provost, Montreal	15	1,005	254
Ken Wharram, Chicago	12	766	252
Cy Denneny, Ottawa-Boston	12	326	250
Eric Nesterenko, Toronto-Chicago	20	1,219	250
Doug Mohns, Boston-Chicago-Minnesota	20	1,287	246
Max Bentley, Chicago-Toronto-New York Rangers	12	646	245

PLAYER	SEASONS	GAMES	GOALS
Bob Nevin, Toronto-New York Rangers-Minnesota	13	893	243
Harvey Jackson, Toronto-New York Americans-Boston	15	633	241
Murray Oliver, Detroit-Boston-Toronto-Minnesota	14	969	238
Syd Howe, Ottawa-Philadelphia Quakers-St. Louis Eagles-Detroit	16	698	237
Don McKenney, Boston-New York Rangers-Toronto-Detroit-St. Louis	13	798	237
Harry Watson, New York Americans-Detroit-Toronto-Chicago	14	805	236
Toe Blake, Montreal Maroons-Montreal Canadiens	13	577	235
Vic Hadfield, New York Rangers	12	762	235
Robert Rousseau, Montreal-Minnesota-New York Rangers	13	862	233
Ted Kennedy, Toronto	13	696	231
Eddie Shack, New York Rangers-Toronto-Boston-Los Angeles-Buffalo-Pittsburgh	16	962	230
Bill Cook, New York Rangers	11	474	229
Milt Schmidt, Boston	16	776	229
Dit Clapper, Boston	20	830	228
Roy Conacher, Boston-Detroit-Chicago	10	490	226
Charlie Conacher, Toronto-Detroit-New York Americans	12	459	225
Ron Ellis, Toronto	9	656	221
Tod Sloan, Toronto-Chicago	12	745	220
Doug Bentley, Chicago-New York Rangers	13	566	219
Elmer Lach, Montreal	13	664	215
Woody Dumart, Boston	15	771	211
Dennis Hull, Chicago	9	606	210
Ken Hodge, Chicago-Boston	8	565	207
Phil Goyette, Montreal-New York Rangers-St. Louis-Buffalo	15	941	207
Herbie Cain, Montreal Maroons-Montreal Canadiens-Boston	13	570	206
John McKenzie, Chicago-Detroit-New York Rangers-Boston	12	691	206
Paul Henderson, Detroit-Toronto	10	608	205
Ron Murphy, New York Rangers-Chicago-Detroit-Boston	17	889	205
Lorne Carr, New York Americans-Toronto	12	566	204
Jim Pappin, Toronto-Chicago	9	562	202
Syl Apps, Toronto	10	423	201
Sweeney Schriner, New York Americans-Toronto	11	484	201
Babe Dye, Toronto-Chicago-New York Americans	10	271	200
Hooley Smith, Ottawa-Montreal Maroons-Boston-New York Americans	17	715	200

WORLD HOCKEY ASSOCIATION

WORLD TROPHY

The league's top award, it goes to the club capturing the play-offs. When first awarded in 1973, it was called the Avco World Trophy.

SEASON	CLUB	GEN. MANAGER	COACH
1972-73	New England Whalers	Jack Kelley	Jack Kelley

DIVISION CHAMPIONS EASTERN

SEASON	CLUB	GEN. MANAGER	COACH
1973-74	New England Whalers	Jack Kelley	Ron Ryan
1972-73	New England Whalers	Jack Kelley	Jack Kelley

WESTERN

SEASON	CLUB	GEN. MANAGER	COACH
1973-74	Houston Aeros	Jim Smith	Bill Dineen
1972-73	Winnipeg Jets	Annis Stukus	Bobby Hull

GARY DAVIDSON TROPHY

This is for the WHA's most valuable player, and is named for the league's first president.

SEASON	PLAYER
1972-73	Bobby Hull, Winnipeg

BILL HUNTER TROPHY

The league's scoring champion takes this trophy, named for the Edmonton Oilers' official who was one of the league's guiding forces.

SEASON	PLAYER	GAMES PLAYED	GOALS	ASSISTS	TOTAL POINTS
1973-74	Mike Walton, Minnesota	78	57	60	117
1972-73	Andre Lacroix, Philadelphia	78	50	74	124

DENNIS MURPHY TROPHY

This honors the WHA's best defenseman, and is named for one of the league's founders.

SEASON	PLAYER
1972-73	J. C. Tremblay, Quebec

LOU KAPLAN TROPHY

Named for one of the Minnesota Fighting Saints' founders, this trophy goes to the rookie of the year.

SEASON	PLAYER
1972-73	Terry Caffery, New England

BEN HATSKIN TROPHY

The man who brought Bobby Hull into the league was honored by having this trophy named for him. It is awarded to the goalie or goalies on the team with the best goals-against average.

SEASON	PLAYER	AVERAGE
1973-74	Don McLeod, Wayne Rutledge and Ron Grahame, Houston	2.74
1972-73	Gerry Cheevers and Bob Whidden, Cleveland	2.98

PAUL DENEAU TROPHY

The most sportsmanlike player receives this award given in honor of the first chairman of the Aeros.

SEASON	PLAYER	TOTAL POINTS	PENALTY MINUTES
1972-73	No award (ballots weren't mailed)		

HOWARD BALDWIN TROPHY

The coach of the year is awarded this trophy, named for Whalers' first president.

SEASON	COACH
1972-73	Jack Kelley, New England

THE ALL-STAR GAME

This game was started in the league's first season and is played between the Eastern and Western divisions.

YEAR	SCORE
1974	East 8, West 4
1973	East 6, West 2

SUMMARIES	WON	LOST	TIED
East	2	0	0
West	0	2	0

THE 50-GOAL CLUB

PLAYER	SEASON	GAMES PLAYED	GOALS
Mike Walton, Minnesota	1973-74	78	57
Bobby Hull, Winnipeg	1973-74	75	53
Danny Lawson, Vancouver	1973-74	78	50
Danny Lawson, Philadelphia	1972-73	78	61
Tom Webster, New England	1972-73	77	53
Bobby Hull, Winnipeg	1972-73	63	51
Ron Ward, New York	1972-73	77	51
Andre Lacroix, Philadelphia	1972-73	78	50

GOAL-SCORING LEADERS EACH SEASON

SEASON	PLAYER	GAMES PLAYED	GOALS
1973-74	Mike Walton, Minnesota	78	57
1972-73	Danny Lawson, Philadelphia	78	61

LEADING GOALTENDERS IN SHUTOUTS

SEASON	PLAYER	GAMES PLAYED	SHUTOUTS
1973-74	Gerry Cheevers, Cleveland	59	4
1972-73	Gerry Cheevers, Cleveland	52	5

ASSIST LEADERS EACH SEASON

SEASON	PLAYER	GAMES PLAYED	ASSISTS
1973-74	Andre Lacroix, New York-New Jersey	78	80
1972-73	J.C. Tremblay, Quebec	75	75

SHOOTING PERCENTAGE LEADERS

SEASON	PLAYERS	SHOTS TAKEN	GOALS	PER-CENTAGE
1972-73	Norm Ferguson, New York	110	28	25.4

SEASON PENALTY-MINUTE LEADERS

SEASON	PLAYER	GAMES PLAYED	PENALITIES IN MINUTES
1973-74	Gordon Gallant, Minnesota	72	223
1972-73	John Schella, Houston	77	239

POWER-PLAY PERCENTAGE LEADERS

SEASON	TEAM	ADVANTAGES	POWER-PLAY GOALS	PER-CENTAGE
1973-74	Houston	223	64	28.7
1972-73	Houston	188	50	26.5